CW00555633

NEVER STOP

NEVER STOP

How Ange Postecoglou Brought the Fire Back to Celtic

HAMISH CARTON

Foreword by Scott McDonald

First published by Pitch Publishing, 2023

Pitch Publishing
9 Donnington Park,
85 Birdham Road,
Chichester,
West Sussex,
PO20 7AJ
www.pitchpublishing.co.uk
info@pitchpublishing.co.uk

© 2023, Hamish Carton

Every effort has been made to trace the copyright.
Any oversight will be rectified in future editions at the
earliest opportunity by the publisher.

All rights reserved. No part of this book may be reproduced,
sold or utilised in any form or transmitted in any form or by
any means, electronic or mechanical, including photocopying,
recording or by any information storage and retrieval system,
without prior permission in writing from the Publisher.

A CIP catalogue record is available for this book
from the British Library.

ISBN 978 1 80150 426 3

Typesetting and origination by Pitch Publishing
Printed and bound in Great Britain by TJ Books, Padstow

Contents

Acknowledgements

LIKE SO many of you reading this, I'm in a loving relationship with Celtic Football Club. I've supported the club from an early age, with my first season ticket arriving at the age of nine in 2005. I'd go to Celtic Park with my dad all those years ago to watch Gordon Strachan's team entertain, win trophies and upset the big dogs in Europe.

Throughout the years since, we've had many great managers who brought different things to the party. Strachan fostered a team greater than the sum of its parts, who punched above their weight time after time. Neil Lennon brought us from despair to the Champions League last 16, while Ronny Deila kept us at number one in the country. With his arrival in 2016, Brendan Rodgers ushered in a period of complete Celtic dominance. The club won every domestic trophy for four years straight, routinely battered Rangers and had the occasional great night in Europe. They were halcyon days that many thought would never return.

As good as the above managers were, I'd never have considered writing a book about their spells at Celtic. Ange Postecoglou has a way of sucking you in. It's almost impossible to describe unless you feel it. Thankfully, I have this book to give it a go.

The inspiration for writing this will sound pretty banal, so apologies in advance. The story goes something like this: one morning in March 2022 I found myself in the sports section at my local bookshop. As I stood gazing at the latest football titles, with the likes of Lionel Messi, Pep Guardiola, and Jürgen

Klopp featured, it suddenly dawned on me that I was in the midst of an incredible football story myself. That morning, just like every morning, Celtic had been on my mind. The team had just beaten Ross County 4-0 at home and were three points clear at the top of the Premiership with seven matches to go. With the Scottish title winners qualifying automatically for the next season's Champions League group stage, my journalistic mind went into overdrive with all the possibilities. I tried to think of reasons not to write the book, and the only one I arrived at was 'it'll be a lot of time and effort'. I wasn't wrong about that.

Of course, this book wouldn't have made much sense had Celtic not got over the line and won the league, so I thank Postecoglou and the players for that. Over the following chapters we'll follow the journey of that remarkable triumph, from a little-known Australian arriving in Glasgow to the same guy standing at Celtic Park with a microphone in his hand and an entire stadium captivated. It's a hell of a journey, and we'll go a little further too, as Celtic return to the Champions League after a five-year absence.

Of course, the finished product is a result of the efforts of more than just me. The book you're reading wouldn't have been possible without Jane Camillin from Pitch Publishing showing blind faith in me to write something worthwhile. So a huge thank you to Pitch for all their support and to Duncan Olner for the cover.

Additionally, I've been fortunate to speak to many valuable contributors, exclusively, during the process. Quite simply, the book wouldn't have been half as good without their insight and stories. In alphabetical order, they are: Aisling Baker-Ford, Andrew Smith, Andy Harper, Ante Milicic, Ben Coonan, John Hutchinson, Lewis Toshney, Matt Smith, Michael Zappone and Ryan McGowan.

I'd also like to thank Scott McDonald for agreeing to provide the foreword to this book. I watched Scott score so many huge goals for Celtic in my younger years, so to have him involved in this project has been a complete joy.

I'd also like to thank my family for their continued support throughout this project and my career. My girlfriend Kimberley for putting up with my changeable moods and weekends spent in front of a laptop. Thanks to my local coffee shop, which will have seen its profits skyrocket over the last six months. Thanks to *Breaking Bad* and *Better Call Saul* creator Vince Gilligan for keeping me sane with his two wonderful shows.

This process has been a demanding but enjoyable one. Given my obsession with the club, the difficulty hasn't been coming up with information but finding a way to process it all.

Also, thank you for buying this book. If you're a Celtic fan, enjoy reliving every minute of our triumph. If not, don't worry. Welcome to a sensational story.

Finally, my most enormous thank you goes to Ange Postecoglou and his fantastic group of players for giving me so many memories and, above all, something to write about. Postecoglou is an elite-level manager – without a doubt one of the best on this planet. The Celtic support and the rest of Scottish football are aware of that now, as are those in the countries where he's worked. The rest of the world is going to find out very soon.

Hamish Carton, September 2022

Foreword

by Scott McDonald

I'VE THOROUGHLY enjoyed watching this new Celtic team, led by an Australian, play over the past couple of seasons, although it hasn't always been easy. Watching Celtic while living on the other side of the world can be challenging because of the time difference involved. You want to be connected to the club as much as possible, but it's often tough to do so with the timings. It's been hard from a family perspective because I want my son to be ingrained in Celtic. He loves the club and spends ages watching videos of the team on YouTube. But it's still a challenge being so far away.

Like him, Celtic have been ingrained in me from an early age. My whole father's side of the family are mad Celtic fans. My grandfather was originally from the Gorbals. He used to go home every year and bring me back the latest Celtic shirt. More often than not it was 'McStay 8' on the back. I remember having the 1994 black-and-green away kit, the one that's the same as the team wears now. I remember Andy Payton on the posters for it.

All these years later, after playing for the Hoops and enjoying so many good times, it's been amazing to see a fellow Australian managing the club. I didn't see that happening, so it's pretty surreal. Surreal but fantastic. It means that there's more attention on Celtic in Australia, which is good.

The journey under Ange has been outstanding, and you can't underestimate the job he's done. When he arrived in

Scotland the club was in turmoil, probably in the worst place since Martin O'Neill took over at the start of the 21st century. Ange's turnaround has been similar to Martin's first year in many ways, in that the club was positioned in a similar place. But let's be fair, Ange has done it on much less of a budget than Martin.

It's been a phenomenal turnaround, especially when everyone was wondering whether the momentum had swung back to the other side of Glasgow. Rangers had won the title, so for Celtic to clinch it back within a year was significant. It was Ange and the football club saying, 'We're going nowhere. We're as strong as ever.' It didn't look that way 12 months earlier.

The 2021/22 season was amazing because nobody had any real expectations going into it. Many people didn't even think winning the league was possible, but it all clicked so quickly after a rocky start. When you think about how little time Ange had with the team to make it work, it's an amazing achievement. I don't think you'll ever see him as emotional as he was when the team got over the line at Tannadice against Dundee United. He knew how much hard work had gone into winning the league and how incredible an achievement it was in those circumstances. I felt a similar thing at the same ground in 2008.

Lifting the Premiership trophy took the team back to the Champions League group stage, and it means everything for us to be back there. It's the special moments, the memories and the connection the club has with the competition, going back to 1967. There's no more special place in football than Celtic Park on a Champions League night. I loved those nights under Gordon Strachan against the likes of AC Milan, Barcelona and Manchester United. It was the chance to embed yourself in history. When you play against the biggest clubs and do that, it's there for years to come. Even now, when I'm on Twitter, I come across videos of some fantastic nights I was part of.

This Celtic team have already made so many memories over the last couple of seasons, and Hamish is the perfect person to tell the stories behind them. He's lived every moment of the journey and been present at most of the important events. I've enjoyed working with him on the *67 Hail Hail* YouTube channel over the last couple of years. His enthusiasm for Celtic and brilliant storytelling will shine through on every page.

This Celtic team now have a chance to make even more memories in the years to come. They're in a strong position to become a force and leave another successful legacy behind. It will be hard to match the domestic achievements of the Brendan Rodgers era, and there were some memorable times under Neil Lennon and Martin O'Neill too, while Gordon Strachan was the first manager since Jock Stein to win three titles in a row. This team are more than capable of doing similar things if they keep progressing under Ange.

Enjoy the book.

Scott McDonald
Queensland, Australia
September 2022

CHAPTER 1

These Are the Champions

*'I just feel the responsibility of bringing this
football club to this level.'*
Ange Postecoglou

*Celtic 0-3 Real Madrid, UEFA Champions League, Celtic
Park, Tuesday, 6 September 2022*

Celtic 0, Real Madrid 3. And yet Celtic Park is bouncing. The
Hoops faithful have been singing songs in support of Ange
Postecoglou and his players for 15 minutes at the end of a frantic
Champions League contest that promised much and, in the end,
delivered little. For 55 minutes, Celtic had more than held their
own against the reigning Spanish and European champions –
going toe to toe with a team featuring some of the best players
in the world and managed by the imperious Carlo Ancelotti.

Celtic Park had been a hostile place an hour earlier
when the hosts were taking the game to a team featuring 10
of the 11 starters from the Champions League Final victory
over Liverpool months earlier. Only Casemiro, the Brazilian
defensive-midfielder, had departed the scene in the 101
days since the Paris showpiece, being replaced by Aurelién
Tchouaméni, the €100m summer arrival from Monaco. And
yet Celtic had created the better chances against this immense
collection of footballers.

Callum McGregor and Daizen Maeda had gone closest, with McGregor thumping the post midway through the first half and Maeda passing up a golden chance shortly after coming on as a substitute. Predictably, they were made to pay for this wastefulness minutes later. Two classy goals in four minutes from Vinícius Júnior and the peerless Luka Modrić took the match away from Celtic. A third from Eden Hazard 15 minutes later ended it as a contest.

The final goal, finished by the Belgium international, came at the end of a remarkable 33-pass move. Ancelotti's team worked the ball from side to side and back to front, keeping possession for a full minute and 38 seconds without a single Celtic player touching the ball. As per stat website The Analyst, the goal featured the third-most-extended sequence of passes since Champions League records began in 2003. The longest on record, scored by Barcelona's Cristian Tello, was also against Celtic. This was an altogether different level for Postecoglou's team.

Despite the unfavourable scoreline, Celtic had produced enough on the big stage to feel good about themselves. While the Spaniards could rely on world-class quality and immense experience – their starting XI with a combined 28 Champions League trophy wins between them – Postecoglou had seven players playing their first minutes in the tournament. Only Joe Hart, Callum McGregor, Jota and Giorgos Giakoumakis had previously played in the group stage, and only McGregor had done it with Celtic. Of the 16 players used in the match, 13 had been brought to the club by Postecoglou. The response from the Celtic support in defeat said as much about their efforts on the night as it did about the overall direction the team was headed.

Die Meister
Die Besten
Les grandes équipes
The champions

14

Before kick-off, the North Curve section unveiled a striking display alongside the words 'back with a bang', signifying Celtic's return to the competition after five years away. The tifo was raised while the iconic Champions League anthem bellowed from the PA system, not that you could hear it above 59,000 Celtic fans roaring at the tops of their voices. Matt O'Riley, one of the many experiencing a Champions League night at Celtic Park for the first time, couldn't help but smile.

Postecoglou had described the Celtic faithful as 'a Champions League support' in the lead-up to the match. Toni Kroos and Thibaut Courtois clearly agree with the sentiment as they turn to applaud all four corners of the stadium on their way off the pitch. Postecoglou shares a brief embrace with Modrić, the chief architect of his team's downfall, while most other smiles are reserved for those wearing black.

The Celtic players look weary as they shuffle around the pitch, applauding a support still singing as loud and proud as ever. They've no real reason to feel downbeat after going toe to toe with the best team in Europe for most of the match, although the final scoreline is a sore-looking one. Postecoglou follows them around in typical fashion. There's no pump of the fist or beating of the chest this time. Celtic's boss has no time for hard-luck stories. He looks gutted after the second-half capitulation.

'I just feel the responsibility of bringing this football club to this level,' he tells the press barely half an hour later. 'That's what these fans deserve. There is no starker reminder of that than the reception they gave us after the game. They deserve to see their football club competing with the likes of Real Madrid on a regular basis, and really competing. I feel that responsibility, and I want to get us up to this level so that this club and these fans get what they deserve.'

There's an argument that Postecoglou has already given the Celtic support what they deserve: a team to be proud of. Celtic Park is buoyant again, the kind of place where fans can escape their daily struggles. Dreams aren't dashed when Postecoglou is around, only made.

'So you want me to burst people's bubbles, do you?' had been his response a day earlier when asked about managing expectations against Madrid. 'You want me to bring a downer to this whole experience? I'm glad our supporters are buzzing about it. I'm sure they get enough of their bubble burst in their normal lives on a daily basis. They don't need me to bring them down.'

The quote is an isolated example of Postecoglou tapping into what it means to be a Celtic fan. As a result, the fanbase hangs on their manager's every word. They believe that his way will bring success. In the lead-up to the Madrid clash, virtually every Celtic supporter fancied them to achieve an improbable result and do it by playing Postecoglou's expansive, attacking way.

Given the Australian's track record in Glasgow, why would any Celtic fan have any doubts? The club is back in the Champions League for the first time since 2017, rubbing shoulders with Europe's elite after a Premiership triumph for the ages. The League Cup is also in Celtic's cabinet, and if there was any doubt about the team's status in Scotland, the 4-0 dismantling of Rangers days earlier proves Celtic are by far the best in the country.

The squad is in the strongest place it has been since the early 21st century, with at least two good players for every position. There are stars in the making, such as Reo Hatate, Jota and Matt O'Riley, and reliable Postecoglou disciples such as Callum McGregor, Cameron Carter-Vickers and Greg Taylor, all buying into the greater good.

The club has a real long-term vision for the first time in decades, and the support fully believes in the manager to get them where they need to be. Postecoglou's masterplan involves turning Celtic into a team that plays in the Champions League every season and can compete with the likes of Real Madrid in one-off matches. Despite the scoreline, he's ahead of schedule. The turnaround since his arrival has been remarkable.

Celtic: *Hart, Juranovic, Carter-Vickers, Jenz, Taylor, McGregor, O'Riley, Hatate, Abada, Giakoumakis, Jota*
Subs used: *Maeda, Kyogo, Mooy, Turnbull, Hakšabanović*

Real Madrid: *Courtois, Carvajal, Militão, Alaba, Mendy, Modrić, Tchouaméni, Kroos, Valverde, Benzema, Vinícius Júnior*
Subs used: *Hazard, Rüdiger, Camavinga, Asensio, Rodrygo*

CHAPTER 2

500 Miles

*'To be fair, I did just say it. I didn't sing it,
just so people are fully aware.'*
Ange Postecoglou

IT HAD been a damaging 24 hours – the perfect encapsulation of one of the most disastrous seasons in Celtic's history. When the wheels came off the club's protracted pursuit of Eddie Howe, it wasn't just those involved in negotiations who would feel the heat. At *67 Hail Hail*, we'd gone big on AFC Bournemouth's former manager from the day his name had first been mentioned. One of our team even purchased a mug with his face on it. Pretty soon, the Celtic support were feeling like mugs.

Howe felt like the ideal choice to get Celtic over Neil Lennon and back to the glory of the Martin O'Neill and Brendan Rodgers days. The Englishman seemed to have a similar profile to O'Neill or Rodgers when they'd journeyed north to take the Celtic gig. While Howe hadn't managed a club the size of Liverpool, like Rodgers, he was a young, highly motivated coach and a sexy name, as Saudi-backed Newcastle United would prove months later in hiring him.

Howe and Celtic felt like the perfect match, and it wasn't like it was just hopeful chat from supporters either. The first reports of the Englishman being a serious contender for the position had arrived on April Fool's Day, an irony not lost on Celtic fans further down the line. Within days, outlets had gone from reporting that Howe had been sounded out to speculating on whether he'd take charge of Celtic's remaining league fixtures or sit it out until the summer. It seemed a matter of when and not if he'd be taking over.

And then silence. And more silence. Interim boss John Kennedy took charge of ten Celtic fixtures, seeing out the season with meaningless matches, bar two Scottish Cup ties, the latter a 2-0 defeat to Rangers that consigned Celtic to a first trophyless campaign since 2009/10. The bleak run of virtual friendlies, played in empty stadiums, couldn't have been more different to the noise and excitement Ange Postecoglou and his players would bring in subsequent months. However, most Celtic fans may not have heard of Yokohama F. Marinos at this stage, never mind Postecoglou. They had their hearts set on Howe. Just like the bid for ten in a row, it all went up in smoke.

Leading Scottish journalists had known about Howe's decision to turn down Celtic's job offer the previous evening but the story wasn't released until they'd firmed up sources the following morning. The *Daily Mail*'s Stephen McGowan was the first out of the blocks, reporting that a deal for Howe, alongside trusted former colleagues Richard Hughes, Stephen Purches and Simon Weatherstone, had collapsed. McGowan cited Howe's inability to assemble the backroom team that he wanted as the reason.

Almost immediately, Celtic, desperate to get their side of the story across, started phoning around fan media outlets. Their version of events was that Howe had told the club weeks in advance that he was willing to become the new manager. He then asked for more time to assemble his backroom staff, with Celtic granting that request. He then informed them that he wouldn't be able to get his team together, with family obligations and contract complications at Bournemouth the main reasons.

The Englishman would later corroborate this at his Newcastle United unveiling, saying: 'I didn't want to take a job of such size, knowing the job needing to be done, on my own. I knew what was needed. There was no change of mind. I was open and honest with everyone connected.'

The conclusion to proceedings between Howe and Celtic was amicable but that was of little consolation to the Celtic support, who had been let down by the club's hierarchy once again. In isolation, it was a damaging affair. The club had put all, or at least most, of its eggs in one basket, waiting and waiting only to be left empty-handed just weeks out from the new season. When added to the list of blunders throughout the 2020/21 campaign, it was a complete disaster.

* * *

Celtic have had some bad seasons in the past. In 1994/95, under the late Tommy Burns, the club finished fourth in a ten-team top flight, winning just 11 of their 36 league matches. More recently, the Tony Mowbray campaign of 2009/10 promised much and delivered little, with the Englishman being sacked after a 4-0 drubbing away to St Mirren. Yet, when expectations are compared with reality, the 2020/21 season takes a fair bit of beating.

Led by club legend Neil Lennon, Celtic had entered the campaign on the brink of history and in a strong position to make the record books. The Hoops were on a run of nine successive league titles and 11 straight domestic trophies. Brendan Rodgers and Lennon had helped the club win three consecutive trebles, and a fourth was soon to be completed. Celtic were odds on to better the triumphs of the club's immortal Lisbon Lions (1965–74) and Rangers (1988–97) and become the first Scottish top-flight men's club to fulfil a decade of dominance.

However, the 2020/21 campaign didn't follow the pattern of the previous nine. For a start, Scottish football was played without fans due to the ongoing threat of Covid-19. The pandemic had cut the previous season short, with an average points per match calculation used to crown Celtic as nine-in-a-row champions. The pandemic would play a defining role in Celtic's bid for ten in a row, although many of the problems were self-imposed. Celtic's troubles weren't unique, but the club did seem to struggle without supporters more than most, as Lennon would be at pains to point out.

The tone for a season of blunders was set when full-back Boli Bolingoli decided to go against the club's pandemic protocols and travel to Spain without anyone's knowledge. His failure to quarantine on his return, playing in a draw at Kilmarnock, created a significant issue. When it became public knowledge, a livid Lennon let loose at the Belgian and maintained that the club couldn't have done more to maintain standards. Scotland's First Minister Nicola Sturgeon also blasted the defender and ordered Celtic not to play for at least seven days. Her message was simple and hit at the precarious nature of the situation as far as Scottish football was concerned: 'Consider today the yellow card; the next time, it will be the red card.' Bolingoli was never a viable option for Celtic again. He featured in just two more matches, both under Ange Postecoglou, and spent time on loan in Turkey and Russia before sealing a permanent move to Belgium's KV Mechelen.

Bolingoli's lapse wouldn't be Celtic's final Covid-related drama of the season. Before then, there would be plenty of on-field disasters that stole the headlines. The club exited the Champions League at the second qualifying round at home to Ferencváros – a team Postecoglou would get the better of a year later. After the damaging loss to the Hungarian champions, a furious Lennon blasted his players' attitudes, saying: 'My message to the players is we have to do better. Get your mentality right. Get your attitude right. If some of you don't want to be here then leave, and let us work with players who want to be here.'

If Lennon's intention was to jolt his team into action, it had the opposite effect. By the time Rangers had won the traditional New Year derby, the gap at the top was 19 points, and not in Celtic's favour. Europe had continued to be a disaster, with successive 4-1 defeats to Sparta Prague the low point in a Europa League campaign that brought just four points. The domestic cup dominance had also been ended by Ross County, who won 2-0 at Celtic Park in the League Cup last 16, after which Celtic fans protested against Lennon and key board members.

Further defeats to Ross County and St Mirren in the league would end Lennon's second spell as manager, but not before more damage had been caused. Somehow, the worst had still been saved for off-the-pitch matters as Celtic continued to lurch from disaster to disaster. If the club weren't taking down fan displays, they were putting out tweets sponsored by debt collectors. The biggest calamity was reserved for January when, at the height of the pandemic, the first team and supporting cast travelled to Dubai for a mid-season break. Winter trips to the United Arab Emirates had been in place since Brendan Rodgers' first campaign in 2017. They'd often worked, with Celtic arriving in the Middle East after bruising derby defeats to Rangers in 2019 and 2020 and soon getting back on track to win the league on their return. It was hoped that the same powers of recovery could be utilised in 2021 after the Ibrox defeat, but the mid-season trip was just as ill-advised as Bolingoli's several months earlier.

Dubai ended up killing off any faint hopes Celtic had of winning ten in a row. Injured defender Christopher Jullien tested positive on his return to Scotland, forcing 13 first-team players, Lennon and John Kennedy into isolation. A shadow team dropped further points at home to Hibernian and Livingston, and chief executive Peter Lawwell was forced into an excruciating apology in front of in-house club media. 'Clearly, it was a mistake,' he said. 'For that, I profoundly apologise to our supporters. Things haven't gone the way we wanted them to. The outcome is clearly very regrettable.'

The disharmony at the club was laid bare just days later when Lennon, fresh out of his ten-day isolation, reopened the wounds and let rip at anyone within a 50-mile radius of Celtic Park. 'We've been held to a far higher standard than any other club,' he said during a press conference. 'As soon as Celtic are deemed to do something wrong, bang, you're all wanting blood. It's absolutely scandalous. The fallout from this has been way too much. My apology is to the fans because 13 players and three staff had to isolate for ten days, which is ludicrous. I'm not apologising for anything else. I'm not apologising for going out there and training for a week. Everybody's negative, the whole squad's negative bar two players.'

The final comment confirmed suspicions that Lennon still didn't understand the gravity of the situation. The Northern Irishman achieved so much in his near two decades at the club, contributing 21 trophies, including ten league titles as player and manager. There's no doubt that the 2020/21 campaign tarnished that legacy, but hopefully in time he'll be remembered for the good rather than the bad.

Lennon didn't see the end of the campaign, leaving the club on 24 February 2021 with Celtic 18 points adrift of Rangers. That gap would extend to 25 by the end of the season, with a new manager tasked with the seemingly impossible challenge of bridging the gap to a Rangers team that hadn't lost a league match all season. On top of the domestic issues, the new boss had to find a way to make Celtic competitive in Europe again.

The task seemed a challenge, even for someone of Howe's standing. When it emerged that he wouldn't be moving to Glasgow, things looked bleaker still. Yet all hope wasn't lost. In frantic calls to fan media outlets, the club had revealed that it was in advanced talks with an alternative candidate. Within hours, it became clear this person was Ange Postecoglou, the Aussie currently managing Yokohama F. Marinos in Japan's J1 League. Amid all of the Howe fallout, Postecoglou was very much an afterthought.

* * *

It was the City Football Group (CFG) link that brought Postecoglou to the attention of Celtic. Long-time Hoops chief executive Peter Lawwell's son, Mark, held an important role at CFG – the multi-club ownership that includes Manchester City, New York City and, crucially, Yokohama F. Marinos. Lawwell Jnr's position as head of CFG scouting and recruitment had helped to create an informal link between Celtic and Manchester City, which allowed several prodigious talents from the City academy to pass through Celtic's door. Patrick Roberts, Jeremie Frimpong and Jason Denayer were just three of the youngsters who became fan favourites in Glasgow and furthered their own careers. It wasn't just a one-way street either. CFG also benefited from the connection, with former Hoops boss Ronny Deila leading New York City to their first MLS Cup in 2021, with another ex-Celt, Efraín Juárez, as his assistant. In September 2021, former Celtic defender Gary Caldwell was appointed as loans coach at Manchester City.

Celtic's version of events is that the Lawwell connection was key in bringing Postecoglou to Glasgow, although it is worth noting that the club were happy for Dom McKay to take the credit during his days in office. Another viable explanation, reported by the likes of Sky Sports at the time, is that Postecoglou had been recommended to Celtic by Fergal Harkin, the Manchester City football partnerships manager who looked destined for a role in Glasgow. Wherever the truth lies, it's clear that Celtic's relationship with CFG was vital.

CFG is all about connections. Established in May 2013, at the time of writing, it has complete or partial ownership of 12 clubs in all corners of the globe: Manchester City (England), New York City (USA), Melbourne City (Australia), Yokohama F. Marinos (Japan), Montevideo City Torque (Uruguay), Girona (Spain), Sichuan Jiuniu (China), Mumbai City (India), Lommel SK (Belgium), Troyes (France), Palermo (Italy) and Club Bolívar (Bolivia). All CFG clubs strive to play an attacking brand of football, which aims to attract supporters, while remaining sustainable in the long term. Postecoglou is a popular figure inside the organisation, given his work with F. Marinos. He's highly rated by many at Manchester City, including manager Pep Guardiola, who praised Marinos' style of play after a friendly in 2019. The group has its fair share of detractors, although not nearly as many as the Red Bull family, but it's hard to argue with the recent domestic success of the likes of Manchester City, New York City and Melbourne City. The story of how Postecoglou ended up in Glasgow is a complex one. Australian broadcaster David Davutovic best clarified it in a May 2022 article for Aussie outlet KEEPUP.

The article explains that, in many ways, it was a perfect storm that led to the ideal appointment. Howe, CFG, AEK Athens and more contributed to the end result – a little known Aussie standing on the Celtic Park touchline in late June holding the doomed 2020/21 home shirt, one final reminder of the previous campaign.

As Davutovic explains, the critical factor was that Postecoglou wanted a change. After success in Australia and Japan, he felt it was time for his family to move to Europe to take on the next challenge. Despite most Celtic fans not being aware of Postecoglou's work at the likes of Brisbane Roar and for the Australia national team, those in key positions inside the club knew all about his exploits and had been tracking him for years. His progressive playing style was closely aligned with Celtic's, while his overall knowledge of the game and high standards were also desirable qualities. When the board started hunting for their successor to Neil Lennon, Postecoglou's name was on their mind. Yet there was an obvious issue: his name wasn't well known in Scotland.

Pressure from supporters looking for a box-office appointment akin to Brendan Rodgers five years earlier had led the board down the Eddie Howe road. In the meantime, Greek giants AEK Athens had shown an interest in taking

Postecoglou back to the city of his birth. The prospect of landing a job at one of the big three clubs in his homeland was enticing for Postecoglou, and it was seen as a good first step back into European football. When the Super League club instead went for Vladan Milojević, someone who would last just three months in the job, Postecoglou's dreams were crushed again. AEK's decision was their loss as they finished a distant fifth in the Greek Super League, missing out on European football altogether. It was also Celtic's gain.

When the club's lengthy pursuit of Howe collapsed, Postecoglou quickly became the new preferred candidate. He spoke to key decision-makers at the club, such as outgoing chief executive Lawwell, his replacement Dom McKay and majority shareholder Dermot Desmond, and impressed every single one. 'We had a list of five, and Ange was on the list,' said Desmond in a rare Celtic TV appearance nearly a year later:

> I had no idea who Ange was. I couldn't pronounce his name. Peter was insistent he was a person we should put on the list, that he had a great record. We pursued another manager in public. He was excellent to deal with, a person of ability and integrity, I couldn't say enough good things about him. But, unfortunately, for personal reasons, he couldn't take up the position. That happened at 12.30pm on a Thursday, and I made arrangements to speak with Ange at 5pm UK time. I should say, prior to that, I researched quite a bit about Ange and what he'd achieved, what his type of personality is. I watched that Craig Foster interview several times. That showed me his determination, integrity, passion and individualism. And that he was a leader. He was a general. I was very pleased to interview Ange.

As his foray on to the infamous Foster exchange proves, Desmond was as unaware of Postecoglou's credentials as virtually every Celtic fan. Yet, after the call, he'd made up his mind. Postecoglou was the ideal choice to lead Celtic back to glory. The deal was sealed with some inspirational lyrics from Scottish music duo The Proclaimers.

Desmond: 'I said to him, "Celtic, as we all know, is more than a club. It can't just be a mercenary role, that you are coming in here, taking the money, using it as a stepping stone, using it as career development rather than a club you want to intimately pursue and manage." He gave this great reply. He said, "In the words of The Proclaimers, I will walk 500 miles, and I will walk 500 more to manage Celtic."' When the quotes were put to Celtic's manager, the response was typically restrained. 'To be fair, I did just say it. I didn't sing it, just so people are fully aware.'

The Celtic gig being Postecoglou's just days after the AEK Athens rejection proved remarkable timing – a genuine sliding-doors moment for the Greek team, the Aussie and his new employers. Celtic agreed compensation with Yokohama F. Marinos, who didn't stand in their manager's way, and on the morning of Thursday, 10 June 2021, a fortnight on from the Eddie Howe collapse, Postecoglou was confirmed as the club's 19th permanent manager.

There wasn't much fanfare following the announcement. Little did the Celtic support know that the day would go down as one of the most momentous in the club's recent history. The overwhelming feeling at the time was one of uncertainty. Postecoglou's lack of top-level European experience made him a risky appointment. Yet his track record of proven success and silverware since taking the Brisbane Roar job in 2009 hinted that Celtic might have found a gem. In hindsight, it's pretty astonishing that no major European club hired Postecoglou before Celtic.

The reports from those who knew him were glowing, with very few people having a bad word to say. Celtic fans were about to get the chance to form their own opinion, with Postecoglou set for his debut in front of the media. It was the start of an improbable period that saw apathy turn to belief. Before then, he had to get himself to Scotland. During the ongoing pandemic, that was more of a challenge than usual.

CHAPTER 3

The Hilarious Takes They Will Now Be Trying to Bury

*'We now know what the Ange in
Ange Postecoglou stands for. Absolutely.
Not. Good. Enough.'*

Hugh Keevins

IN THE period between Ange Postecoglou's name first being mentioned in connection with Celtic and his team picking up some momentum, everyone had an opinion. Scottish football's most notorious pundits chimed in with their thoughts on Postecoglou, Celtic and what was to come. Many wrote off the Aussie because they'd never heard of him. Others simply underrated his abilities.

Some are still guilty of that. Most people commented on anonymous forums or down the pub, with little accountability. Unfortunately, those included in this chapter were speaking more publicly.

* * *

John Hartson was a terrific Celtic player. He netted 110 goals for the club over a five-and-a-half-year period and contributed to six domestic league titles. Since retiring, he's fought Celtic's corner regularly as part of the Scottish media. He's a genuinely decent man, adored by supporters, so regretfully we include an early assertion he made on Ange Postecoglou:

> No disrespect to Ange Postecoglou. He comes with some raving reports. He's a disciplinarian and plays on the front foot and attacking football, which sounds great if you're going to manage Celtic. I look at the situation and think he's managed the Australia youth side. He's managed the national side. He's currently managing in Japan. I just think Celtic need to be thinking bigger in terms of their next manager.
> (Go Radio)

To be fair to Hartson, many felt the same way when Postecoglou's name was first discussed. Weeks later, another ex-Celt, Kris Commons, was conceding the title to Rangers. Celtic had just lost their league opener at Tynecastle, and Commons reckoned that Postecoglou had little chance of turning things around:

> This is without question the worst Celtic team we've seen in well over 20 years. You would need to go back to the dark days of the early to mid-90s for anything to even get close. Celtic had an abundance of time to prepare for the summer rebuild. Yet, eight months down the line, they have handed Postecoglou a donkey in what already looks like a one-horse race once again. I would be astonished if Celtic got anywhere near Rangers this season. I felt like things couldn't get any worse after last season, but now I'm not so sure.
> (*Scottish Daily Mail*)

In hindsight, Commons' remarks after just one league fixture were premature. They haven't aged well, but it's important to remember the doom and gloom surrounding everything Celtic were doing at the time. Six months later, the former Celtic attacker's view had changed entirely:

> There's now a ruthlessness to this Celtic team. A relentless streak which, from their position at the top of the table, means it's now their title to lose. They have all the momentum. Celtic are now the pacesetters. They are the best team in the league right now, and it's up to Rangers to catch them.
> (*Scottish Daily Mail*)

Unsurprisingly, the most infamous case of sheer Postecoglou ignorance was found on talkSPORT. The radio station specialises in bold ill-informed claims that tempt listeners into phoning up or sharing their clips on social media. In the days after Postecoglou's name was first mentioned, a clip showed footballer turned broadcaster Alan Brazil mocking his credentials. At the time, there had been reports of the Aussie not having the required licence to manage in Europe.

> Is this a wind-up? Breaking news from Scotland as Celtic have applied for an exemption with UEFA for Yokohama Marinos boss Postacoogloo [sic] to manage in Europe. He does not hold the required UEFA Pro Licence. Oh, this has got to be a wind-up. Dear oh dear. He'll be a great manager. Where do they come up with these guys from?
> (talkSPORT)

The former Scotland international had played against Postecoglou's South Melbourne years earlier, not that he'd be likely to recall. As with virtually everyone in this chapter, he was found apologising at some stage over the following 12 months. A similar story of reprieve occurred with another former footballer who enjoyed his heyday in the 1980s – Charlie Nicholas:

31

There's nothing wrong with having a plan B – but this is not plan B. This is desperation. I will give Postecoglou a chance because I'm a supporter but is the former Australia boss really the height of the club's ambitions? It has nothing to do with his lack of knowledge of the Scottish game or me looking down on football in the southern hemisphere. It scares me just how unambitious the club has become, going from a position of strength to where they find themselves now. Luring Postecoglou from Yokohama F. Marinos is not quite the same as when Arsène Wenger left Japanese football to join Arsenal in 1996.

(*Daily Express*)

Nicholas was at it again in late September. Celtic had just been held to a 1-1 draw at home by Dundee United and had three league wins from seven matches. The knives were out for Postecoglou, with many reaching some wild conclusions:

Ange Postecoglou looks to me to be the new Ronny Deila. I am not sure Postecoglou has realised how big Celtic really are before he came in. I believe he has missed a pitch. I think Ange thought he would just come in here, and his playing style would get him over the line, no problem. But it is not about style. It is about winning.

(*Daily Express*)

Nicholas and Postecoglou would meet by chance in Glasgow months later. By that stage the Aussie had won the former Celtic striker over. Just as well:

We had a wee five-minute conversation where I thanked him for the job he is doing and what he is building at Celtic.

(*Daily Express*)

Former Rangers and Scotland forward Kris Boyd is perhaps the most controversial pundit currently operating in Scottish football, so it was pretty likely that he'd have something to say in Postecoglou's early weeks. After Celtic exited the Champions League to Midtjylland, he didn't disappoint:

> Ange Postecoglou has no authority at Celtic, no backing, no support from the board, and virtually no chance of being successful. Unless things change, there's no point in him being there.
> (*Scottish Sun*)

Boyd at least has media inexperience on his side. Veteran journalist Hugh Keevins has no such excuse after he delivered perhaps the most remarkable lack of foresight around the same period:

> At the very least, we now know what the Ange in Ange Postecoglou stands for. Absolutely. Not. Good. Enough.
> (*Daily Record*)

CHAPTER 4

Believing in Ange

'You're assuming I was second choice.
I might have been fifth choice.'
Ange Postecoglou

ANGE POSTECOGLOU may not have expected such a warm welcome from the Celtic faithful. It's about 7pm in the east end of Glasgow, and Celtic's new manager is walking along the touchline at his new home. It's a roasting hot summer evening in Paradise, so warm that the club has been handing out complimentary cartons of water to supporters. Postecoglou has just completed his obligatory pre-match television duties with broadcasters Premier Sports and is making his way back to the inner parts of the stadium. He stops in his tracks. Everyone inside the ground is standing and showing support for him. There are only 9,000 in attendance due to pandemic-enforced restrictions, yet Celtic Park may as well be full given the noise. The stadium is making its first collective noise in nearly 18 months. Postecoglou raises a single fist to the sky.

His Celtic team are preparing for their first competitive match of the season: a Champions League second qualifying round clash against Danish Superliga runners-up FC Midtjylland. New season hopes are high, yet they're matched by a realisation that the tie may have come too soon for a team in transition. The weeks prior to Postecoglou's Celtic Park bow had been filled with concern and uncertainty. As Celtic fans wrestled with the idea of an unfancied name taking over their club at a critical juncture and fans of rival clubs poked fun, those from Postecoglou's homeland offered some much-needed hope for the future. To them he was a known quantity, someone who had coached their greatest club side ever and led their national team to their first major trophy. Those who knew of Postecoglou believed in his ability to make a success of it at Celtic, although few would have expected it to happen so quickly. Their optimism was vital amid heaps of local cynicism.

Unlike Brendan Rodgers and Rangers pair Steven Gerrard and Giovanni van Bronckhorst, Postecoglou didn't arrive in Scotland with a high-profile reputation. As a result, inaccuracies such as him not holding the necessary UEFA Pro Licence to coach in Europe, newspaper exclusives with disgruntled former players and badly misjudged tirades from media personalities were rife. When Alan Brazil claimed news of Postecoglou's appointment 'had to be a wind-up' live on radio station talkSPORT, he had Ally McCoist and an entire studio in fits of laughter. Months later, he apologised.

Other nonsense from various outlets, such as the *Daily Record*'s Keith Jackson claiming Postecoglou 'could be the best thing to come out of Australia since Kylie Minogue's hot pants' didn't feel particularly helpful. Yet, the media's job wasn't to help. Postecoglou maintains that he wasn't bothered by the initial negativity, but his resolve may have been strengthened by the refreshing perspective from down under. Celtic supporters were frantically trying to find out more about their new manager from those who knew him, and virtually every report was glowing.

The issue of support towards Postecoglou in his early days isn't a black-and-white matter despite many being keen to portray it that way. Celtic fans weren't outside the stadium with pitchforks following his arrival, nor were they completely overjoyed at the club hiring a man with little experience of European football. Despite all the uncertainty, season tickets sold out again. By the time the Midtjylland tie rolled around, they were on board with their new leader. Part of that backing was a lack of other options. When Postecoglou was appointed, there was a feeling that the only productive option was to fully back him and see how things went. The media's brutal assessment of his credentials also fuelled the fire. Then Postecoglou opened his mouth, and belief soared. It became clear that high standards had returned to the club.

When you look at the authority Celtic's boss exudes from the dugout nowadays, it's hard to fathom the level of doubt that existed early on. While we'll investigate Postecoglou's impressive spells at Brisbane Roar, Australia and Yokohama F. Marinos in more depth in later chapters, an initial look at his pre-Celtic CV showed a respectable track record. He'd achieved wonderful things in some jobs, while others hadn't gone quite so well. Despite the good times being more frequent than the bad, there was always a niggling doubt. If Postecoglou was so good, why had no one else in Europe taken a punt?

Of course, the details were vital in understanding the complete picture. While many may debate the merits of footballing success in a country like Australia, the A-League salary cap rarely allows for sparkling success stories like Roarcelona – the affectionate name given to Postecoglou's Brisbane Roar team of 2009 to 2012. As his close mate Andy Harper put it to me: 'You're trying to make a silk purse out of a sow's ear in Australia.' Postecoglou had succeeded in making a team that was different from anything the league had seen before and probably ever will.

In Japan, leading Yokohama F. Marinos to the J1 League title in 2019, 15 years after their previous success, was probably an even more significant achievement. In one of the most competitive leagues on the planet, in terms of different champions, it was seen as one of the most outstanding achievements by an Aussie coach. Yet, while those two magical club stories and the 2015 Asian Cup win had taken place firmly away from the gaze of European football, the displays of Postecoglou's Socceroos at the 2014 World Cup were evidence that he could manage at the highest level.

Despite reports to the contrary, Postecoglou was well aware of what Celtic had encountered over the previous year. He'd started work from the minute he knew his future lay in Glasgow, even though his journey to the city had been challenging. After sorting contractual issues, Postecoglou's arrival from Marinos was confirmed by Celtic on 10 June 2021. He arrived in England and underwent a period of quarantine through the UK government's Test to Release scheme. During the spell in isolation, he was introduced to more key figures at the club via Zoom, and gave an interview for Celtic TV, saying: 'Ultimately, the people there have got to believe in me before they believe in any of my ideas. I'm trying to meet as many people as I can before I get there. The sense I get is that everyone's looking forward to it. It's a fresh start, a new beginning, and I think when that happens, it gives me a chance to set a tone from the beginning.'

In any normal world, arrival from Japan would have been a straightforward exercise. During the pandemic and an era of testing and quarantining, it would take until 18 June before an image of the Celtic boss emerged. Even then it came from London in the form of a first meeting with newly appointed chief executive Dom McKay. Postecoglou and McKay were meeting to 'continue working on preparations for the new season' as the club put it. That evening they were at Wembley as Celtic's Callum McGregor put in a sumptuous display in Scotland's Euro 2020 clash with England. We'll never know what early discussions Postecoglou and McKay had or what the former thought of the match as the Scots held Gareth Southgate's eventual runners-up to a 0-0 draw. But McGregor's performance must have given Postecoglou food for thought, with the Celtic captaincy up for grabs following Scott Brown's move to Aberdeen.

Postecoglou's mind was far from the Euros, though. In the days after Scotland were eliminated by Josip Juranovic's Croatia, despite a brilliant McGregor goal, Celtic's boss visited the club's Lennoxtown training complex for the first time. 'The last thing people would have wanted to see when they first met me, particularly at the stage we were in, was to see a guy who was in a panic,' he'd later tell Sky Sports. 'I felt that it was really important that when I came in they saw somebody who was ready to get on with it and pretty clear about the direction we were going.'

He met the squad, at least what was left of it, and immediately let them know what would be expected of them. Of the 15 or so players in attendance at that first session, only Anthony Ralston, Stephen Welsh and Nir Bitton would go on to play any meaningful part in the coming season. 'The key thing for me is that people believe in me,' he reiterated to *The Scotsman* in his early weeks at the club. 'I don't say that in an egotistical way. Whatever message I'm trying to give, whatever I'm trying to do, it won't happen unless people believe in me. That's what I've found in management.'

If belief was what Postecoglou craved, there was soon plenty of it to be found. There was a belief in the air when he got his ovation before the Midtjylland match. It was the same when he strolled into his first meeting with the media three weeks earlier.

* * *

There was nervousness as we sat together in a vast function room inside Celtic Park. The iconic stadium was a vastly different place from the last time most of us had visited. On that occasion, Leigh Griffiths had netted a hat-trick to seal a 5-0 win over St Mirren to move Neil Lennon's team 16 points clear at the top of the Premiership. The points were to be Celtic's last of the campaign, with the world shutting down six days later. Celtic had been declared winners of the curtailed 2019/20 season two months later, equalling the Scottish men's record of nine titles in succession, but had seen their bid for the historic ten go up in smoke. Players had been signed by the club, failed miserably and departed without ever being seen in the flesh by a single supporter. Unsurprisingly, the club was just as keen as us to look to the future amid a genuine hope that the coming season would be far more fruitful than the last.

On this Friday afternoon in late June, Celtic were holding a series of media events to unveil Postecoglou as the club's new manager. The Aussie had only arrived in Scotland a couple of days earlier and was about to be thrown in at the deep end. He'd meet the Scottish broadcast media in a conference streamed live by the club before taking on fan media in the main event downstairs. The written press and photographers would also be taken care of later in the day.

Many will try to rewrite the history surrounding Postecoglou's announcement and arrival. The truth is that it was an exciting time to be a Celtic fan. There was work to be done, but also genuine hope in following Celtic for the first time in over a year. That only increased when the Australian first opened his mouth in front of Scotland's renowned media outlets. As we watched Postecoglou's debut from upstairs on a large television, it immediately became clear that he'd suffer no fools in Scotland. If the country's leading football journalists had undertaken anything close to the same research route as Dermot Desmond, they'd have become aware very quickly that Postecoglou can give as good as he gets in front of the media. Ignorance and ill-advised assumptions wouldn't wash with Celtic's new leader. They were about to get an experience first-hand. His first victim was the BBC's Chris McLaughlin.

McLaughlin: 'Much has been made about the jump this is for you, perhaps. How big a jump do you think this is in terms of your career? Also, quite a lot has been made about the pressure of being the Celtic manager. What are your expectations of that?'

Postecoglou: 'I'm not sure what you mean by "jump", but I'm assuming you're saying I worked at a lower level. I guess that's a matter of opinion. I've coached at a World Cup, I've coached against some of the best teams in the world, so that's not how I look at it. You talk about pressure. If I didn't want pressure I'd probably be doing a different kind of occupation or would have stayed coaching my local club with my friends. I'm here because this is where I want to be, this is where I want to coach, this is where I want to have success. I think I'll get judged on what happens moving forward rather than what's happened in the past.'

The dignified demolition of the journalist's question was a sign of what was to come. It wouldn't be the last time Postecoglou put one of Scotland's leading reporters in their place. Downstairs, the chatter was intensifying. Celtic's new manager was impressive. Postecoglou also dealt expertly with the Eddie Howe-shaped elephant in the room. Given that Celtic's pursuit of Howe had been so public, with the Englishman even named in the club statement confirming a breakdown in talks, it was only natural that Postecoglou would be quizzed.

Sky Sports reporter Mark Benstead: 'I'll ask this question as delicately as I can. I hope you won't take offence to it. The club spoke to another candidate before turning to you. On face value perhaps you weren't their first choice. Does that put you out, or does that act as extra motivation to prove them right now?'

Postecoglou: 'That was very delicate, the way you put it. You're assuming I was second choice. I might have been fifth choice. It doesn't really bother me. For me, what's important is that I've been given the responsibility and the opportunity. That fact alone shows that the people who made this decision have faith in me. That's all I need.'

The conference lasted just over 30 minutes. Postecoglou batted away questions on various issues, with mentions for the 25-point deficit to Rangers, his backroom team and even, bizarrely, Gordon Strachan. His message was simple and consistent throughout: people would be in no doubt about how his team played football, and that style would give them the best chance of success. The common feeling among my Celtic media colleagues, huddled downstairs, was that Postecoglou had passed his first test with flying colours. As he entered the vast room where we were situated, alongside Dom McKay, minutes later, it was perhaps no surprise to hear a smattering of applause.

Notably, under-fire chairman Ian Bankier, who had joined the pair in the upstairs conference, was absent as fan media got their chance to ask some crucial questions. McKay and Postecoglou were the forward-thinking faces of Celtic Football Club. A pair of outsiders, one from another continent and the other from an entirely different sport.

The appointment of McKay as Celtic's chief executive had been announced in late January, at the end of a torrid month. The club had won just one of their six matches in the period, a run that could be attributed to the ridiculous decision to venture to Dubai for a mid-season training camp during the height of the pandemic. The excursion to the Middle East had been widely condemned, including by the club's supporters, with long-serving chief executive Peter Lawwell forced into an embarrassing apology shortly before announcing his exit from the role. By the time Celtic had announced Lawwell's departure and McKay's arrival, it felt more like a desperate attempt to ease fan pressure than a proactive move. While many still hold Lawwell in high regard for the 18 years of mainly domestic dominance he presided over, the final months of his time in the role certainly tarnished his legacy.

McKay was a 'long-term season ticket holder' at Celtic Park, as the club was keen to point out in its statement. His background was in rugby, as the chief operating officer of the Scottish Rugby Union (SRU). He'd helped transform the fortunes of Scottish rugby and its two professional clubs – Glasgow Warriors and Edinburgh Rugby – and it was hoped that he could do the same at Celtic. McKay had forged a reputation as a pioneer, with his ability to think outside the box particularly desirable given the rut Celtic found themselves in. He'd presided over a period of substantial growth for rugby in Scotland. Under his stewardship, Murrayfield, the largest sports stadium in Scotland, had become one of the hottest tickets in town, with Scotland selling out all three Six Nations home matches for the first time in 2017. The SRU had sold the 67,000-seater arena's naming rights to telecoms giant BT in 2014, and the stadium had found ways to make money away from the sport as well. Madonna, One Direction and Robbie Williams played to sold-out crowds during McKay's time at the helm, while the stadium had also made its mark in football.

McKay ticked many boxes, with the only obvious flaw his lack of experience in football. Time would prove that McKay and Celtic weren't a good fit. He lasted just 72 days in the role, with the club citing 'personal reasons' in a shock mid-September announcement. While the finer details of the split are unlikely ever to be made public, numerous respected journalists reported that McKay was pushed to quit before he was sacked. It had become very clear from the early days that the appointment was a mistake, and club chiefs were forced to act.

McKay came across as a warm, genuine person in any private interactions we shared. He was a strong proponent of fan media, which continues at Celtic today. In the weeks after his arrival, he phoned around every fan media outlet just to introduce himself. He also helped make some improvements to the football structure at the club, with several specific roles created that would pay dividends for Postecoglou in the long run. Like every board member at Celtic, he'd been damaged badly by the Eddie Howe fiasco. It's perhaps no surprise that he was keen to attach himself to Postecoglou in the early days, despite what we now know about how Ange wound up in Glasgow.

Postecoglou would form a closer bond with McKay's replacement Michael Nicholson, someone he'd been working with in his early days at the club. 'It didn't really disrupt me,' he told the press months later. 'Michael was pretty integral in all of that, anyway. He was somebody I already knew, and we were already working together. He was one of the key people in all transfers we did. He's the one that does all the legal work, all the paperwork, and a lot of the negotiating. So there was no real change there. From my perspective, there was nothing that would hamper us moving forward.'

Back in late June, with McKay by his side, Postecoglou spoke for the best part of an hour with various Celtic fan media outlets. Fan media doesn't tend to rely on the shock or scandal factor to turn a profit in the way newspapers or mainstream broadcasters are forced to. Many fan media platforms make little or no money, while others have loyal fans who pay monthly subscriptions to hear what fellow supporters have to say. As a result, there was no mention of Eddie Howe or the supposed 'jump' Ange had or hadn't taken in moving to Glasgow. Celtic fans just wanted to know more about the two men their club had employed, and fan media gave each party a chance to connect. That's not to say that the questions were soft. The opener quizzed McKay on whether events and better communication with supporters would continue once season ticket money had been gathered. Issues such as the return of fans to Celtic Park and recruitment were also tackled, while Postecoglou addressed the reaction he'd received since coming to the country. Celtic's new boss ended the event with the declaration: 'Best press conference ever.'

McKay was pleasant and charming and had done this kind of thing before. In contrast, Postecoglou didn't offer the world. As comfortable as he was dealing with the media, you got the impression that he'd much rather be out on the Lennoxtown surface coaching his new players and gearing them up to do their talking on the pitch. Walking away from Celtic Park that day, the overwhelming feeling was that Celtic had a manager who would take responsibility and give his all for the furtherment of the club. Postecoglou had some of the belief that he craved.

It was no longer just the Aussies who understood him, even if it was still early days.

* * *

For all of the talk of Celtic having time on their side in their pursuit of a new manager, Postecoglou's first meeting with the media arrived just three and a half weeks before the first competitive match of the season against Midtjylland. By this time, fans knew a lot more about Postecoglou's methods, with the club's decision to release footage of a mic'd-up Lennoxtown training session one of their best they made all season. 'Just get it into your heads, we never stop,' Postecoglou was heard saying to his players. 'We never stop. We'll stop at half-time, and we'll stop at the end of the game when we celebrate. But during the game, we don't stop.'

Few could have foreseen how prophetic the words would prove to be over the following seasons. The footage gave supporters a peek behind the curtain at what Postecoglou was like and added to the growing sense of excitement. Opposition fans mocked, but they weren't laughing the next time Postecoglou uttered the three vital words in public at the end of the season.

A squad not even close to resembling the one that would lift the Premiership trophy that day ventured to Wales for an intense training camp and some friendly matches. They trained hard, almost always with a ball, and showed bright glimpses in wins over Sheffield Wednesday and Charlton Athletic at Newport's Dragon Park. A dull goalless draw with Bristol City, marred by an ankle break to Karamoko Dembele, and a 1-0 home loss to Scott Sinclair's Preston North End reminded the Hoops faithful that there would be no quick fix under their new boss.

Progress was slow in the transfer market. For all the ridicule that Celtic's stars had been subjected to during the failed 2020/21 campaign, there was still a lot of quality that walked out of the club around the time of Postecoglou's arrival.

Kristoffer Ajer and Odsonne Edouard were sold to Premier League teams Brentford and Crystal Palace, respectively. Shane Duffy, Jonjoe Kenny and Moi Elyounoussi returned to their parent clubs in the same league, while Ryan Christie signed for a Bournemouth team that were promoted to England's top tier ten months later. Scott Brown's decision to leave the club after 14 years of service to become a player-coach at Aberdeen left an even more significant void.

A summer of upheaval followed. Brown was succeeded as captain by Callum McGregor. Ajer's direct replacement was Carl Starfelt, with the capture of the Rubin Kazan man announced minutes after the Norwegian's departure. Edouard wasn't sold until the final day of the summer window. By then, Kyogo Furuhashi had already become Celtic's main man after sealing his move from Japan's Vissel Kobe. Shane Duffy and Moi Elyounoussi were arguably upgraded by the deadline-day signings of Cameron Carter-Vickers and Jota, initially on loan from Tottenham Hotspur and Benfica, with permanent deals concluded a year later. Josip Juranovic was a sizeable improvement on Jonjoe Kenny, while the further signings of Joe Hart, James McCarthy and Giorgos Giakoumakis added experience and quality. Long-term contracts were a theme, even with older players such as Hart and McCarthy.

Yet, by the time the Midtjylland first leg had rolled around, only teenage Israeli winger Liel Abada was signed and available to play. In truth, Postecoglou would probably have been worthy of a statue on the Celtic Way had he been able to oust the team that had missed out on the Danish title by a single point just weeks earlier. While the previous season had been extremely damaging, it allowed Postecoglou to take the squad in a new direction with very little resistance from the players. Amid all the negativity, he was supremely confident in his ability to turn Celtic's fortunes around. Deep down, even at this early stage, Postecoglou felt he had to deliver something tangible in his first season at the club. Vague progress wouldn't be enough, and the prospect of the Premiership winners gaining automatic entry to the following season's Champions League group stage was extra motivation.

CHAPTER 5

The Journey, Part 1: Rollercoaster

*'If this is your idea of relaxation, I'd hate
to think what would happen if you went
on holiday.'*

Ange Postecoglou

STANDING AT an immense 456ft, the Kingda Ka is the tallest rollercoaster in the world. Thrill-seekers who venture to New Jersey encounter one of the craziest coasters in the world – a ride that goes from 0–128mph in just three and a half seconds. The entire experience lasts just under a minute but features tremendous highs and sickening lows, all on an upside-down 'U' more than 100 metres high in the sky. Willing participants experience a ride unlike any other in the world.

If Ange Postecoglou views the journey of his football team as a rollercoaster, then the early weeks of the 2021/22 season saw Celtic riding the Kingda Ka. At times, the start of the Postecoglou reign felt even more chaotic. Celtic's first 18 matches brought disappointment, hope, frustration and dismay, then, finally, a reason to be optimistic.

The most recent result dictated entire opinions on players, staff and board members. Celtic went from apparent title contenders to a team occupying the bottom half of the table. Players went from being the next big thing to plainly not being good enough. Some staff members didn't even make it out of the period with their jobs intact. At the front of it all was Postecoglou, trying to build an exciting, winning team while facing his own questions.

There was an understanding among the Celtic supporters that change wouldn't happen overnight. Early defeats would have to be taken on the chin, as former Hoops boss Tony Mowbray would regularly say during his tenure. Losing wasn't made any easier by this realisation, yet a sense of the bigger picture was key amid the erratic nature of results. Around this period, the phrase 'trust the process' first entered the consciousness of the Celtic support. The expression would be muttered regularly during Postecoglou's first campaign and beyond, often offering comfort in times of need.

The expression wasn't used solely in the stands either. Midway through the season, defender Osaze Urhoghide revealed that Postecoglou had uttered the words when addressing the team in his early weeks. The message had been to ignore the external noise and focus on the fundamental principles that would bring about improvement. Control what you can control and embrace the topsy-turvy journey on the rollercoaster. Postecoglou told me early on in his second season:

> It's not like I walk around with a Maxwell Smart cone of silence on me. I need to be intuitive as to what people are thinking around the place, whether that's outside our organisation, what our fans think, what the media may think, what other coaches or teams may think about us. I think it's important. Does that affect my mindset or what I think? Not really, because ultimately, what's really important is the group that are before me, what we say and the way we conduct ourselves. What you find is that when there's a singular focus, people then understand that the really important communication channels are the ones that they see and hear on a daily

basis within the four walls rather than what's on the outside.

There was perhaps no time when Celtic needed that singular focus more than after the 4-0 loss at home to Bayer Leverkusen in the Europa League. The defeat to the Bundesliga high-flyers was a painful one, made worse by the attacking performance being largely encouraging. Celtic had created several clear-cut opportunities, perhaps as many as the Germans, but a combination of poor finishing and lax defending had created the sobering four-goal gap.

As Celtic's bruised players walked around the Parkhead surface after the loss, many fans stayed to applaud them, not too dissimilar to the Real Madrid defeat 12 months later. The big picture was that the Celtic supporters were still on board with the project, and the players were still buying into what their manager wanted. The aftermath of the match would prove to be the turning point in the season, with the squad using the defeat as part of the journey that would lead them to two trophies and the Champions League group stage.

* * *

Celtic 1-1 Midtjylland, UEFA Champions League qualifying, Celtic Park, Tuesday, 20 July 2021

Postecoglou's first experience of the UEFA Champions League could hardly have been more different to the visit of Real Madrid. The starting line-up that the new Celtic boss fielded in his first competitive match against the Danish league runners-up Midtjylland barely resembled the one that would take to the pitch against Carlo Ancelotti's European champions more than a year down the line. Only Greg Taylor, Callum McGregor and Liel Abada started both matches, with David Turnbull the other to feature in each match. Taking gradual steps can often cloud the overall sense of progress. If you ever want an accurate measure of the improvement Postecoglou has made, imagine how his first starting line-up, with Vasilis Barkas and Ismaila Soro, would have fared against Real Madrid.

The playing personnel wasn't the only difference on this first experience of the Champions League either. UEFA doesn't deem the early qualifying rounds worthy of their sleek branding or iconic pre-match anthem. The scorching summer weather, bright sky and pandemic-restricted crowd made the occasion feel more like a pre-season friendly than a crucial Champions League qualifier. Everyone has to start somewhere.

Despite the circumstances, there was still the fresh hope that only the first match of a new season can bring. Supporters flocked to Celtic Park, many for the first time in over a year, with a feeling of promise. In retrospect, Postecoglou would probably have been worthy of a statue on the Celtic Way had he found a way to oust the Danes.

Midtjylland were hardly elite-level European opposition, but they'd been playing in the Champions League group stage just seven months prior, holding Atalanta and Liverpool to draws. They had the familiar face of former Celtic defender Erik Sviatchenko at the back and the talented Denmark international Pione Sisto. Postecoglou knew all about the opposition due to an Aussie connection: attacker Awer Mabil.

'There's no doubt you're not going to see the team flying like I want them to in the first Champions League game,' had been his message to me at the unveiling weeks earlier. 'At the same time, that's not to say that we can't make significant progress quickly.'

What followed was an entertaining match featuring two goals and two red cards shared equally between the teams. Debutant Liel Abada gave Celtic the lead five minutes before half-time when he latched on to a rebound from a Ryan Christie shot. The instinctive finish from Abada was the kind fans would get used to seeing from him. Postecoglou's high-fives with his backroom team John Kennedy, Gavin Strachan and Stephen McManus would also become a theme of the season.

The goal had been a reward for an impressive attacking showing from Postecoglou's men. Celtic's attack wasn't the issue, though. The problem was the team continuing to shoot themselves in the foot at the most critical times. When Abada struck, Celtic had control of the tie. Minutes later, his international team-mate Nir Bitton was sent off when he inexplicably shoved a finger into Anders Dreyer's face while on a yellow card. The Midtjylland attacker was also booked for the incident after a dive left Bitton incensed. Yet the damage was done, and Celtic had gone from a position of strength to one of jeopardy.

When former St Mirren loanee Dreyer was dismissed ten minutes into the second half for another dive, Celtic had the control back that Postecoglou craves. Then an error from Vasilis Barkas allowed an Evander free kick to nestle into the top corner and earn Midtjylland a positive result. The mistake would cost Celtic dearly a week later in Denmark. By that time, Scott Bain was between the sticks, with Barkas only ever seen again in the case of emergency.

The basic goalkeeping error and Bitton's indiscipline cast a shadow on a generally heartening performance. There was a sense that the team had something to work with but that Postecoglou needed severe help in the transfer window. If he got that and some time, then he could be on to a winner. The Midtjylland opener was far from perfect, but at least Celtic were rolling under their new boss.

After the match, Postecoglou took full ownership of the team's position, telling the BBC, 'I don't think we will ever be as badly prepared as we were tonight, and that's on me. I haven't done a great job so far because, with the disruptions we've had, we haven't been able to bring the players in. My role is to try and reinforce and prepare this squad. To their credit, the players didn't look for excuses. They put in a solid shift, and I'm just disappointed they didn't get the rewards for what I thought was an outstanding performance.' The rewards were just around the corner.

Celtic: *Barkas, Ralston, Welsh, Bitton, Taylor, Soro, Turnbull, McGregor, Abada, Edouard, Christie*
Subs used: *Murray, Ajeti, Rogic*

Midtjylland: *Lössl, Dalsgaard, Sviatchenko, Høegh, da Silva, Anderson, da Silva, Onyedika, Dreyer, dos Santos Júnior, Sisto*
Subs used: *Mabil, Madsen, Hansen, Andersson*

* * *

Jablonec 2–4 Celtic, UEFA Europa League qualifying, Stadion Střelnice, Thursday, 5 August 2021

There were more likely places for the start of the Ange revolution than Jablonec nad Nisou. The northern Czech city of around 45,000 inhabitants couldn't have been further away from the hustle and bustle of Glasgow or the glitz and glamour of the Champions League nights that the club would experience a year later. Maybe the tranquil surroundings were what Celtic needed. Some quiet time away in a popular skiing region to do some soul-searching and find an identity. Holidays were on the manager's mind too.

'You think I should be relaxed?' joked Postecoglou during a press conference at the start of the month. 'You think that's the situation I'm in right now? If this is your idea of relaxation, I'd hate to think what would happen if you went on holiday. I'm no more relaxed or no more anxious than I was last week. The goals and the determination to get things right doesn't change.'

July had been a tough start for Postecoglou. Champions League elimination had stung but not nearly as much as defeat to newly promoted Heart of Midlothian days later. John Souttar's 89th-minute winner had consigned Celtic to their first opening-day defeat in 24 years. In time, these bad results and undesirable records would prove to have been pretty unavoidable, given the state of the Celtic squad.

Postecoglou had been forced to throw in new signings almost immediately at Tynecastle. Kyogo Furuhashi only had lunch with his new team-mates before coming on as a substitute.

Carl Starfelt hadn't even trained but started the match. Months later, following Celtic's Premiership success, Callum McGregor was asked by Sky Sports for the most pivotal moments in the regaining of the title:

'I think the first one was against Hearts. Off the back of a difficult season, it was very easy for everyone to be negative again after game one. At that point, we had to get the group together and understand we had to change this. We're the only ones who can change it. It's very easy to put your head down and say it's going to be the same again, but the group of players were strong.'

At the time, patience was already thin with a support that had endured a torrid 12 months. The capitulations to Midtjylland and Hearts felt like a continuation of the bleak days under Neil Lennon, yet there was something different under Postecoglou. In the days after the Tynecastle loss, Dermot Desmond called the Australian to give him a vote of confidence. Celtic's principal shareholder could see something was building. He told the Hoops boss that his first assessment would come at the end of the year.

'Our performances haven't been too bad,' Postecoglou said after the Tynecastle loss. 'In all three games we've played we've had opportunities to win. It's about improving our performance and turning that performance into a result.'

Postecoglou may have been much calmer than most of the Celtic support, and it's vital that he was. The team didn't have long to stew over the disappointments. The coming weeks offered them the chance to get back on track in the Premiership, progress in the League Cup and qualify for the Europa League group stage. The first breakthrough arrived in Czechia.

Jablonec had finished third in the Czech top flight the previous season, just five points behind Sparta Prague, who had battered Neil Lennon's Celtic 8-2 over two horrific Europa League encounters. They'd been leading the Prague outfit going into the final four matchdays of the campaign and would surely smell blood against an unsettled team that had made a slow start to the season. It seemed far from an easy game for Celtic, who still had to navigate another round of qualifying just to make the group stage, even if they got past Petr Rada's team.

Before August, only Liel Abada and Carl Starfelt had started a match as new Celtic signings. The trip to Czechia gave Postecoglou a chance to double that number instantly. A first start was handed to Kyogo Furuhashi with Odsonne Edouard benched. Joe Hart, signed two days prior from Tottenham Hotspur, made his Hoops debut between the sticks with Starfelt and Abada also included. Of the team that started, only Ismaila Soro would fall completely out of Postecoglou's plans over the following months, with every other player contributing something towards Celtic's title triumph. Even at this early stage, the manager had a good idea of who he could trust.

Celtic had played some good stuff at points in their early outings. But it was in match four, in the sparsely populated Stadion Střelnice, where things first properly clicked. Wearing their new all-white third kit, Celtic raced into a 2-0 lead inside the first 16 minutes. Abada notched the opener, his second for the club, again on the rebound after his original shot was blocked. Kyogo then opened his account, latching on to a Nir Bitton pass and chipping the ball past goalkeeper Jan Hanuš like he was a six-year-old schoolkid. Barely a minute later, Jablonec reduced the deficit. Neither Bitton nor Starfelt looked convincing, and Hart could do little as Václav Pilař slotted home. With the heat turned up a little, Celtic kept playing their football. Callum McGregor drilled just wide, Hanuš denied Abada, and Kyogo blazed over when it looked easier to score. James Forrest soon added a third after some dynamic running from Abada before more lax defending let Jablonec reduce the deficit to 3-2.

After failing to win from leads in their past four European away matches, Celtic could have folded in the early evening sunshine. In the absence of a settled defence, the strength came from the attackers. With just minutes to go, the natural tendency may have been to protect the narrow lead ahead of the return leg at Celtic Park a week later. Under Postecoglou, the idea of retreating would be as welcome as Eddie Howe picking the winner for the Paradise Windfall half-time draw. The scoreboard wouldn't define Celtic's game plan. Bournemouth-bound Ryan Christie's final goal for the club sealed a 4-2 win. Ange's lesson about moving forward at all times was being heard.

'It's great to get a win,' he said afterwards. 'Especially for the players who have worked hard without getting the result. It's a reward for the players and hopefully gives them confidence and belief. There are definitely areas we can improve. We started really well, but there were periods where we lost control, particularly in the second half.'

Postecoglou was right about there being areas where Celtic had to improve. The defence had allowed Jablonec to score two cheap goals in a match that had posed little danger. Joe Hart hadn't looked completely convincing for the second Jablonec strike, while Carl Starfelt and Nir Bitton didn't inspire much confidence in the centre of defence. Yet there was a quiet optimism developing. Kyogo and Abada were real finds. Callum McGregor, Anthony Ralston and Greg Taylor looked far better than they had the previous season. More new signings would be arriving. It may only have been Jablonec in front of fewer than 5,000 spectators, yet supporters could get a little excited about what was to come for the first time in a long while. Something was building.

Jablonec: Hanuš, Surzyn, Martinec, Zelený, Krob, Pleštil, Kratochvíl, Považanec, Kubista, Pilař, Doležal
Subs used: Malínský, Houska, Holík, Čvančara, Hübschman
Celtic: Hart, Ralston, Bitton, Starfelt, Taylor, Soro, Turnbull, McGregor, Abada, Kyogo, Forrest
Subs used: Christie, Rogic, Edouard

* * *

Celtic 6-0 St Mirren, Premiership, Celtic Park, Saturday, 21 August 2021

If the Celtic support needed evidence that things were different under Postecoglou, the sight of Albian Ajeti charging 30 yards to dispossess a St Mirren player in the closing stages of a 6-0 win was a pretty good sign.

Signed for a reported £5m from West Ham in the summer of 2020, Ajeti was one of the many late Neil Lennon signings who failed to make it at Celtic. Injuries, the pandemic, an ailing team on its last legs and numerous other factors contributed to a frustrating period under the Northern Irishman. Things didn't get much better when Postecoglou arrived.

Other than a run of matches in the early days, when both Kyogo and Giorgos Giakoumakis were injured, Ajeti was a largely peripheral figure in the Celtic squad. When his season-long loan move, with an option to buy, to Austrian side Sturm Graz was confirmed in August 2022, Postecoglou explained the situation fully. 'Albian was probably one of a number of players who got caught in between periods,' he told BBC Radio Scotland. 'They came in at a really difficult time for the club, through the Covid experience as well. I can just imagine it would have been very hard for new players to settle in at that time. Then I came along, and we changed direction again. Albian's a good player. He just needs an opportunity.'

Despite a promising start, Ajeti never seemed to be a good fit for Celtic's style of play. His attitude was called into question on occasion and the sight of him wearing sunglasses as his team-mates celebrated with the Premiership trophy at the end of the season did little to dispel the feeling that his heart wasn't quite in it.

Yet his heart was most definitely in it when he charged over to former Celtic youth Marcus Fraser in the closing minutes of the St Mirren match. Ajeti dispossessed Fraser and set up David Turnbull's third goal of a profitable afternoon that had also seen Liel Abada grab two and Odsonne Edouard net his final goal for the club. St Mirren had looked like a beaten team ever since midfielder Alan Power was red-carded for a frustrated lunge on Turnbull near the corner flag. Celtic scored four before the break, with Saints keeper Jak Alnwick questionable for every single one, while Turnbull and Edouard also struck the woodwork in a scintillating display.

The game was the culmination of a remarkable run of home matches that had seen momentum build for Postecoglou's team. A bizarre scheduling quirk had led to five Celtic Park fixtures in succession, with Celtic going on to greater heights with every passing match. The gradual phased return of supporters to the stadium also heightened the feeling that something was building.

A crowd of 24,000 had taken in the 6-0 thrashing of Dundee, where Kyogo Furuhashi struck a stunning hat-trick on his home debut. Celtic Park returned to full capacity, save for the Main Stand, days later as the team completed the job against Jablonec in the Europa League. A 3-2 revenge cup victory against Hearts, which hugely flattered the Edinburgh team, followed before a sold-out Celtic Park saw the first genuinely impressive result of the Postecoglou era: a 2-0 win over Eredivisie high-flyers AZ Alkmaar. When St Mirren left Glasgow battered and bruised the following weekend, Celtic had suddenly gone from a team in crisis to one others should fear. Postecoglou's team hadn't been able to buy a victory weeks earlier. Now they were on a run of six in a row.

Ajeti's improved work rate was a single example of Celtic players buying into Postecoglou's methods. If an out-of-favour attacker, probably never suited to a Postecoglou team, was showing such a desire to impress, what about those who could really make an impact?

The captain, Callum McGregor, had quietly found his role at the base of the midfield, providing a brilliant option for a rearguard that was getting used to playing out from the back.

Joe Hart had already emerged as a big presence, while Anthony Ralston had suddenly turned into a player worth talking about. Carl Starfelt was improving with every passing match, Abada and Kyogo looked like utter diamonds, and Turnbull was weighing in with his share of goals as well. There was a sense that St Mirren wouldn't be the last team to leave the east end of Glasgow with their tail between their legs. Not when players like Ajeti were showing such a hunger for more even when the result was far out of sight.

The demolition of St Mirren moved Celtic to the top of the Premiership for around 24 hours. Postecoglou's team looked like early title challengers based on their home form at least. Rangers' surprise exit from the Champions League and early league defeat at Dundee United added to the sense that Celtic weren't a million miles away. The following month would tell a different story. Bigger challenges were ahead.

Celtic: *Hart, Ralston, Starfelt, Welsh, Taylor, McGregor, Turnbull, Christie, Abada, Edouard, Kyogo*
Subs used: *Rogic, Soro, Ajeti*

St Mirren: *Alnwick, Fraser, McCarthy, Shaughnessy, Flynn, Power, McGrath, Erhahon, Tanser, Kiltie, Main*
Subs used: *Brophy, MacPherson, McAllister*

* * *

Celtic 0-4 Bayer Leverkusen, UEFA Europa League, Celtic Park, Thursday, 30 September 2021

Jeremie Frimpong looks a little embarrassed. His Bayer Leverkusen team has just battered Celtic in their second UEFA Europa League fixture. The Bundesliga outfit sit top of Group G after the 4-0 win in Glasgow, alongside La Liga's Real Betis. Both have six points, with Celtic and Ferencváros yet to register one.

Frimpong stands in the Celtic Park centre circle, looking for familiar faces. He only left Glasgow nine months earlier but finding former team-mates is a struggle. He hugs Vasilis Barkas and Stephen Welsh, then shakes the hand of a dejected Tom Rogic. There aren't many other faces he knows. Minutes later, he's live on BT Sport. In typical Frimpong style, he smiles his way through a charming interview. 'It was amazing to be back home. Celtic are always a good team. They made it tough for us, especially at the start. You've always got to be ready against Celtic.'

The Dutch wing-back would have known better than most about the dangers a trip to Celtic Park poses. Frimpong was the poster boy of Neil Lennon's Celtic not long before – the infectious personality who represented everything good about the club on nights like this. If he'd stuck around a little longer, he might have become a crucial part of Postecoglou's team. As it is, he's dressed from head to toe in blue, having just dished out a damaging blow to the Aussie's hopes.

Celtic hadn't even played badly. They'd just been picked off by an ultra-efficient team – the best they'd face all season. This was the kind of team they had to aspire to be.

Celtic: *Hart, Ralston, Carter-Vickers, Starfelt, Montgomery, McGregor, Rogic, Turnbull, Abada, Kyogo, Jota*
Subs used: *Bitton, McCarthy, Ajeti, Giakoumakis*

Bayer Leverkusen: *Hrádecký, Frimpong, Tah, Hincapié, Bakker, Aránguiz, Demirbay, Diaby, Wirtz, Paulinho, Alario*
Subs used: *Amiri, Bellarabi, Adli, Retsos, Schick*

* * *

Aberdeen 1-2 Celtic, Premiership, Pittodrie, Sunday, 3 October 2021

'This is the day, this is the day, that we win away. We will rejoice and get mad with it.' The Celtic support enjoys a well-earned party in the South Stand at Pittodrie. The self-mocking chant is usually reserved for big away wins on the Continent. It has been heard in the likes of Trondheim and Anderlecht over the years but never in Aberdeen. Callum McGregor and the rest of the team come over to the corner where the Hoops support are housed. There's plenty of fist-pumping and clapping. Then Ange Postecoglou walks across the pitch. He clenches his fist and the away section erupts.

'I thought that was a bigger moment for the players rather than the fans,' he'll later tell Darrell Currie and Chris Sutton on BT Sport's *Currie Club* podcast. 'I sensed even before then that the fans could see something happening. We'd had a couple of big wins at home before that, 6-0 and Kyogo had scored a hat-trick, so they could see some seeds. I thought the supporters were getting on board, and that game was really important for the players winning away. That's when I felt the pendulum shifted for the players.'

Celtic aren't a club that can go eight months without a league win away from home. When the team finally managed to get over the line, in dramatic circumstances at Pittodrie, everybody felt a fair amount of relief. For all the pressure heaped on Postecoglou, the team's struggles on the road pre-dated the arrival of the majority of his squad. Celtic had been struggling away from home since midway through the previous season.

Yet under the Aussie, the disparity between home and away levels of performance and result had become a real cause for concern. The trip to face Aberdeen was the eighth match of Celtic's Premiership campaign and the fourth away from home. Before kick-off, all ten of their points had been earned at Celtic Park. In a matter of weeks they'd gone from the apparent title contenders who hit Dundee and St Mirren for six to a team sitting in that position in the table. Eight matches had followed the thumping win over the Saints: two wins, one draw and five defeats. Yet, even during such a horrendous run, Postecoglou still seemed to be the calmest man in Glasgow, telling the press, 'I love this. This is what I'm passionate about, and I'll make sure that we get to where we want to get to. This part of the process is not new to me.'

Days before the Pittodrie visit, Celtic had been left battered by Bayer Leverkusen. Like after the defeat to Real Betis, there had been a sense of perspective as to where the team were in relation to their lofty opponents. A dire loss to Livingston and more dropped points at home to Dundee United a week later had been harder to compensate for. Postecoglou would later comment on the period after the Leverkusen loss, saying, 'When we lost to Leverkusen 4-0 in the Europa League at Celtic Park, it wasn't a 4-0 game. We played some good football on the night against a very good team. But we lost 4-0, and when you lose 4-0 at home, that's never good. I think the players saw that "okay, we're going to persist with this, it's not going to change, this is who we are going to be". That helped me build trust with the boys.'

At full time less than three days later, Celtic's players and supporters were celebrating the feeling of winning on the road. There are plenty of pivotal moments in the Postecoglou reign, many of which can be viewed positively with the benefit of hindsight. The dramatic victory over Aberdeen at Pittodrie is almost certainly the biggest, and it felt big at the time.

Football is so often defined by the big moments. We'll never know how events would have transpired had Jota not slid in at the back post to divert Adam Montgomery's cross into the net, or had Cameron Carter-Vickers not made such a crucial clearance to prevent Christian Ramirez from scoring minutes earlier. The pressure on Postecoglou would undoubtedly have increased, with the post-international break fixtures taking on an even greater meaning. Games at Fir Park and Easter Road would have become even more precarious, with fans and players having doubts. As it was, winning ugly was the making of this new Celtic team.

The timing was perfect, with Celtic heading into the break off the back of a huge victory. When the team returned to action, they'd be a completely different animal. The wait for a league win on the road was over. The irony of it being achieved against a team captained by former great Scott Brown wasn't lost on many. A new team was in the process of being assembled. The rollercoaster was calming down.

Aberdeen: Woods, Ramsay, Bates, McCrorie, MacKenzie, Hayes, Longstaff, Brown, Samuels, Ferguson, Ramirez
Subs used: *McGeouch, McLennan, Campbell*

Celtic: Hart, Ralston, Carter-Vickers, Starfelt, Montgomery, Bitton, Turnbull, McGregor, Abada, Kyogo, Jota
Subs used: *Ajeti, Rogic*

CHAPTER 6

Kyogo Furuhashi: Inspiring Hope

*'My old clubs were great, but this
is on another level.'*

Kyogo Furuhashi

'SUBSTITUTION FOR Celtic. Coming off, number 17, Jota. And coming on, we welcome back number 8 … KYOOOOOGO.'

The roar inside Celtic Park is deafening. Celtic are six goals ahead against St Johnstone and Kyogo Furuhashi is about to make his long-awaited return from injury. The Japanese star was last seen in action 104 days ago, limping off minutes into the previous meeting with the Perth club. He steps on to the surface, does a hop on his left foot and then sprints to the top of the pitch. Minutes later he picks the ball up inside his own half and lofts a stunning pass over the Saints defence for Daizen Maeda to chest down and Liel Abada to rifle into the roof of the net. *The Magnificent Seven* theme blares out at Celtic Park.

Celtic have gone from title chasers to champions in waiting during the three months the forward has missed. The team hasn't lost a single domestic match while he's been away, with points dropped in just one league fixture. Yet, everything only truly feels perfect once Kyogo is back.

It's hard to explain to a non-Celtic fan what Kyogo means. He has an effect on the support that you can only experience. When he's not fit and available it's like there's a dark cloud hovering menacingly above Celtic Park. The atmosphere is uneasy and something is missing. When Kyogo is playing at full flight it feels like life is complete. It becomes hard to imagine how the club even functioned in the 133 years prior to his arrival.

* * *

Kyogo was inspiring hope before he'd even touched down in Scotland. If you were to put your finger on the moment the entire mood among the Celtic support changed, it might have been somewhere around the morning of 16 July 2021. An era-defining signing isn't often announced before you've poured your cornflakes. At 8.26am, Celtic announced they'd 'reached an agreement to sign Japanese internationalist Kyogo Furuhashi'.

Kyogo signed a four-year deal, and joined from Vissel Kobe for a reported £4.6m in a deal arriving entirely out of the blue. Nobody, apart from a few optimistic tweeters looking at the Japanese market after Postecoglou's arrival perhaps, had foreseen Celtic being able to sign the top scorer in Japan on a long-term deal. Like his manager, few in Scotland had heard Furuhashi's name. The obligatory YouTube highlights package suggested that he had plenty to offer. With explosive speed, clever movement and clinical finishing, it was genuinely exciting news to wake up to.

Postecoglou had, of course, encountered Kyogo during his days in Japan. The pair had regularly crossed paths in meetings between Yokohama F. Marinos and Vissel Kobe. 'Kyogo was the least risky out of all the summer signings,' he'd later tell BT Sport's *Currie Club* podcast. 'I was so confident about him. Even though I didn't coach him, I'd watched him. Even when we won the championship, I remember talking to our players, and the defenders always said he was the one player they couldn't handle. He was the first one I said as soon as I got the job, I said, "I have to sign this guy.'"

Kyogo's move to Scotland was a significant moment in his career. Years earlier, at 21, and still to make his professional debut, he'd been ready to give up the game, telling *Tokyo Weekender*: 'In my final year at university, I had trials at different teams but I couldn't find a team. Fortunately, I had many supportive people around me, especially my parents who were brilliant. That helped me keep going and I eventually got my chance at FC Gifu.'

Furuhashi joined the second division club in 2017 and excelled before securing a move to top-flight Vissel Kobe a year later. The Kobe outfit had been bought by the electronic commerce company Rakuten four years earlier, creating a link with FC Barcelona, who they sponsored. The partnership saw several former Barcelona players, such as Andrés Iniesta, David Villa and Thomas Vermaelen, all head to Japan. Former Germany star Lukáš Podolski was another who signed up.

Playing with Iniesta and Villa took Kyogo's game to new levels. In the summer of 2019 he received offers from Dutch clubs AZ Alkmaar and FC Groningen but stayed in Japan to help Vissel Kobe win the 2019 Emperor's Cup. In the 2020 season, he netted 17 goals, and then scored 16 more in the first half of the following campaign. Then Postecoglou and Celtic came calling.

'It's a unique club with special fans,' he told *Tokyo Weekender* after his first season in Glasgow. 'Getting those supporters off their feet when you hit the net, there's no feeling like it. Before flying to Glasgow, Andrés [Iniesta] told me about the atmosphere when he played against Celtic for Barcelona. He said it was intimidating and I can see why, as it can get very loud. My old clubs Gifu and Vissel Kobe were great, but this is on another level.'

With Celtic fans excited by the announcement and keen to see their new forward in action as soon as possible, Kyogo still had some business to conclude in Japan. A short behind-the-scenes documentary was filmed by Vissel Kobe, covering the final days before his move to Scotland. On day one he netted in his last match for the club, a 1-1 draw away to Cerezo Osaka. The documentary shows the moment the forward was told about Celtic posting the goal on social media. 'I really look forward to playing for Celtic,' he says while trying to hide a smile. 'I want to do what I can to get results for Celtic, and I aim to become the type of player that can excite the fans.'

With no away supporters allowed inside the Yodoko Sakura Stadium for his final match, a special farewell event was organised for the following day. An emotional Kyogo addressed the Vissel fans, with Iniesta and others also in attendance. 'First of all, thank you all for being here today,' he said. 'Thank you as well to the people watching online. All I have for you is gratitude. At all times you were both kind and passionate. Words cannot describe how thankful I am. It pains me to leave this wonderful city of Kobe and to leave this club, but I will go to Celtic to give my all and stay true to myself.'

Iniesta was next to address the crowd. 'Today is a sad day for us. Losing an important team-mate mid-season is not easy. But at the same time, he is fulfilling his dream of playing in Europe. I would like to wish Kyogo a wonderful life going forward, not just as a football player but as a person.' Behind Iniesta, another ex-Barcelona man, Sergi Samper, was in tears.

The brilliant film also showed an intriguing conversation about squad numbers between the Scotland-bound attacker and an unnamed figure at the club. 'Number 11 was taken. 7 and 8 are still open,' Kyogo says. 'Apparently, number 7 is a legendary number there. Larsson used to wear it,' says the other person. 'He went from Celtic to Barcelona. You will have to choose between 7 and 8.'

Ten days later, with the No. 8 on his back, Kyogo made his Celtic debut in a totally different environment at Tynecastle. He'd only just met his team-mates for lunch, but a lack of other attacking options forced Postecoglou to introduce him with ten minutes to go. Kyogo made his entrance on the left wing, a position he'd occupy on occasion in his early days at the club, but was unable to prevent Celtic from going down to a 2-1 defeat.

While many claimed he'd be too small and lightweight to succeed in Scottish football, Kyogo did his talking on the pitch. Like fellow newbie Liel Abada, he made an explosive start, netting his first goal during the team's first competitive win under Postecoglou against Jablonec. The goal was straight from the YouTube compilation – an intelligent run behind the defence and a neat, dinked finish beyond the goalkeeper.

If his first start had shown promise, his second was simply astonishing. The most staggering thing about his 67-minute hat-trick against Dundee was that he could have scored six. Before his opening goal, he'd slotted wide from a Tom Rogic cutback when it looked easier to score. Two further clear-cut chances were passed up between his second and third strikes. It was an astonishing performance of intelligent movement, pace and instinct. An opposition defence has rarely looked so lost at Celtic Park.

Kyogo was already the most hyped player at Celtic in years, and he'd only played two matches. In the following weeks, his fairy tale start continued with goals in a League Cup tie against Hearts and in both legs of the Europa League play-off against AZ Alkmaar – a crucial contribution that saw Celtic through to the group stage of the competition.

For all his scoring exploits, it was the hard work and thrilling attitude that caught the imagination of the Celtic support. Celtic had never had a forward who pressed the opposition defence quite as well as Kyogo. His desire to chase every lost cause and not stop running until half-time or full time was a perfect fit for both Postecoglou and the supporters.

Together with Abada and Jota he formed the sparkling new-look front three that would define the first half of Celtic's season. All three encountered injury troubles in their debut seasons, with Kyogo spending the most time on the sidelines. Celtic's form plummeted when he missed a month near the start of the season after picking up a knee injury on international duty. With Giorgos Giakoumakis still getting up to speed, Celtic looked laboured in the final third. When he returned, the team's form took an upturn. A goal at Pittodrie in his second start back proved to be crucial, as did strikes away to Hibs, a double at Dundee to heap more pain on James McPake, and goals in both matches against Ferencváros. The stunning goal at home to the Hungarians showcased everything great about his play and was eventually named the UEFA Europa League goal of the group stage with 43 per cent of the vote.

The goals dried up a little for Kyogo in the winter months, with only three arriving, all against Edinburgh clubs. Yet every one was enormous in the context of Celtic's season. The first, the only goal in a tense Thursday night win over Hearts in early December, was vital in keeping Celtic in touch at the top. The other two, in a dramatic League Cup Final against Hibernian, secured the first trophy for Postecoglou and his new-look team. Kyogo wasn't even close to being fully fit for the Hampden showpiece, it later emerged, with Postecoglou telling Premier Sports, 'He was just determined, even on one leg, to get out there today and help the boys out.'

The willingness to put himself on the line for his team-mates is an underrated part of the forward's game. When words like 'committed' and 'bravery' are bandied around, you're more likely to think of a player like Anthony Ralston or Cameron Carter-Vickers. Kyogo is the epitome of bravery, as was showcased when winning Celtic a penalty in the BayArena after being clattered by Leverkusen keeper Lukáš Hrádecký.

The vital two-goal contribution in the League Cup Final came at a cost. Kyogo missed Celtic's next match, against St

Mirren, but returned for the Boxing Day visit to St Johnstone, lasting just 15 minutes before limping off. At first the prognosis was good, with Postecoglou saying, 'It's nothing major, nothing that's going to keep him out anyway.' But Kyogo would be kept out for months at the start of 2022, missing 17 matches before his eventual return. Unlike his previous spell on the sidelines, Celtic coped, with the likes of Giakoumakis, Maeda and Reo Hatate rising to the occasion and firing the team to the brink of the title by the time he returned.

The reaction of the Celtic Park faithful when he was brought back into the fray in the closing stages of the match against St Johnstone told you everything you needed to know about how he's viewed in Glasgow. Kyogo is loved as much as anyone at Celtic Park in recent years. Whenever the Celtic starting line-up is aired through the stadium PA in the minutes before kick-off, the two loudest cheers are reserved for Kyogo and Postecoglou. The Celtic boss even revealed in an interview with *Open Goal* that the Japanese forward is the preferred player of his two youngest sons.

There's perhaps an argument that Henrik Larsson was the last player to receive such adulation on a weekly basis, although the forward still has a lot to do to live up to the King of Kings' legacy, despite a stunning start to the 2022/23 season. Simply being considered 'the best since Larsson' is evidence of Kyogo's status in Glasgow. He'll move on from Celtic one day, probably in the not-too-distant future, but he'll leave a lifetime of memories.

CHAPTER 7

Roarcelona

'He just told me he wanted to build a team that would do something special in Australian football.'

Matt Smith

ANGE POSTECOGLOU demands three things from those around him at a football club: high standards, hard work and continual improvement. If you show a thirst for all three, he'll back you to the hilt, even when times are hard. Celtic's manager wants to win more than anything – something often overlooked amid the charm of his attractive playing style. He doesn't enjoy losing in the slightest. Yet, as long as he can see his people doing the right things, he's content that they'll get to where they need to be, even if it takes time. It's what he calls the journey. 'This journey is a rollercoaster,' he regularly tells his players and staff.

Matt Smith knows as much about the journey as anybody. As captain of Postecoglou's celebrated Brisbane Roar team of the early 2010s, Postecoglou trusted him to carry his message on to the pitch. Much like Celtic skipper Callum McGregor, he was perfectly suited to the role as someone who gave his all and, by his own admission, 'never stopped'.

'I'm not the most technically gifted player,' the three-time Australia cap tells me. 'I was never the best player in the group.

But I had that continual work ethic and hunger to never stop. I was so determined as a kid to play professional football, and I never got the chance. So I would've died to continue being a football player. I would like to think that I was one of the hardest-working players and led by example.'

Our chat clearly shows that Smith still holds his former manager in high regard, even all these years later. The feeling seems mutual when I mention Smith's name to Postecoglou during a press conference barely a week after our chat. 'Ah, Matty Smith,' he says, perking up at the mention of the name. 'How is Matty Smith? He's too nice to be a centre-back, let me tell you.'

It's not difficult to see why there would still be so much affection between the pair more than a decade after Smith's arrival at Suncorp Stadium. Roarcelona – as Postecoglou's history-making team came to be known, given their similarities with Pep Guardiola's Catalan giants – are widely understood to be the greatest team ever to grace the A-League.

Smith was a massive part of the Roar journey. Celtic's stars, too, will have heard countless times about the journey they find themselves on. It then became their decision whether they want to be part of it. A challenge thrown down by Postecoglou without the need to say so directly. On the journey, expectations can be met but never exceeded. Postecoglou doesn't talk about endings because he doesn't want to set limits for what can be achieved. The minute a level is reached, the bar rises again and everyone is forced to up their game.

Postecoglou doesn't mention the goal of becoming champions at the start of the season. His theory is that if you do the right things and continually improve, these achievements will arrive naturally. As he put it to me with a championship medal around his neck on the final day of the season: 'We hold the pen to our story and those words are written by us.'

To understand the Celtic that the Aussie now presides over and what may happen in the future, it's essential to look back at Postecoglou's all-conquering Roar team and what led him to that point. Away from an obvious bias surrounding anything Celtic-related, the Roar story is perhaps still the most magical of Postecoglou's managerial career. What made it even more remarkable was that he'd built the team from the ground up while also restoring his own managerial reputation. Postecoglou had been on one hell of a journey himself.

* * *

Football became an important part of Postecoglou's life shortly after his move to Melbourne in 1970. He'd been born in Athens five years earlier, with his family emigrating after his father, who specialised in furniture-making, lost his business amid government nationalisation in Greece. A young Postecoglou would rarely get to spend time with his dad throughout the week but on Sunday afternoons the pair would watch South Melbourne Hellas – a club formed in 1959 by Greek migrants. As well as watching the team in the years before the launch of the National Soccer League (NSL) – Australia's first national football competition – Postecoglou also played in their youth teams, where he'd be driven to training by his father.

Often seen sporting a mullet, Angelo Postecoglou broke through to play for and captain the South Melbourne first team. The club twice won the NSL Championship, in 1984 and 1991, with Postecoglou as a player. He was a good player too, an underrated one who earned four Australia caps. His real talent, however, was always in coaching, and in 1996, shortly after retiring, he became the South Melbourne head coach.

It was here that Postecoglou took his first steps in management, earning back-to-back NSL Championships and the Oceania Club Championship in 1999. Victory in the final over Fijian hosts Nadi secured a spot in the inaugural FIFA Club World Championship the following January, alongside some of the world's biggest clubs. In a significant step up, Postecoglou led his team into battle against Mexico's CONCACAF winners

Club Necaxa, Copa Libertadores holders Vasco da Gama and the recently crowned European champions Manchester United. In strikingly similar scenes to the World Cup 14 years later, also held in Brazil, Postecoglou's underdogs failed to register a point from three matches but came away from the tournament with plenty of credit. Amid the rubbing of shoulders with footballing elite such as the great Sir Alex Ferguson, this period of Postecoglou's life also allowed him to meet his future wife Georgia, the marketing manager at South Melbourne, who he credits with helping him through the hard times.

His success with the Melbourne outfit alerted national bosses and he was soon asked to coach Australia's youth teams. While the under-17s and under-20s lifted numerous Oceanian titles under Postecoglou, Australia always wanted to measure itself on a grander stage. When the country left Oceania to become a member of the Asian Football Confederation in 2006, and both under-17s and under-20s teams subsequently failed to qualify for major competitions a year later, Postecoglou was under immense pressure. When his infamous on-air argument with Craig Foster was broadcast by *The World Game*, Postecoglou's game was up. He was gone three months later, two months after he married Georgia.

As the A-League, Australia's brand-new elite football division, was getting started, Postecoglou found himself completely out of the picture. His reputation had suffered significant damage after the failure of the Young Socceroos teams and the car-crash Foster argument. His next opportunity arrived back in Greece – his only European-based gig before Celtic. Panachaiki FC, hailing from the city of Patras, were owned by an Adelaide businessman and gave Postecoglou a platform to regain his confidence away from the spotlight of the Aussie media. He spent one year in Greece's third-largest city before returning to Australia.

On his return he still couldn't seem to land a job. He became a football pundit, working mainly for Fox Sports. After one broadcast he bumped into Archie Fraser, the Scottish-born A-League chief executive. Postecoglou chanced his arm, looking for a route back into the consciousness of Australian football, and shortly afterwards got a call from Brisbane Roar. Frank Farina had just been sacked as Roar manager after a drink-driving charge, and Postecoglou was soon announced as his replacement.

Ironically, the pair had worked together in the early 2000s when Farina was Socceroos boss and Postecoglou was in charge of the youth teams.

Postecoglou was going to do things his way in Brisbane – a different way to every other team. 'I've had just about everyone in Australia tell me what's wrong with the Roar,' he said in his first press conference. He wasn't lying either. The club was in crisis when Postecoglou arrived midway through the 2009/10 campaign. Farina had been well-liked by the players, and they hadn't taken the news of his dismissal well.

Brisbane Roar, who had only taken on that name during the inaugural season of the A-League in 2005, were having trouble establishing themselves as one of Australia's top clubs. Their struggles continued in Postecoglou's maiden campaign, with the Roar unable to string together a consistent run of results at any stage of the season. They finished ninth in the ten-team division with only Adelaide United below them.

Despite all the negativity enveloping the club, Postecoglou was steadfast in his beliefs. He had a master plan that involved changing the way the sport was played in Australia. Postecoglou had grown up as a massive fan of Johan Cruyff and the Dutch legend's Ajax team. Around the time of his arrival in Brisbane, Pep Guardiola's Barcelona were reaching new heights with their spectacular, attractive football, and Postecoglou wanted his new team to do the same. He moved on some key members of the underperforming old guard, such as former Rangers men Bob Malcolm and Charlie Miller, and replaced them with younger, hungry stars like Matt Smith.

The defender had endured a challenging career until Postecoglou came into his life. Smith had just left the now defunct North Queensland Fury after an ownership change – the latest disappointment in a career of unlucky breaks. Born in England, he'd started with dreams of making it as a professional footballer at local club Portsmouth. Failure to land a pro deal at Fratton Park led him to a crossroads in his life. He made the ambitious decision to move to Australia, working for his uncle's finance company while trying to plot a career as a professional footballer. He started with semi-pro Brisbane Strikers and was soon picked up by the Fury, making his professional debut at 27, before Ange came knocking.

Smith says:

> The conversation probably only lasted 15 or 20 minutes. I don't think we even negotiated my contract. He just told me he wanted to build a team that would do something special in Australian football. The game tended to be quite transitional and long, but his approach was 'why can't Australian-based players play possession-based football?' He explained how I would fit into the system and what he expected from me. It was about selling his ideals and beliefs about how football should be played and where he wanted to take the team. Part of his messaging all the time was: 'Let's do something beyond what we see on the pitch.' It was always about the bigger picture. 'What's the journey and how are we doing?' He had a 'why' to everything, which was so believable. For the players that were there, he just wrapped them in that. It was like a snowball that kept rolling and rolling. It shaped how I spent the next ten years of my playing career.

Playing in a Postecoglou team is demanding but extremely rewarding. You must put in the graft, as Jota and Liel Abada have learned. Hard work is non-negotiable, as the boss would put it, but the rewards are being part of a team trying to achieve something special. While attackers are asked to put in the hard yards, defenders like Smith don't have it easy either. They're required to pass the ball out from defence under pressure when every instinct is telling them to go long. Postecoglou would prefer his players make mistakes with the right intentions rather than succeed by going against his principles. Smith got a good indication of that in one of his very first training sessions: 'I received the ball from the left-back and made this beautiful 80-yard pinged pass. Straight on the button. I was happy with it. Then Ange came over and spoke to me. He said, "Smithy, we don't do that here."'

Smith would eventually get up to speed with Postecoglou's demands, although not before an uncomfortable learning period:

In matches, I've got the ball, forwards and wingers are trying to press me and midfielders are pushing in. It's petrifying. But it's petrifying until it becomes normal. How many times do you see a central-defender open up his body and go long, even though he had an option to pass? We used to rewatch the games, and the commentators would be mad because we passed the ball along our six-yard line. But that was how we trained so it just became the norm. In training, your opposite number knew exactly what you were going to try and do with the ball. So they're pressing you and they know how you will play. To try and unpick that in training was actually harder than the games. How we trained and how we prepared just became the norm. When it came to matches, we were so prepared because we trained harder than we played, believe it or not. The training sessions were so intense every day that when it came to the games, you didn't think about anything other than angles, space, movement, and rotations. It was more about your team-mates than yourself. If I played out and made an error, it wasn't necessarily my fault. It was the people moving off me.

Celtic goalkeeper Joe Hart would echo Smith's sentiments in the early part of his second season at the club. Hart was in the midst of his first proper pre-season at Celtic and had been asked to play a slightly different role when his team were in possession. Often playing as another ball-playing centre-back, 40 yards from his goal, the change was further evidence of Celtic evolving under Postecoglou. Like Smith, Hart had been put firmly out of his comfort zone, telling the *Glasgow Times*:

I couldn't just come in and play as high as that as I'd never done it before, so I had to learn and I'm still learning. That's why I absolutely love being here and playing under the manager. It's becoming less uncomfortable to be that high. Before, to be that high, I always thought 'danger, danger'. But now I understand the reasons why I am there. I am not there for any reason other than to help the team to progress and move forward. I understand the reasons better, so I feel more comfortable.

Postecoglou takes pleasure in seeing his players out of their comfort zone because that's where he believes real improvement is made. Again, mistakes and errors aren't necessarily bad, as long as players learn and continue with the right intentions. He told me when I put Smith's comments to him:

I think it's the only way you improve. I'm constantly on at the players about that. Sometimes people will say, 'That was a perfect training session. No one made a mistake.' That sends a signal to me that maybe the training session wasn't challenging enough. I'm constantly talking about players not being in their comfort zones because comfort means that you're doing something that is not really testing you. That's why I'm constantly talking about the improvement of us as a team. When people say, 'How much improvement is there in the team?' Well, there's always improvement because once I see that players have got to a level where they can excel at something, my job is to test them again and make them uncomfortable.

* * *

Back in Brisbane, Postecoglou's methods were starting to bear fruit. The team had made a solid start to the A-League season, winning two and drawing two of their first four matches while not conceding a single goal. That defensive fortitude came crashing down on matchday five when the Roar were thumped 3-0 away to Melbourne Victory. Postecoglou was travelling back to his hometown with a point to prove and saw defender Luke DeVere cost his team two goals while trying to follow orders and play out from the back. The defeat stung but Postecoglou's reaction in the days after the loss surprised his players.

'He was very encouraging even though Luke DeVere was at fault for two of the goals,' says Smith. 'I remember going in and watching the video analysis after training on the first session back. He went through the phases of play. It was more words of encouragement than anything. He said minor errors cost us the goals, but everything was about the process. Don't worry about the outcome, because that will come. Just worry about the process. After that, I guess the rest is history.'

DeVere would become an important player for Postecoglou's Roar and was called up for the Socceroos by his old boss in 2015, making his one and only Australia appearance against world champions Germany.

Comparisons between Roar's 3-0 loss in Melbourne and Celtic's 4-0 defeat suffered at home to Bayer Leverkusen in Postecoglou's first campaign can be made. The Hoops hadn't performed badly in the Europa League clash but had been undone in brutal fashion by the Germans. The drubbing arrived on the back of several disappointing domestic results – with Celtic having won just three of their seven league matches. A sink or swim moment had arrived. Postecoglou reflected months later:

> People will look at the 4-0 scoreline and say it must have been a thumping. But that doesn't really tell the story of the night. Yes, we conceded four but we could have scored four ourselves, which gives us confidence that, even against the best teams, we can still create good chances and play our game. I think copping four against Betis and Leverkusen helped build some trust between me and the players. They were probably looking at me and wondering, 'Is he going to change his approach? Are we going to have to take the blame for this?' That never happened, and it has been a lot better the last four or five weeks with results following the performances.

Smith has first-hand experience of what Postecoglou is like in these defining moments. He reckons the idea of 'the journey' would have been at the centre of the conversation after the Leverkusen loss:

> Ange is all big picture. There's always a focus on the here and the now but he's more interested in where you're going. I don't know for sure, but I reckon Ange would've said, 'That's part of our journey.' If players weren't trying to follow and do what he was asking them to do, they wouldn't be there. We had players within the group that came and went. If you didn't buy into what he was doing, you didn't last too long. He blocks out everything. That playing group will be so invested in each other that they won't hear the noise, they won't hear the media, they

won't hear all the external factors because he's so good at blocking that out.

While Postecoglou offered encouragement after punishing losses because he could see his players following his message, that's not to say he doesn't get angry on occasion. Celtic fans have witnessed his true fury on a few occasions, most notably midway through the first half of a Scottish Cup clash against Raith Rovers. The Hoops led the match through a spectacular Liam Scales strike, but their overall play had been ponderous and lacking in imagination. A backwards series of passes featuring Nir Bitton and Stephen Welsh was the final straw for the frustrated boss. 'Stop passing it back,' he roared, with broadcasters Premier Sports forced to apologise for the series of expletives accompanying the tirade.

Smith explains:

> He gets angry when you don't follow the principles. He doesn't care about you making mistakes. If you make mistakes trying to do the right thing, he'll back you one million per cent. If you start not being brave, not showing, not working hard enough, if you're cheating or cutting corners, he won't be happy. That's what makes Ange so passionate about his beliefs. If you stop doing that, the system breaks down. Whereas, all the time you're doing that, it's like a wave you keep riding. He's very determined about how he wants his teams to build and play and his cultural ethics within that group. If you step outside that, he's there to support you, bring you in, and educate you.
>
> There was one occasion when he pulled me to the side. He told me that my performance the previous week had not been up to my standards and that I'd been playing the easy game. It focused me completely. He never let anyone get comfortable and drop their standards. On the

flip side, he would praise you when things went well. We would walk into analysis on a Monday, and every player would be absolutely petrified of not having their name called out. He had that uncanny way of knowing what certain players needed at the right time.

The Melbourne Victory match turned out to be a significant turning point for Postecoglou and the Roar. Together they embarked on a 36-match unbeaten run stretching from matchday six of one campaign to matchday nine of the next, including the end-of-season finals. Roar won the regular season A-League title by eight points and backed it up in the Grand Final, beating Central Coast Mariners on penalties in one of the most remarkable Australian football matches ever. Roar had trailed their opponents 2-0 going into the last five minutes of extra time but scored twice in quick succession and won the shoot-out to end the season on the highest of highs.

Postecoglou had played an uplifting video to his players on the day of the match. The Brisbane Roar media team had been tasked with making the video, a compilation of Roar's best moments, under precise instruction from the boss. He even chose the background music: 'Revolution' by the John Butler Trio, a fitting choice.

* * *

The following season, as Neil Lennon was guiding Celtic to their first title of a nine-year run that would only end months before Postecoglou's arrival, Roar were winning the Grand Final for a second successive campaign, but only after finishing as runners-up in the regular season.

Smith had been made captain at the start of the year, with Postecoglou looking for a new leader after former captain Matt McKay moved to Rangers of all places. Smith certainly didn't expect to be in the running for the vacancy:

There weren't many conversations. I had just finished my first full season as a professional footballer. We were a new team, just being formed, with a great captain in Matt McKay. Ange put a leadership group in place; I wasn't even in that. There had been lots in the media about who would replace Matt, and my name wasn't even mentioned. One evening, I got a phone call from one of the journalists in Brisbane. My son had just been born, so I assumed he was phoning about that. He said, 'I hear you're the new captain.' I almost spat my coffee out and didn't even think about it after that. Then when I walked into training the next day, Ange asked me for a word. He would very rarely call you for a one-on-one before training, so I assumed I was in trouble. He said, 'Matt, you're the new captain. Are you okay with that?' I replied, 'Absolutely. I'm not going to let you down.' That was it.

Smith's maiden campaign as Roar captain wasn't nearly as successful for the team, with a bizarre run of five straight defeats following the end of the 36-match unbeaten run. Roar finished the regular season two points behind Central Coast Mariners but gathered themselves to reach the Grand Final, where they saw off Perth Glory.

By the time Postecoglou had departed for his next challenge with Melbourne Victory, Roar were the best team in Australia and Postecoglou was the biggest name. Yet that success hadn't been brought about because of a close relationship between the boss and his players. Postecoglou doesn't follow a style guide when leading his team. While other managers cosy up to their charges to form close bonds, Celtic's boss gives them room to breathe. He doesn't mingle in the dressing room or ask what they got up to at the weekend. His interactions are almost always football-related and usually on the training pitch or on matchdays.

'It's just me, mate,' he told me midway through his first season in Scotland. 'I've always said that you've got to be yourself. I think the dressing room is the players' domain. They should feel comfortable there. They shouldn't have a cranky old guy walking around telling them they should pick their rubbish up or change their music.'

Later in his career, while managing the Australian national team, players would dread getting the 'death seat' – the berth next to Postecoglou on long-haul flights. Ten-hour journeys would pass without their manager saying a single word, as Socceroo Ryan McGowan explains:

> You didn't want to get the seat next to him on the plane. I had it once and from Sydney to Dubai – a 15-hour flight – he didn't speak to me once. Nothing. Even when the flight hostess handed over the food, he didn't ask what I'd picked or nudge me. It's just his way of distancing himself. His main focus is winning football games, and he doesn't want anything to come between him and doing that. He's approachable in a way. You wouldn't go up to him and say, 'Hey boss, what did you get up to yesterday?' But if it was something game-related, he'd be very open. He likes to keep that distance because his main job is to pick a squad. It's human nature that personal relationships can come into your thinking, so he does put a barrier between the players and the coaching.
>
> I worked with him for four or five years, 15 of my caps probably came under him, and I'd have been lucky if he said five words to me outside of the pitch. Then, when I was at Sydney, we played Yokohama F. Marinos in the Champions League, and I spoke to him for about 20 minutes before the game. It totally freaked me out.

Smith agrees:

He's a personable guy. You could have a conversation with Ange, but you could see that there was never any click. He would hold the conversation to a point and then keep his distance. The players respected that. There were some very good times with Brisbane Roar in the dressing room and on the training pitch, but there was always a line. His coaching staff were the same. In football, there are often different relationships between players and certain coaches. Under Ange, you could talk to any of the coaches, and they would all have a unified response. They'd have the same feedback and messaging as him.

The approach has many benefits. It allows Postecoglou to cut the cord if the situation requires it. It's far harder to make a rational decision about a player's contract when you know all about his life at home. That's not to say that Celtic's boss isn't a caring man who thinks deeply about every facet of his football team. In the man's words, it's just the way he is.

Players seem to enjoy being given the space to operate with their team-mates, without their manager casting an intrusive eye over them – or so they think. To say that Postecoglou doesn't miss anything would be a gross understatement. He's always watching and gathering as much information as possible to make that next crucial decision.

CHAPTER 8

The Journey, Part 2:
Netflix and Thrills

*'We've got to build our house, make sure it's
nice and beautiful, then see how it stacks up
to the rest of the neighbourhood.'*

Ange Postecoglou

'WITHOUT SOUNDING arrogant, I've never doubted myself or wavered in my own self-belief. All of you were probably running a book on how long I'd last. A few of you probably had December, but that's now out the window.'

Ange Postecoglou is sitting proudly in the vast auditorium at Hampden Park in front of the media. Celtic have just won their first trophy under his stewardship, a nerve-shredding comeback victory over Hibernian to seal the League Cup, and he can't resist a dig at those who have written him off.

The Kyogo Furuhashi-inspired victory comes at the end of a pulsating six months, which has delivered glorious highs and depressing lows. The trophy win is vindication for the Aussie, his methods and the players who have bought into his way of doing things. After all the summer chat of Celtic being in crisis, it's they who once again find themselves picking up the major honours as the rest of Scottish football watches on enviously.

Celtic's 21st century has been dominated by silverware. The Premiership success Postecoglou and his players would enjoy months later would be the club's 36th major trophy: 16 league titles, 10 Scottish Cups and 10 League Cups in 22 seasons since the turn of the century. In the final 22 years of the previous century, Celtic won only 12. After going without a trophy in 2020/21, for only the third time this millennium, Celtic needed to come out on top in at least one tournament in Postecoglou's first season.

Brendan Rodgers, who contributed seven trophies and laid the groundwork for many more, would often speak about the importance of the League Cup. Often overlooked in comparison to the league and Scottish Cup, he felt the trophy was vital in giving the players something tangible to show for their early season endeavours. Postecoglou must have felt the same way as he sat in front of the media barely an hour after full time, having watched his team show all their battling qualities to get over the line.

Celtic's final victory was a fitting encapsulation of the first six months of the Ange era. Setbacks, like Paul Hanlon's 51st-minute header, seemed to have everyone questioning everything. But if belief existed, then answers could be found. Having Kyogo in the team was a help, even if he was nowhere near fully fit.

In this period, the Japanese star had become a talisman for the club, netting big goals at big moments, often out of nowhere. Like at Hampden, he'd been the match-winner on a sticky Thursday night two and a half weeks earlier, when a single goal had seen off Heart of Midlothian. That night, I was at the post-match press conference when Postecoglou cut a far less content figure in front of the media. Irritated by the line of questioning, he fired back at suggestions that his team had been fortunate to win the match. Of course, there had been other things going on in the background. There were distractions aplenty for Celtic in this turbulent October to December period. Some were enforced, while others were completely avoidable.

To say that the Hoops squad had the blinkers on would be an understatement. As far as they were concerned, they were the only horse in the race and nobody else would matter as long as they did the business. Having that attitude in April or May when the league is in your hands is one thing. That belief when trailing Rangers by as many as seven points on multiple occasions was more evidence of the squad buying into their manager's mindset.

The early months of the season had been interrupted by multiple international breaks. Celtic entered the first two FIFA windows in a precarious state, with individual results affecting how the entire support felt about Postecoglou and the project. By the November break, the debate had moved from whether Postecoglou was the right man to lead the club to how quickly he could get things right. Celtic had built up real momentum for the first time and had a reason to feel good. But Postecoglou could park any plans for a quieter time while international football took centre stage.

Distractions are never far away in Glasgow, as he'd tell fan media months later. 'In this city, with this football team, a thousand things happen every day that will try and take away your focus from what's important. You can get distracted by other clubs, stories, people saying things, and expectations. What we've tried to do is come in there with real concentration to be the best we can be and chip away and chip away. Don't look at the Premiership table, don't look at how many games are left, who's above and below us. Just focus on what's in front of us.'

The first distraction didn't actually affect Celtic, except it did. Rangers manager Steven Gerrard had decided to join the Premier League's Aston Villa, replacing Dean Smith on a three-and-a-half-year deal. The news that Gary McAllister and Michael Beale would also be joining him in the West Midlands was an extra blow for the Ibrox club, who hadn't made a great start to the season themselves. Given that they'd won the league by 25 points the previous season, there was always a fear that, even if Postecoglou improved Celtic's fortunes dramatically, he might still be unable to bridge the gap in his debut season. Rangers' failure to navigate the Champions League qualifying rounds and the early defeat to Dundee United gave Celtic fans hope that they weren't far off the pace. Gerrard's departure to Villa suddenly made Celtic the stable Glasgow club, something that would have been unthinkable months earlier.

Postecoglou was asked about the upheaval across the city, as is custom in Glasgow, and played down the distraction with two great analogies:

> We're trying to build something here, and when you're trying to build something and be successful, you can't afford to be looking over your fence to see what other people are doing. We've got to build our house, make sure it's nice and beautiful, then see how it stacks up to the rest of the neighbourhood. It's like when we watch TV these days. People binge a series in one night because they don't want to sit another week and wait for an episode, which is what I used to do in the old days, as you'd know. I feel like people want to binge this season as well. One result and it's over, a good result and it's done.

If the Aussie was building a neat new house while his neighbour's one fell apart, he could have done without any discontent in his own camp. Postecoglou had managed to silence, or at least quieten, the frustration among his supporters towards the boardroom with his team's impressive start. However, the board versus fans feud had never gone away. It was ignited again when Celtic's intention to appoint the controversial Bernard Higgins to a senior security role at the club became public knowledge.

Higgins, Assistant Chief Constable at Police Scotland, had played a significant part in implementing the infamous Offensive Behaviour at Football and Threatening Communications

(Scotland) Act 2012, which unfairly targeted football fans. The act was repealed in 2018 after tireless work from Labour MSP James Kelly but left a bitter taste in supporters' mouths. When reports of Higgins landing a job at Celtic emerged, several supporters' groups protested. Protests were addressed to Celtic chief executive Michael Nicholson and ranged from the launching of tennis balls, alongside a banner that read 'Nicholson, the ball is in your court', an open letter signed by over 130 fans' groups, to silent protests at home matches. The demonstrations were always peaceful, and the support for the team was never in question. Yet this was a distraction Celtic could have done without at such a challenging point in the season. The blame fell at the club's door rather than the supporters, and the sight of chairman Ian Bankier being jeered at the club's AGM weeks later must have been an unwelcome sight for Postecoglou.

Finally, and most sadly, the passing of club legend Bertie Auld at 83 left the club in mourning. Auld, a midfielder from the famous Lisbon Lions who won the European Cup in 1967, had been diagnosed with dementia just months earlier. Tributes would be paid to the iconic figure when Celtic returned to action after the international break, with the upcoming matches no longer seeming quite as important.

* * *

Celtic 2-0 Ferencváros, UEFA Europa League, Celtic Park, Tuesday, 19 October 2021

European matches aren't meant to kick off at the same time as *Countdown*. The charm of even UEFA's second competition – the Europa League – is lost a little when the Thursday night lights are replaced by the chime of the Tuesday home-time bell. Not that any Celtic-supporting youngsters would have been at school this Tuesday, nor their parents at work.

'I apologise to all the employers who had little productivity today as they were missing people and schools may have been empty,' Postecoglou would say. 'But they come here, create an energy, and we have to match that with our football.'

Celtic fans certainly faced a conundrum when it emerged that the matchday three clash against Ferencváros would be moving from the usual Thursday night slot to a Tuesday afternoon. As Glasgow opened its doors to the world's leaders for COP26 – the 26th United Nations Climate Change Conference – Celtic were left in a difficult position.

The effect of the conference on police resources meant that both Celtic and Rangers would have to play their second home match on matchday three. The clubs couldn't play at home simultaneously due to police, steward and service requirements, ruling out a blockbuster Thursday. Additionally, UEFA doesn't allow other continental fixtures to take place during Tuesday or Wednesday Champions League matches so, with the earliest of those taking place at 5.45pm, a 3.30pm Tuesday solution was the only remaining option.

Celtic went public with their frustrations, saying they'd 'exhausted all avenues' amid the 'unfortunate and unique set of circumstances driven by COP26'. They needn't have worried about supporters finding a way to make the match. Fans took short-notice holidays, announced sick days and flocked to Celtic Park. The crowd of 50,427 was the fifth-highest of all the European fixtures that took place that midweek. Only Atlético Madrid vs Liverpool, Ajax vs Borussia Dortmund, Benfica vs Bayern Munich, and Manchester United vs Atalanta attracted more. All of those took place in the Champions League. Crucially, all were in the late evening.

That's not to say that the Celtic support was happy that a vital European clash occurred during working hours. There were protests at the match – the wittiest banner reading 'FCUKUFEA. Conundrum clue: Fans before TV'. You didn't have to be Susie Dent to work that one out.

Their efforts weren't lost on Postecoglou. 'I just wanted to take this opportunity to thank so many supporters for committing to next week's match,' he said in a club statement in the lead-up to the game. 'We fully understand that this is a highly unusual time for a European match. However, I can assure our fans that we will be doing all we can to make it a good occasion for us and do all we can to get a positive result for our supporters.'

Postecoglou's team succeeded in making it a good occasion against a team that had eliminated Neil Lennon's Hoops from Champions League qualifying a year earlier. The irony of the Tuesday afternoon clash was that it almost certainly featured the season's most iconic goal. The scores were level approaching the hour mark, with little goalmouth action, when Celtic's two attacking forces combined to score a goal fit to grace any ground in Europe. Jota started the move virtually on his own goal line, working a one-two with Adam Montgomery and galloping into space. From 20 yards inside his half, he heard a roar from the crowd and spotted Kyogo Furuhashi making a trademark run behind the Hungarian defence. To say Jota's pass was on the money would insult the pound sterling. It couldn't have been more perfect, and neither could the Japanese forward's touch as he cushioned it into his path without breaking his stride and slotted past Dénes Dibusz.

Celtic Park went wild, then got even louder when Bálint Vécsei diverted the ball into his own net to seal the three points for Postecoglou's team. It could have been more emphatic, too. Callum McGregor had earlier missed a penalty on an afternoon when Celtic had delivered, just like the fans. That was hardly a coincidence, with Joe Hart saying, 'A 3.30pm kick-off on a Tuesday afternoon. To have the place full, we could only win. Otherwise, we'd have really let the people down.'

Ferencváros hadn't been great. They'd finish their group campaign with just three points. Yet these were early signs that Postecoglou's way of playing could bring success for Celtic in Europe. Callum McGregor and Jota had been excellent, while Carl Starfelt had played his best match. Celtic hadn't lost control of the match like in previous continental clashes under Postecoglou.

It was a significant moment, and Postecoglou's celebrations showed it. Celtic Park had rocked, and there was a sense that it was only the beginning. Tuesdays were when Celtic could be playing their European football the following season, only several hours later. Winning the league would afford them that luxury. The chase was on.

Celtic: *Hart, Ralston, Carter-Vickers, Starfelt, Montgomery, McGregor, Rogic, Turnbull, Abada, Kyogo, Jota*
Subs used: *Bitton, Giakoumakis, Scales, Johnston*

Ferencváros: *Dibusz, Wingo, Blažič, S. Mmaee, Ćivić, Laïdouni, Vécsei, Uzuni, Tokmac, Zachariassen, R. Mmaee*
Subs used: *do Rosário Calmon, Loncar, Mak*

* * *

Celtic 0-0 Livingston, Premiership, Celtic Park, Saturday, 30 October 2021

Nir Bitton couldn't even look as Giorgos Giakoumakis stepped up. The Israeli was facing his own goal, watching events on the giant screen attached to the top of the Lisbon Lions stand. At the other end, Giakoumakis and Celtic were about to pass up a massive opportunity.

Celtic had risen from the ashes after their worst start to a league season in 23 years. The team had found a way to win on the road, with the vital Aberdeen victory backed up by further successes against Motherwell, St Johnstone and Hibernian. Celtic had won the latter three with a bit to spare, while poor form across the city had allowed the gap to shrink from six points to just two. With Rangers not in action until the following day, victory for Celtic over Livingston would put Postecoglou's team back on top of the pile.

Yet things weren't going to be that straightforward. What followed was an extremely frustrating afternoon against a team that knew how to limit more talented opposition. Livingston didn't offer much, but neither did Celtic, despite having a remarkable 85 per cent of possession. Ninety dull minutes passed with virtually all of the drama saved for stoppage time. Celtic's golden chance arrived in strange circumstances – referee Bobby Madden awarding a penalty and sending off Ayo Obileye for slapping Kyogo on the back of the head.

Given that Josip Juranovic had confidently dispatched a penalty just seven days earlier, it was a major surprise to see Giakoumakis step up. The Greek forward had a good record from the spot in his time with VVV-Venlo, netting nine from his last ten, yet Juranovic seemed the more secure option. Postecoglou would later say that he'd made the decision weeks before the Livingston match and that Giakoumakis simply hadn't been on the pitch a week earlier. The Croatian was soon back in as the first choice. Giakoumakis's short run-up hardly inspired confidence, and his weak penalty was saved and then grasped by Max Stryjek.

What often goes under the radar on this late autumn afternoon is that Celtic still had two more major chances to win, even after the penalty. One fell to a combination of James Forrest and Giakoumakis, but the pair both scuffed efforts wide. Then, even later in the day, David Turnbull skied from around the penalty spot after being picked out by Anthony Ralston.

Of course, as many teenage girls would have you know, everything happens for a reason. Giakoumakis certainly redeemed himself and more in the final seven months of the campaign, finishing as the Premiership's joint-top scorer with 13 goals. Celtic's eventual ascent to the top of the table, courtesy of a 3-0 win over Rangers in February, was far more memorable.

At the time there was plenty of discussion about the team lacking bottle in the big moments. That would be answered in spades in the coming months. Bitton would have a better view of that.

Celtic: Hart, Ralston, Carter-Vickers, Starfelt, Juranovic, Bitton, McGregor, Turnbull, Abada, Giakoumakis, Jota
Subs used: Johnston, Kyogo, Forrest

Livingston: Stryjek, Devlin, Fitzwater, Obileye, Parkes, Kelly, Bailey, Holt, Omeonga, Shinnie, Anderson
Subs used: Forrest, Panayiotou, Longridge

* * *

Bayer Leverkusen 3-2 Celtic, UEFA Europa League, BayArena, Thursday, 25 November 2021

'No more nights like this.' Joe Hart's message was clear. There would be no more hard-luck stories in Europe.

Celtic have too proud a history to indulge in tales of glorious failure or defeats snatched from the jaws of victory. Yet a pattern of close calls had been forming for several years. Under Neil Lennon just a year earlier, Celtic had led eventual French champions Lille 2-0 away from home, only to draw 2-2. More remarkably, they'd been two goals up at the San Siro against AC Milan inside 14 minutes, only to fall to a 4-2 loss. Under Postecoglou, a two-goal lead had also been earned away to Real Betis before the home team came back to win the match. Remarkably, Celtic had netted the first goal in 11 straight European away matches, of which only four had been won, with two drawn and five lost from winning positions.

Copenhagen 1–1 Celtic (Europa League round of 32)

Riga 0-1 Celtic (Europa League qualifying)

Sarajevo 0-1 Celtic (Europa League qualifying)

Lille 2-2 Celtic (Europa League group stage)

Sparta Prague 4-1 Celtic (Europa League group stage)

AC Milan 4-2 Celtic (Europa League group stage)

Midtjylland 2-1 Celtic (AET) (Champions League qualifying)

Jablonec 2-4 Celtic (Europa League qualifying)
AZ Alkmaar 2-1 Celtic (Europa League qualifying)
Real Betis 4-3 Celtic (Europa League group stage)
Ferencváros 2-3 Celtic (Europa League group stage)

The ending was predictable. Celtic would start well but eventually come unstuck amid a flurry of home pressure. Often the home team wouldn't even have to produce anything special. Celtic would implode of their own volition.

The Europa League matchday five trip to Bayer Leverkusen felt different. For a start, Celtic hadn't scored first. They trailed through Robert Andrich's early header on a dreich evening in North Rhine-Westphalia. They'd then rallied to lead through a Josip Juranovic 'Panenka' penalty and a thrilling Jota counter-attack goal. The scenes when the winger dispatched the driven effort past Lukáš Hrádecký felt just as euphoric as the goals in Milan and Lille, but not with the same menacing danger attached. Yet, the inevitable still happened. Postecoglou's team had their hearts broken in the final ten minutes.

Andrich struck again to equalise, and then Moussa Diaby fired in a terrific volley. The reaction of the Celtic players when the France international's effort hit the back of the net said it all. At the time of the goal, ten Celtic players were inside their 18-yard box, a worry in itself. Only David Turnbull didn't display some sort of anguish when the ball hit the net. The exasperation from the rest, even usually tranquil figures like Callum McGregor and Juranovic, gave an insight into how they felt at being so close yet so far once again.

Quickfire conceded goals were nothing new for Celtic in Europe. Setbacks habitually rattled the team, with further blows arriving shortly afterwards. Against Betis, Celtic conceded in the 32nd and 34th minutes, then the 50th and 53rd. A year earlier, 67th- and 75th-minute strikes had been shipped in Lille, while AC Milan had scored in the 24th and 26th minutes.

'[We can take] loads of positives, of course, but I think we've got to be real,' Hart said to Virgin Media Sport. 'We're trying to create something where we're not here to take part, and we're here to really compete. There were probably only 10/15 minutes of that game in fragments where we were second best, and look what happened to us. Very frustrating. We're learning as a group. I feel like the supporters are with us, and we appreciate that, but we can't take that for granted. No more nights like this.'

As far as the supporters were concerned, the issue had been Postecoglou's substitutions, not that the boss was being blamed. The match seemed to hinge on the departures of Jota and Kyogo from the pitch, and their replacements Mikey Johnston and Albian Ajeti offering a fraction of their quality. Nir Bitton was also an impressive performer on the evening and was replaced by the less effective James McCarthy. Postecoglou was pretty blameless. The four subs he made, including Liel Abada, were the best he could bring off a 12-man bench that also included two goalkeepers, Ismaila Soro, Osaze Urhoghide, Dane Murray, Liam Shaw and others.

The defeat in Germany ended Celtic's hopes in the Europa League, parachuting them down to the newly launched Europa Conference League after Christmas. Victory in a matchday six dead rubber against Real Betis would mean Celtic ended a respectable group stage campaign with nine points. With leads lost in Seville and Leverkusen, it was a case of what might have been.

The players travelled back to Scotland and attended the funeral of legendary Celtic figure Bertie Auld at St Mary's Chapel the following morning. If they needed inspiration for what the club could achieve in Europe, they needn't look very far.

Bayer Leverkusen: Hrádecký, Frimpong, Kossounou, Tah, Hincapié, Diaby, Andrich, Palacios, Paulinho, Adli, Wirtz
Subs used: Amiri, Sinkgraven, Tapsoba

Celtic: Hart, Ralston, Carter-Vickers, Welsh, Juranovic, Bitton, Turnbull, McGregor, Forrest, Kyogo, Jota
Subs used: *Abada, Johnston, Ajeti, McCarthy*

* * *

Celtic 1-0 Hearts, Premiership, Celtic Park, Thursday, 2 December 2021

Ange Postecoglou didn't take kindly to the assertion that his team had been fortunate to win. The Hoops had just beaten the third-best team in the country, Heart of Midlothian, on a Thursday night fraught with danger. It hadn't been pretty against Robbie Neilson's team, especially in the closing stages, but Kyogo Furuhashi's contentious first-half strike had been enough for victory.

The three points moved the Celts five ahead of the Jambos, with a match in hand and, more significantly, back to four behind Rangers. On the face of it, Postecoglou had little to be concerned about. His team had taken 22 points from the last 24 available. Yet injuries had given him plenty to contend with.

Throughout the season, Postecoglou's players would be plagued with muscle injuries. Similarly energetic teams such as Jürgen Klopp's Liverpool and Marcelo Bielsa's Leeds United had encountered the same issues in the first years under their managers, with players' bodies struggling to cope with the demands put on them. Celtic lost virtually every summer signing to a muscle injury at some stage early in the season. When Postecoglou added strength in depth in January and beyond, the injuries lessened.

Celtic started the Hearts match without Cameron Carter-Vickers and Greg Taylor, while starting trio Anthony Ralston, Stephen Welsh and Jota all limped off on a damaging night, regardless of the result. The match had been a gruelling one. Hearts had given as good as they got for large swathes of the second half, with Stephen Kingsley and Barrie McKay passing up clear-cut opportunities. Postecoglou was delighted with the character his players had shown but took exception to the media's negative slant after the match.

Reporter: 'Their manager feels as if you have to come here and play double what you normally play because they didn't get big decisions in the game [sic].'

Postecoglou: 'You should be asking him. You're asking me. What's the question for me? Did I feel that the referee made the difference today? Is that the analysis here? [laughs] It's not my analysis. We were the better team, and we deserved to win.'

Reporter: 'Are you worried about the second half when they started to come into the game? They had a couple of really big moments.'

Postecoglou: 'Which moments? James Forrest didn't have a chance? If you're talking about big moments, who had the more big moments? You can manufacture a story any way you want. The reality is that we dominated that game. It was 1-0, and they were always in with a chance, which is fair enough. But if we had been more ruthless in the final third, it would have been a different scoreline.'

Remarkably, Postecoglou's comments seemed small-fry a few minutes later when Jambos boss Robbie Neilson strolled into the media room and claimed he'd be sent to jail if he said what he really thought of referee Bobby Madden's performance.

Nevertheless, it was special to witness Ange on the charge that December evening, unwilling to accept an unfair summary of the match. Postecoglou had the bit between his teeth and he'd need every bit of that fight for the harsh winter months when Celtic simply had to dig in and stay as close to Rangers as possible.

To their eternal credit, the Celtic players did just that in a challenging period where they battled injuries, a brutal fixture schedule and various distractions. Of the eight domestic wins they chalked up between the final international break in

October and the winter break at the end of December, six were by a single goal, with just two won by a bigger scoreline. All but the 3-0 defeat of Dundee United, inspired by the red-hot Tom Rogic, were in doubt going into the final ten minutes. Celtic were rarely at their free-flowing best in these stuffy winter months, but they didn't have to be. They just had to win. It could all have been over if they hadn't.

For all of the upheaval across the city, Rangers were flawless in the league from Giovanni van Bronckhorst's appointment until the winter shutdown. The Ibrox team won nine straight league matches between Halloween and Boxing Day – a longer winning run than Celtic managed at any point in the campaign. Rangers won at traditionally troublesome venues such as Fir Park, Easter Road and Tynecastle. Just like Celtic, it was rarely by a hefty scoreline.

As a result, Celtic regularly entered challenging fixtures well off the pace. On four consecutive matchdays, the Hoops took to the pitch seven points behind their rivals. The fact that some of these matches were against eventual top six opposition such as Hearts, Dundee United and Motherwell added further pressure. Victories in all four showed that Celtic had the mettle to be champions, even when it looked like a long shot.

It regularly felt like Celtic were pushing a truck uphill during this period. If it wasn't the fixture list putting Rangers in the earlier kick-off slot, it was being forced to play a midfielder up front with all three strikers injured simultaneously. In a rebuilding season, it would have been so easy for Celtic to let all these distractions force their eye off the ball. But Postecoglou doesn't believe in excuses. He only sees opportunities.

Postecoglou: 'This group of players don't want excuses. They want to go out there and prove they can overcome every challenge. We have had plenty of them since I got here, and we will keep tackling them in the same way. We had challenges right from the moment I came here. Throwing guys in without training, throwing guys in who hadn't had a pre-season, throwing guys in from the other side of the world. Through it all, we haven't made excuses, we haven't tried to make allowances, we haven't said "give us time".'

Perhaps that's why he was taken aback by the cynical tone of questioning after the Hearts match, Celtic's tenth win in 12 matches. The form was immense but the rocky start to the campaign had left little room for error. Celtic finished 2021 six points off the pace, with dropped points at St Mirren the only black mark in an otherwise flawless period. Staying in touch would prove vital in 2022, as Rangers started to drop points regularly. But the final month of 2021 would be remembered most for Hibernian, Hampden and a half-fit Kyogo.

Celtic: *Hart, Ralston, Welsh, Starfelt, Juranovic, McGregor, Rogic, Turnbull, Forrest, Kyogo, Jota*
Subs used: *Montgomery, Johnston, Bitton*

Hearts: *Gordon, Smith, Souttar, Halkett, Kingsley, Devlin, Haring, Woodburn, McEneff, McKay, Ginnelly*
Subs used: *Boyce, Mackay-Steven*

* * *

Hibernian 1-2 Celtic, League Cup Final, Hampden Park, Sunday, 19 December 2021

The power of Kyogo Furuhashi was felt before a ball was even kicked at Hampden Park. Talk of whether Celtic's talisman would be fit to start the League Cup Final had dominated proceedings since he hobbled off against Real Betis. The Europa League fixture had been a dead rubber, with Celtic already eliminated from the competition, and Postecoglou had initially decided to rest the forward and the ten other players who started the 3-0 win over Dundee United. An early hamstring injury to Albian Ajeti led Postecoglou to introduce Kyogo to the action, only for the Japan international to pull up with the same problem. It was terrible luck, and Postecoglou surely regretted the decision to put the forward on.

He missed the narrow wins over Motherwell and Ross County, with Liel Abada and David Turnbull playing up front in his place, and seemed sure to sit out the Hampden showpiece too. Then, in the days leading up to the final, social media rumours claiming that Kyogo was fit started to circulate. When the team was announced and the forward was in it, it felt as if Celtic couldn't lose. Almost every tweet and Facebook comment centred around one man, with the other ten starters and Postecoglou a mere afterthought.

'Of course there is a risk,' Celtic's boss said at the time. 'But good luck trying to keep him out. There was no chance. He would have snuck on the bus or snuck on to the field at some point.' Quite simply, Kyogo wasn't fit, but his determination to overcome the hamstring injury had led Postecoglou to trust him. The consequences were that he'd miss the early part of the following year, yet most fans wouldn't change things now.

Celtic's form hadn't suffered in the two matches he'd sat out. Anthony Ralston's 97th-minute winner days earlier against Ross County had been the breakthrough moment many had hoped to see. Everything seemed to have conspired against Celtic in Dingwall, with the starting front three of Josip Juranovic, Liel Abada and Adam Montgomery saying it all. Things started well when Abada struck from close range midway through the first half, but a Jack Baldwin equaliser and a red card for Carl Starfelt left Celtic staring down the barrel. Yet the ten men continued to play their stuff and eventually worked the golden opportunity for Ralston right in front of the euphoric Hoops fans. The goal made belief soar, and Celtic would score many more crucial late goals, most notably Abada's against Dundee United seven weeks later.

The fact that they'd managed to win despite missing six forwards – including Giorgos Giakoumakis, Jota and Kyogo – was another good sign. The team had learned that when presented with such obstacles, the answers lay in their football.

Four days later at Hampden, the team had a more settled look, with Kyogo and Mikey Johnston back involved.

Hibernian had problems of their own, having just parted company with Jack Ross after a run of one league win in nine. The sacking seemed a little harsh, given that Ross had just led them to the cup final with a stunning 3-1 win over Rangers less than three weeks earlier. The hero from their other recent Hampden success over the Ibrox team, David Gray, was put in temporary charge and led the team out alongside Postecoglou at a boisterous Hampden.

When the smoke eventually cleared from both ends of the national stadium, an entertaining match emerged. Hibs frustrated Celtic for large parts of the first half, and when Paul Hanlon lost Starfelt to score from a corner shortly after the break, it felt like one of the Hampden days Celtic used to experience under Neil Lennon and Ronny Deila. Then Celtic struck when Hibs were most vulnerable.

Postecoglou wants his teams to use every minute of the 90 to score goals. He demands that his players go forward as soon as possible from kick-off. There were 11 seconds between Tom Rogic restarting and Kyogo slotting the ball into the Hibs net. In that time, Nir Bitton, Greg Taylor and Callum McGregor all touched the ball. McGregor's lofted pass for Kyogo was immense, and the touch to control and finish was even better. As the half-fit forward wheeled away clothed in dark green – both teams were strangely wearing their away kits – Postecoglou must have had a massive smile on his face.

There was a real hint of the Aussie in the winner too. Again, Hibs were napping as Tom Rogic took a quick free kick, lifting the ball over the defence for Kyogo to lob over Matt Macey and into the net. The Hibs defenders were incensed at referee John Beaton for allowing the free kick to be taken while they were waiting to make a substitution. Their frustrations would have been better directed at themselves for stopping against a team that never does. The strike would later be named Celtic's goal of the season at the club's end-of-season awards. Commentator Rory Hamilton saw the beauty at the time. 'A phenomenal finish from an unbelievable player,' was his line.

Celtic survived some late scares to get over the line. Kyogo was the hero of the first cup win of the season, but there had been other vital contributions. Tom Rogic's quick thinking had been the making of the winner, while Joe Hart had made several impressive saves, including from Joe Newell in stoppage time. Callum McGregor's influence had also been important. It hadn't been pretty, in keeping with Celtic's November and December schedule, but it would have felt out of place if it had been. The team had found a way to get over the line, giving supporters a memorable day amid a period of uncertainty, with lockdowns and closed-door matches back on the agenda due to the rise of the Omicron variant.

While Celtic didn't have to see off Rangers to win the trophy, they'd beaten double cup holders St Johnstone, Hearts and Hibernian, and Raith Rovers, who had just dispatched Aberdeen. With a rough month ahead over the festive period, this new Celtic team led by McGregor had delivered silverware at the first time of asking.

Kyogo's contribution had been immense, but it came at a cost. The forward would play just 14 more minutes for Celtic over the next four months, arguably only returning to form on the final day of the season against Motherwell. When Celtic next faced Hibernian, in the first match of 2022, there would be no shortage of Japanese influence, despite their talisman's absence.

Hibernian: *Macey, McGinn, Porteous, Hanlon, Stevenson, Newell, Doyle-Hayes, Boyle, Campbell, Murphy, Nisbet*
Subs used: *Allan, Doidge, Doig*

Celtic: *Hart, Juranovic, Carter-Vickers, Starfelt, Taylor, McGregor, Rogic, Turnbull, Abada, Kyogo, Johnston*
Subs used: *Bitton, Ralston, Moffat, Scales*

CHAPTER 9

Callum McGregor: Fuel the Fire

'I love the intensity about the
club – having to win Saturday,
Wednesday, Tuesday, Thursday.'
Callum McGregor

THERE WAS a moment at Tannadice that summed up Callum McGregor. Celtic were level with Dundee United and minutes away from regaining their Premiership crown. A draw was also the desired result for the home team in their pursuit of European football after the summer break. The match was threatening to peter out with both teams happy to take their lot and move on – Celtic to the title and Dundee United to the Conference League.

With time ticking down, the ball worked its way back to Hoops goalkeeper Joe Hart. Rather than start a quick attack like he'd been programmed to do all season, he hesitated and began to run the clock down. 'Joe,' came the shout from the masked man in the centre circle. 'Let's go.' McGregor wasn't happy with his lot from the match. He wanted Celtic to find the winner to top off the triumph, even if that meant risking everything when there was no real reason to.

McGregor's journey from an academy graduate with an uncertain future to the very epitome of an Ange Postecoglou captain is one of the finest stories in modern Celtic history. He's benefited mainly from three accomplished Celtic managers and a sensational captain in Scott Brown. But it's McGregor's hard work and continual desire to improve himself – key traits of a Postecoglou player – that's led him to heights many doubted he'd ever reach. That night at Tannadice he was at the centre of every celebration photo. After being part of Celtic's 2020/21 failure, this one was personal to him. He was going to enjoy every moment.

* * *

McGregor is a shining example of what the Celtic academy can produce at its very best. A player coming through the youth set-up to become captain, winning numerous honours and spending the vast majority of their career at the club, all while being adored by the supporters.

McGregor first donned the Hoops at the age of eight. The late Tommy Burns played a prominent role in his development in the early days, helping to establish the mindset that's made McGregor such a leader for Postecoglou. As a youngster he was so talented that he regularly played in older age groups, with most training taking place at Barrowfield, in the shadow of Celtic Park and under the watchful eye of the iconic Burns.

'Tommy was a real role model for the academy,' he said in an interview with Celtic TV in early 2022. 'He was the first-team coach, but he would come down to Barrowfield at 5pm. Jimmy, the groundsman, would be saying, "Right, lights off, the boys have school in the morning." But Tommy would go, "No, more corners, more free kicks." He just wanted to be on the training pitch constantly and, for us, who better to be coaching you and watching your session?'

McGregor was always considered a potential first-team player, although his current role as club captain may even have surprised someone like Burns. As he reached his teenage years, he often took in first-team matches as a ball boy in a move designed by the club to give hopeful youngsters a taste of the big matchdays. At 16, McGregor was photographed, alongside team-mate Marcus Fraser, celebrating a late Scott McDonald header against Rangers. While Tony Mowbray's hapless Celts went on to lose their lead minutes later, the moment registered with McGregor and gave him even more hunger to make his own memories in a Celtic shirt.

McGregor: 'When that goal goes in and the players are celebrating, you want that to be you. You try and envisage yourself being there later down the line. You were just there to enjoy the game and the atmosphere of watching the first team play. The first team was really strong at that stage. There were loads of guys coming through like Aiden [McGeady] who really inspired me to try and complete the journey from the youth team to the first team. Watching Aiden week in, week out was my fuel.'

While McGeady was laying on goals for the likes of McDonald and Jan Vennegoor of Hesselink, McGregor was turning professional and excelling in a youth team that was having success. Under Stevie Frail and John Kennedy, the young Hoops won the Scottish Youth Cup in four successive seasons at the start of the 2010s. McGregor played in every final, even scoring a hat-trick in the 8-0 demolition of Queen of the South in 2012.

Lewis Toshney was a team-mate of McGregor in two of the Hampden finals. As a lifelong Celtic fan, he now watches 'Wee Cal' captain his team up and down the country. Toshney told me:

> He was a year younger than me, but he always played above himself. He was always a very good player. I've been trying to get his number for so long, but our mutual friends know that I'll just pester him. In our dressing room, he was a quiet guy. We were older so it would have been a little daunting for him at times. Nowadays, you can see that he's become a real leader. I'm so happy for him.

We won the double three years in a row at under-19s, and I think only a few guys got full-time contracts with Celtic. Only me and James Keatings from my age group. Then Callum and James Forrest in other years.

When I was at Celtic, he went to Notts County under Neil Lennon. I was shipped out to Dundee at the same time so we were in the same boat. To be honest, I thought Cal was finished at Celtic at that stage because he wasn't getting a sniff. But he got his chance under Ronny Deila and just took it.

For all of McGregor's success at youth-team level, his real breakthrough was to come at Notts County. Having just turned 20, the midfielder was in and around the Hoops first team but yet to make his first appearance. Despite scoring in a friendly win at Brentford, quality midfielders such as Victor Wanyama, Joe Ledley and Scott Brown meant that McGregor's chances of playing time were slim. An opportunity at the League One outfit emerged.

While a loan move can often spell the end of a player's time at the club these days, McGregor's did the opposite. His intention was always to return to Celtic. 'It was so important in my development as a young player, going into a men's environment,' he told Sky Sports. 'When a lot of people think about going on loan, think "that's me done". But I didn't see it like that. I saw it as a challenge to go and play and learn about life in men's football and what it meant to these guys to win. That's the main thing that stood out to me. These guys were playing for their livelihoods. I'll always be grateful to Notts County for giving me the opportunity to go and play men's football.'

McGregor joined the Magpies on an initial six-month loan, but his early season form led to the move being extended until the end of the campaign. He caught fire in the East Midlands, finishing as the club's top scorer with 14 goals from midfield. While on loan, he developed a strong relationship with an 18-year-old Jack Grealish, also at the club on loan from Aston Villa.

McGregor was a changed man when he returned to Glasgow in the summer of 2014, the perfect time to make an impression on new Hoops boss Ronny Deila. He made his debut in Deila's first competitive match – a Champions League qualifier in Iceland against KR Reykjavík. McGregor struck the only goal of a frustrating encounter six minutes from time and then repeated the feat in Celtic's following two European away matches against Legia Warsaw and NK Maribor. He continued his impressive start by netting in the opening league fixture of the season – a 3-0 win away to St Johnstone.

McGregor had spectacularly burst on to the scene, and the signing of a new five-year contract signalled Celtic's intent too. However, he scored just one more goal in the rest of the campaign and dropped out of Deila's plans just as Celtic found form. McGregor didn't feature in any of the final 19 matches of the campaign, although he did suffer a broken ankle in late April. Despite that, he was kept around for the following season, weighing in with six goals, including a memorable solo strike against Ajax in the Europa League. McGregor had shown an ability to rise to the big occasion in Europe, but a lack of consistency and defined position were costing him.

Like many of his team-mates, his fortunes improved with the arrival of Brendan Rodgers in May 2016. Deila had laid the foundations for a successful team but the Northern Irishman took Celtic's stars to new heights. McGregor had gone up against Rodgers' Liverpool in a frantic League Cup tie during his time down south, and fans hoped he'd be precisely the kind of player the new boss would improve.

Rodgers did improve McGregor. He contributed seven goals in Celtic's 'invincible' campaign, all from December onwards. However, unlike team-mates Stuart Armstrong and James Forrest, McGregor's proper rise didn't come until the next campaign. Until that point, the midfielder still had the hint of a nearly man: the guy who was injured for his first title-winning celebration and spurned a golden chance for Celtic to win away to Borussia Mönchengladbach. That was all about to change.

As Celtic struggled to live up to the previous campaign at the start of 2017/18, McGregor became the shining light. He quickly became a vital part of Rodgers' team, striking 12 times in all competitions, including five in his first eight league matches. His goals against Bayern Munich and Zenit Saint Petersburg once again proved he was a man for the big stage in Europe, while his most spectacular strike was saved for the last match of the season – the Scottish Cup Final victory over Motherwell.

Around the same time, McGregor received international recognition for the first time, becoming a big part of the Scotland set-up under Alex McLeish and Steve Clarke. He quickly became an indispensable member for club and country, perhaps to his cost. In 2018/19, McGregor played more minutes of competitive football (5,894) than any other player in the world. He'd featured in 69 matches – 59 for Celtic and 10 for Scotland – with only Philippe Coutinho and Jesús Gallardo playing in more different fixtures throughout the season.

While Celtic were keen to shout from the hills about the achievement, there was a sense that this over-reliance on McGregor may not be a good thing. Fellow academy graduate Kieran Tierney had also been heavily overplayed in his early years and has endured several injuries since. Thankfully, McGregor's condition didn't seem to falter and he played an increasingly prominent part, especially in the 2019/20 campaign under Neil Lennon, when he netted 13 goals. McGregor looked as good as ever at the start of 2020, with a sublime performance at Motherwell a particular highlight.

Like everyone else at the club, the 2020/21 season was difficult for the midfielder. His tally of four goals was the lowest in seven seasons – strangely, he only matched that in Postecoglou's first season – while a crazy red card in the final derby of the campaign at Ibrox had many questioning whether he had the mentality to succeed Scott Brown as captain.

Amid all the doom and gloom of the Covid-hit season, McGregor had benefited from one thing: more exposure as Celtic skipper. With Brown starting just 25 of Celtic's 38 league matches, many of McGregor's appearances had come in the leading role. He'd been earmarked as the next Hoops captain a few years earlier, with his appearance in a behind-the-scenes video posted by the club after a cup tie against Partick Thistle signalling his future role. With Brown rested but still in the matchday squad, McGregor was seen leading the warm-up, almost identically to the legendary skipper.

When the bid for ten in a row had blown up in Celtic's faces and Brown announced his departure, McGregor was still the leading candidate to replace him. Yet it's not accurate to suggest that every single supporter was on board with the idea of him becoming the captain of this new era. Some reckoned that McGregor had been weighed down by the pressure of being Celtic's stand-in captain in the previous campaign. They felt it would be better for him not to be burdened by that responsibility in order to get back to his consistent best.

Of course, the notion of McGregor being weighed down by anything seems pretty laughable now. The scepticism towards his credentials was nothing more than blowback from a disastrous season where Celtic had completely capitulated. On 19 July 2021, 39 days after his appointment, Ange Postecoglou made McGregor his Celtic captain. While the Aussie had deliberated for several weeks, the decision was never really in doubt.

In the club announcement, McGregor said, 'I know I'm following in the footsteps of some great names in the club's history, and I've been able to learn from one of the best in Scott Brown over the past few years. I'm delighted that the manager has put his trust in me by giving me the captain's armband.

It's a new era for the club, and I'm looking forward to playing my part.'

The captaincy and an impressive Euro 2020 display, amid a generally disheartening tournament for Scotland, seemed to rejuvenate McGregor as he headed into his eighth season as a first-team Celtic player. From the outset it became clear that the old McGregor was back and that he'd play a pivotal role in an ambitious playing style.

Presented with a blank canvas, you'd struggle to design a more ideal captain for a Postecoglou team. McGregor's ability to always be an option for goalkeeper and defence and to link the play is key to Celtic beating the opposition press. He's adept at protecting the ball in tight areas and passing forward. He sets the tone in every training session and match and has the stamina required to carry out an intense game plan. Postecoglou probably couldn't believe his luck when he turned up at Lennoxtown and first cast eyes on the midfielder.

After a sparkling start to the season, Celtic faltered when McGregor missed several matches after picking up a knock against Ross County. He sat out four matches, with Celtic losing two, drawing one, and beating lower-league Raith Rovers. When he returned to the team alongside Kyogo Furuhashi for the 4-0 reversal against Bayer Leverkusen, there was an immediate improvement in the team's fluidity. With McGregor back in the heart of the midfield, Celtic soon embarked on a 13-match unbeaten run, including 12 wins, until the next meeting with the Germans.

While McGregor's footballing ability improved Celtic as a team, his leadership was also coming to the fore. Minutes after the 6-0 thumping of Dundee in Postecoglou's second league match, he gathered his team-mates in the centre circle and delivered a message. 'It is just good to show the togetherness,' he told the press afterwards. 'It is just important that they feel the importance of winning at Celtic Park in style, and we just continue to work ever so hard in training, perform as best as we possibly can in games, and try to send the supporters home happy every week.'

McGregor would do similar in defeat too. Later in the season, after the Scottish Cup semi-final loss to Rangers at Hampden, he gathered his dejected team-mates together and said his piece. He did the same in the aftermath of Real Madrid's 3-0 victory at Celtic Park months later. He also walked the walk, leading by example at times of real jeopardy.

Shortly after the 2021/22 winter break, McGregor suffered a severe facial injury after a clash with Alloa Athletic winger Adam King. While tabloids claimed the Hoops skipper could miss months, McGregor miraculously sat out just two matches, returning to the Celtic line-up for the derby against Rangers, wearing a protective mask and putting in a sensational performance. The sacrifice of putting himself into the heat of battle while not fully fit spoke volumes and set the tone on a night of redemption for Celtic. That hunger to make it on to the pitch for the derby despite the circumstances was matched by Daizen Maeda, who flew back to play a part despite featuring for Japan in an international hours earlier. The pair's determination to play was in stark contrast to new Rangers signing Aaron Ramsey, who watched the match from the Main Stand at Celtic Park.

'I'm not going to ditch it [the mask] if I still need it,' McGregor told me after several more sublime performances. 'It's healing well. The general day-to-day stuff is fine, but I still need it for the contact, training and matches. But it is getting better, which is positive.'

Celtic's skipper would wear the mask for the rest of the season, next featuring without it on his return to pre-season in July. By that stage Celtic were champions and McGregor had lifted two trophies in his first season as captain. His gesture to Hart just minutes before the title was won against Dundee United was a testament to the impact Postecoglou had made. But even without the Aussie in the dugout he may have been doing similar.

It was fitting that McGregor's first league title was clinched at Tannadice, the ground where Celtic had surrendered their crown a year earlier. 'We've been so used to success, and when you experience this, it's sore,' he told Sky Sports at the time. 'To watch them lift the trophy will be sore and will fuel the fire for next season.'

While McGregor's words may have been perceived as false optimism at the time, they'd soon prove fairly prophetic. Like his boss, the skipper rarely says things to fill air time. Almost everything that comes out of his mouth is well thought out and with meaning.

Fourteen months later, the meaning was found as thousands celebrated Celtic's latest success. The scene couldn't have been more contrasting to the sparse Tannadice the previous season. 'The players deserve it so much,' he told the same broadcasters. 'The fans were unbelievable again tonight. They have been all season. I'm so proud of the lads and everyone at the club. It's a new group and we've been absolutely relentless since day one.' Then, his finest quote, given to BBC Radio Scotland: 'We had a good run at being champions. You take a slap in the face. Then you've got to show your personality.'

As well as two domestic trophies in season 2021/22, McGregor scooped numerous individual prizes, including the PFA Player of the Year and Celtic's in-house version. He also penned another new long-term contract, keeping him at the club until the summer of 2026. By then he'll have been on Celtic's books for a quarter of a century. While his contemporaries, such as Stuart Armstrong and Ryan Christie, have jetted south for big money and competitive Premier League football, McGregor has thrived while going all in as Celtic captain, just like his predecessor Brown.

'I've been here for nearly 20 years now, and it's been a part of me growing up,' he told me after signing the deal. 'To come from the academy and make the breakthrough and now to be club captain is something I'm hugely proud of. I've had conversations with the board and several guys around it, and we see the club progressing in a positive way. I love the intensity about the club – having to win Saturday, Wednesday, Tuesday, Thursday. I love winning trophies and I think this club can provide the best platform to do that.'

There haven't been many in recent years who have understood Celtic better than McGregor. Nor many who have led the club with such distinction. In the hour after Celtic lifted their first Premiership title under Postecoglou, he was one of the few players who gave up time to speak to fan media. As most of Celtic's stars jetted off to sunnier climes at the end of the season, McGregor was at a Lisbon Lions lunch organised by Celtic to celebrate the 55th anniversary of the European Cup triumph.

This current Celtic team are McGregor's in the same way the previous one was Brown's. He's immensely respected by his team-mates, constantly setting standards and leading the way in anything from warm-ups to trophy celebrations. When Joe Hart was tasked with choosing a Celtic song while on a summer holiday, his choice of McGregor's 'He's like me and you, he loves Celtic too' seemed pretty apt.

When the new season swung around, McGregor was given the honour of unfurling the championship flag to commemorate the previous title win. He told club media: 'When you think about the people that have done it over the years, for the club to ask me to do it is a huge honour personally, and for my family to watch that.' In the following weeks, he led Celtic back into the Champions League, performing admirably in the opener against Real Madrid.

It's telling that, even when Postecoglou made nine changes for the League Cup trip to Ross County, McGregor remained in the team. When all is said and done, he'll go down as one of Celtic's most decorated players. He'll also be remembered as one of the most underrated to pull on the Hoops. Between now and then, there's a lot more improving to be done. Who knows where the true ceiling of Celtic's golden academy bhoy sits?

CALLUM MCGREGOR: FUEL THE FIRE

Callum, Callum McGregor
There's no one better
He's like me and you
He loves Celtic too

CHAPTER 10

Socceroos

'These are just small details but he continually drums it into you that they will make a difference.'

Ryan McGowan

WHEN ANGE Postecoglou grabbed the mic and addressed the Celtic support on the final day of his debut season in Glasgow, he had every single person inside the stadium captivated. The previous 90 minutes had been a joyous celebration of Celtic's title triumph, with singing, pyrotechnics and even tears dominating a lovely mid-May afternoon. When Postecoglou took centre stage, he quickly became the only thing that mattered.

'I've got a group of players who have been unbelievable,' he said while shuffling from side to side, almost like a stand-up comedian. 'Champions of Scotland, and well deserved. And for you, the best on the planet. You've embraced me, you've embraced my family, you've embraced this jumper. I want everyone to enjoy today, enjoy the summer, and we will come back bigger, better because we never stop.' The loudest roar of the day, perhaps the season.

While we'll look at Postecoglou and Celtic's post-season messaging later on, let's just appreciate an elite communicator performing at the top of his game. The address to supporters on the Celtic Park turf lasted 1 minute and 47 seconds, from the first word to the last. In that short period, in an unfamiliar environment, Postecoglou gave fans exactly what they wanted without overstaying his welcome. Sure, Celtic's achievement of wresting back the title from Rangers was immense, and the speech reflected that. But what people wanted at that moment was one last jolt to send them into the summer in a buoyant mood. Postecoglou supplied that, with players, staff, supporters and worldwide television viewers all present. There were no secrets. Celtic would be better next season.

Postecoglou's speech hitting the perfect note was no accident. Celtic's boss is an immense communicator, one of the very best working in the game right now. That shines through on grand occasions like that sunny afternoon and in more intimate surroundings. He's a master of the motivational team talk. Players end his speeches pumped up to the max and ready to commit minor offences just to earn their boss's praise. It's little wonder that Celtic so often score early in big matches, with the boss's inspirational words still ringing in the players' ears.

Defender Ryan McGowan witnessed plenty of stirring Postecoglou speeches while playing for the Australian national team, telling me with a big smile:

> His team talks were incredible. The best I've heard by far. He could be Al Pacino in the movies. On game day, we would have a meeting just before lunch and he would name the team and do this talk. Typically the games were at night, so you would have your meal and go back to your rooms. A lot of us would be trying to get a pre-match sleep and our heads would just be buzzing from his talk. I've spoken to Tommy [Rogic], and he says they did a couple of those talks before games at Celtic. Some managers can try and do it and it doesn't work but Ange can get everyone going.

While McGowan's words paint a fascinating picture, fortunately for Celtic fans footage of at least two Postecoglou Socceroos speeches are readily available online. In one clip, he laments the lack of coverage football in Australia receives compared to some of the country's more traditional sports.

'I wanna wake up tomorrow morning, and the papers are not talking about the next AFL player that f***** farted or the f***** NRL who did something stupid, or some f***** rugby union thing. I want them talking about our f***** game. I want them talking about us.'

Postecoglou takes immense satisfaction from proving people wrong. A large part of him enjoys it when he, his team or even the entire sport is written off or not given the credit it deserves. It gives him extra ammunition to achieve the impossible, like overturning a 25-point deficit to make Celtic champions or winning a historic Asian Cup title with the Socceroos.

While footage of Postecoglou's Socceroos talks show a unified group all pulling in the same direction, things weren't like that before he took over. Much like his first stint in the A-League with Brisbane Roar, Postecoglou inherited a mess with the national side.

He'd been building a strong Melbourne Victory team back in his hometown, albeit without any success, while the Aussies were imploding on the world stage. The Socceroos had reached their rock bottom under German coach Holger Osieck, with two results that looked more at home in tennis than football – consecutive 6-0 losses to Brazil and France. When Osieck was removed, and Football Australia chairman Frank Lowy announced that his successor would be an Aussie, it was down to two men: Postecoglou or Graham Arnold. It was always more likely to be the former.

Victory didn't stand in Postecoglou's way. However, they weren't thrilled with how events transpired as Postecoglou became the first man to jump from the A-League to manage Australia. Privately, his main ambition was to win the 2015

Asian Cup on home soil. Before then, there was the small matter of a World Cup in Brazil a year earlier, and Australia had to be competitive with the world watching.

Much like his arrival at Roar, Postecoglou inherited an ageing squad still hanging on to past glories. Australia had named the oldest party of any team at the 2010 World Cup. When Postecoglou joined eight months from the 2014 edition, not much seemed to have changed. The country still relied on stalwarts from the celebrated 2006 World Cup campaign, such as Mark Schwarzer and Lucas Neill, while other veterans such as Brett Emerton and Harry Kewell had only recently called it a day.

Postecoglou was about to usher in a fresh era for the Socceroos. He went out with the old and in with the new, casting the net far and wide to identify untapped talent, looking at players who hadn't been considered previously. His final 23-man squad for Brazil, minus the injured Tom Rogic, saw unlikely call-ups for Massimo Luongo and Bailey Wright, both playing in the lower leagues of English football. McGowan was also included in the final party for South America. He was a familiar face to Postecoglou but someone he hadn't encountered for several years.

'Ange was the first coach outside of my club that I got in contact with,' he says. 'I'd come from part-time football and was selected for the Aussie under-17s. He was also the under-20s manager, and he brought three of us up from the 17s to the 20s. He was my first coach that was well known in Australia. From a coaching perspective, he's definitely the one I hold in the highest regard.'

Time wasn't on Postecoglou's side as he tried to mould together a group of weary individuals with a brutal group of Spain, the Netherlands and Chile on the horizon. The challenges of international management and not having the chance to work with his players every day added further pressure. According to McGowan:

He said all along that if you fully commit to his way of playing and immerse yourself in it, you would reap the rewards. It's only human nature to go against that at first when you've been told to do things a different way your entire career. If it's the last five minutes and you're chasing a goal, you want to get it into the box as quickly as possible, but he's against that. He wants you to keep passing out from the back and into midfield and keep doing the things you have been doing all game.

Even if you're 1-0 up, he wants you to keep passing out from the back. A lot of fans and players get stressed out, but when you realise that he won't hang you out to dry if you make a mistake, you start to believe in him. Back then, he was a totally different coach to where he is now, but he still had a lot of things that he's kept. He's very strict, knows what he wants, and you know where you stand.

* * *

McGowan is a likeable guy, the kind of player you could imagine Postecoglou getting on well with, in a strictly football sense of course. Born to Celtic-supporting parents from Coatbridge who had emigrated to Australia in their early 20s, McGowan was scouted by former Heart of Midlothian defender Dave McPherson while playing for the Young Socceroos. He moved back to Scotland in 2006 to join the Hearts youth set-up, arriving at a time of real crisis at the Edinburgh club. Just months after McGowan joined, the infamous 'Riccarton Three' episode took place, as future Celtic trio Steven Pressley, Paul Hartley and Craig Gordon publicly criticised Jambos owner Vladimir Romanov for his reckless leadership of the club.

Pressley, Hartley and Gordon soon departed, and the likes of McGowan were tasked with making the step up. The Aussie had been the captain of the Jambos under-19 team but had to earn his first-team spot, developing during loan spells at Ayr United and Partick Thistle. Eventually he made his breakthrough, scoring his first goal in an Edinburgh derby against Hibernian. More notably, he netted the fourth goal in the Tynecastle team's famous 5-1 triumph over their rivals in the 2012 Scottish Cup Final – a result that will be forever etched in Jambos history.

After 73 appearances, McGowan departed the capital for Chinese club Shandong Taishan in a six-figure deal. He soon returned to Scotland to play for Dundee United under Celtic favourite Jackie McNamara, whom he knew from his loan spell at Thistle. McGowan went on to play for the other team in Dundee, Bradford City, Sydney FC and a host of other clubs in Kuwait, the United Arab Emirates and China. In the summer of 2022, shortly after Postecoglou had lifted his first Premiership title, he moved back to Scotland, signing for St Johnstone.

Back in 2014, during his spell in China, McGowan was included in the 23-man Socceroos squad for the World Cup. He was joined by more recognisable names from the club scene, but that didn't seem to matter to his boss, as McGowan explained:

> It wouldn't matter if it was me, Tim Cahill, Tommy Rogic, Mile Jedinak, it was just a yellow marker on the board. He respected everyone but it was a case of having to do what was asked of you. If you didn't, he'd get somebody else to do it instead. That's good for a player because if you do what you've been told, you'll continue playing. There were numerous times when I maybe played in front of somebody who a lot of people felt should play. But he said I was doing the right things, so I got the nod. If Ange believes in what a player is doing, he'll keep them in until their performance drops.

This idea of equality is crucial in the way Celtic's boss manages. Players, coaches and staff members are treated equally, regardless of their reputation. In the Celtic dressing room, Postecoglou is just as likely to call out 75-time England cap Joe Hart as he is an emerging youth prospect. As he told me during an enlightening press conference, 'Every player and every staff member knows that I treat them equally with the same respect. I have the same care and love for them all. There are no favourites and they understand that.'

At the forefront of this approach is the desire to keep players on their toes. In other dressing rooms, a hierarchy may exist, leading to complacency among senior players. At Celtic, Postecoglou expects the same of every player. Captain Callum McGregor doesn't get an easier or a more challenging time than Stephen Welsh, regardless of where they may sit in supporters' minds. As a result, players never slip into a comfort zone. They're constantly challenged to improve, adapt and buy into the philosophies set out for them.

Postecoglou found several McGowans – players who carried out his message and were rewarded as a result – in his first year at Celtic. Anthony Ralston and Greg Taylor were both in a tough place when he arrived. Ralston had failed to shine in loan spells at Dundee United and St Johnstone and looked set to leave, while Taylor was yet to deliver on the £3m Celtic paid Kilmarnock three years earlier. While there was a severe lack of options at the time, a lesser manager may still have disregarded both as players of the past. Instead, Postecoglou relied on the duo heavily in his initial weeks at the club, with Ralston and Taylor starting at full-back in each of his first ten matches. It wasn't a surprise when both were handed lengthy new contracts just months into Postecoglou's reign.

David Turnbull was another Scottish youngster Postecoglou warmed to in his early days. The midfielder started every single one of Celtic's first 30 competitive matches – the run ended only by the Europa League dead rubber against Real Betis when Postecoglou changed his entire team. Turnbull was one of the many players who bought into Ange's philosophy in the early days, laying the foundations for what was to come.

'He's one of those managers you instantly respect,' says McGowan. 'The way he carries himself and the way he communicates. He just has that way with words. He has that charismatic and mean streak through him. You definitely don't want to get on his wrong side. You like playing that brand of football because you have the ball the majority of the time and you're attacking. Every footballer wants to win games, and once you see his style is successful, it adds to the belief.'

Australia needed all the belief they could get back in 2014. Drawn in the competition's 'group of death' alongside 2010 winners Spain, 2010 runners-up the Netherlands, and Chile, ranked 15th at the time of the draw, they had their work cut out. Things looked bleak when they went down 2-0 to Chile within 14 minutes of their opening match. However, the Aussies rallied through Tim Cahill's goal and were unfortunate not to find an equaliser before Chile netted a late third. Defeats also followed in the next two matches, but the 3-2 loss to the Dutch almost felt like a victory for an Aussie public who had been enduring back-to-back six-goal hammerings less than a year earlier. Just like South Melbourne at the FIFA Club World Championship 14 years earlier, Postecoglou's unfancied team had gone up against some of the world's best and come away with credit.

Even more remarkable was that this thrown-together squad, featuring players from the A-League, English lower divisions, South Korea, China and Qatar had rattled their distinguished opposition while playing the Postecoglou way. The Aussies had kept the ball from the Dutch, fresh off a 5-1 win over Spain, for extended periods and fearlessly attacked both in and out of possession. There were sure-fire signs everywhere of the team buying into their manager's way of doing things. You just had to know where to look.

McGowan, who assisted the strike voted the sixth-best goal of the tournament in a FIFA poll, says:

Holland scored first and then Tim Cahill scored a minute later. That's because Ange wants to go right at the opposition from kick-off. It doesn't matter if they've just scored or it's at the start of the game or after half-time. He wants his teams to go and score a goal as fast as they can. It was like that for Celtic in the League Cup Final after Hibs scored.

In most football games, the ball is only in play for between 50 and 65 minutes. He used to look at that after every match, and if it was under 60, he would be raging. His feeling was that the longer the ball was in play with our intensity, the quicker the opposition would tire. A lot of Celtic fans picked up quite early on about Joe Hart getting the ball off the ball boys or when it goes out for a throw. Again, in the League Cup Final, Tommy Rogic takes the quick free kick and Kyogo scores the winner. These are just small details but he continually drums it into you that they will make a difference.

Sometimes you're absolutely knackered trying to carry out his gameplan. He always used to say, 'If you're knackered then just imagine how tired the opposition are.' There was that famous clip of him in training during his first week at Celtic. That's just what he's like. He feels that if you play his style you'll win more games than you lose.'

Postecoglou knew he had his Socceroos stars in a good place. As soon as the World Cup was over, he switched the focus to the Asian Cup, taking place six months later. As much as the Aussies had done their nation proud in Brazil, Postecoglou wanted genuine success on home soil: winning the competition.

The Socceroos thumped Kuwait and Oman in the group stage but finished second behind South Korea after a matchday-three defeat in Brisbane. In the knockout rounds, a favourable draw saw them beat China in the quarters and the United

Arab Emirates in the semis to set up a rematch with the South Koreans in the final at Stadium Australia – the venue Celtic visited in their 2022 Australia tour.

The final was an occasion fraught with nerves. A superb Massimo Luongo strike looked to be enough for Australia before Son Heung-min broke their hearts with a stoppage-time equaliser. Lesser teams may have buckled after the crushing blow but Postecoglou's Aussies were made of stern stuff. As his players stood before extra time, he glanced over at the South Koreans, all hunched over or lying down due to exhaustion. 'This will make it a better ending,' were his final words as he sent his players back into battle. James Troisi netted the winner as Australia lifted their first-ever Asian Cup. The next day, Postecoglou's focus turned to the next challenge: winning the World Cup in Russia or, at least, getting out of the group.

'He used the Asian Cup win as a reference point for what we could achieve,' says McGowan. 'He's very careful with how he speaks in front of the media. If you study his words closely, he's always looking to improve and hit that next target. He was very clear that, as well as Celtic did in his first season, it was just the beginning. That's what you want as a player. You never want to feel like you're resting on your laurels, and he has real strength and belief behind him.'

Postecoglou never got to take his country to another World Cup, resigning a week after qualification for Russia was secured. 'It has been a privilege for me to coach my country's national team,' he told Aussie media. 'To lead them at the 2014 World Cup, to win the Asian Cup in 2015 and now to have qualified for the World Cup next year. I said we would do it and we have done it. All this, however, has taken a toll on me both personally and professionally. I have invested all I can knowing how important a period it was for Australian football. It is with a heavy heart that I must now end the journey.'

While Australia competed well in Russia, running the eventual winners France close, and reached the last 16 of the

2022 World Cup in Qatar, it's fair to say that the national team has missed Postecoglou's influence on occasion. If nothing else, they no longer play with the same fearless intent.

* * *

Midway through Postecoglou's first season at Celtic, footage re-emerged, via Optus Sport, of him addressing his Australia players in a meeting, hours out from a big match. As Postecoglou paces around the room, the microphone picks him up telling his players to remember who and what had brought them to that moment.

'You think about the person in your life who believed in you. It could be your mum, dad, brother, sister, uncle, grandfather, partner, friend, coach. Somebody in your life that, when you started, believed in you more than anyone else. Think about that person. Think about how that person's going to feel when we win tonight.'

Celtic played 60 competitive matches during season 2021/22. Before every one of them, Postecoglou had a different pep talk. Every single speech was carefully curated to fit the occasion. The Celtic boss's ability to say the right thing at the right time was uncanny. Australia players regularly commented that someone should be filming when Postecoglou was in full flow. Renowned producer Ben Coonan put that into practice and recorded some team talks in his media role at Football Australia, as he tells me of the viral Optus Sport clip:

> That was from my camera. The documentary that it was lifted from was one I helped to put together. He must plan them and study them fairly intensely because for a football coach to have that level of quality in his communication is something I've not experienced with anyone else. Every talk I was privy to was so theatrical and on point. The themes were universal, yet they were still so pointed. There wasn't one person in the room that

wasn't totally moved by what he had to say. To do that camp after camp, week after week takes some skill. As far as I'm concerned, Ange is a communicator without peer.

In some speeches it's just Postecoglou and his players. In others he displays presentations or videos on projectors, or brings objects into the room. Some themes, like family, are evident in most of his speeches.

Coonan added:

> I remember one in the camp before the 2014 World Cup and our group with Spain, the Netherlands and Chile. His talk was along the lines of, 'You will have heard all of the chat that we've got no chance. That we're 100/1 to get anything out of this tournament. Let me give you some other odds. What do you think the odds would be on a Samoan kid born into a low socio-economic house in the west of Sydney to become one of the leading players of the Premier League and a Ballon d'Or nominee? What are the odds of a kid born to Croatian migrants without a contract at 24 years old then being the captain of his national team eight years later? So don't read into those odds because you've overcome odds far greater before.' That's just one of a hundred that he gave over that time. They were all different.

In his digital production role with the Socceroos, Coonan would often be tasked by Postecoglou to come up with presentations or short films that would augment his message. He'd be given the space to go away and produce something but, with Ange around, the pressure was always on.

> You wouldn't really get many words out of him in camp. He'd tell me what he was planning for his speech and ask me to put together a video that hit on certain points.

Then I'd be left to my own devices to come up with something to present to him. He'd sit in front of a laptop with his headphones on. He'd be motionless throughout the video. Then when it was over, he'd put down the headphones and say, 'Yeah mate, that'll do.'

If Coonan had the job of filming Postecoglou's speeches, then Ante Milicic had a more old-school approach. The former Socceroos coach, most famous for playing with Sydney United in the 1990s, was such a big fan of the pep talks that he wrote down the best bits for his own use:

> I used to write notes at the back of the room. I wanted to be able to refer back to what he said. The way he would find a theme for a game and the way he would deliver that message. The way he delivered it with eye contact, the variation in tone of his voice, and the way he captured the whole room. I felt it was such an advantage for us as a team.
>
> He gave a great one in June 2017. We were in Russia for the Confederations Cup playing Chile, and it was Tim Cahill's 100th game. He was talking about Timmy's career – how it started, where he came from, the people who were along for the ride throughout his journey, what he's become, what he means to the game in Australia, and how he defied the odds. Let me tell you, what a reaction we got. If you ever want to watch the first half of football where we've taken the game to an opponent who were a top ten side back then. We played some really good games under Ange with the national team against some really good opponents. He has to have practised the talks at home because you can't deliver that. There was always a message and a theme, and he always got you.

Postecoglou's pre-Chile speech was a work of art. Lasting just shy of 20 minutes, he worked his way through Cahill's career in remarkable detail, only pausing occasionally to move the accompanying slideshow on. At the end, he embraced the former Everton man as the room applauded.

Of course, these team talks alone didn't worry the Chileans, Dutch or Real Madrid. Nor did they lead Celtic or Australia to glory. But Milicic is right about Postecoglou's communication skills being a real asset to his teams. If Celtic lose a big match, it's unlikely ever to have been a motivation issue. As for Ryan McGowan, the one that sticks out in his mind again involves family. He admits to not doing it justice.

> He was saying if you were walking along one side of the street, and on the other side of the street you see an elderly lady being robbed, you'd maybe shout or check the traffic to see if you can cross. If you saw it happening to a friend or someone you know, you'd run over, but you'd still be wary. But if it's your mum, your grandma, or your wife or daughter, you're running across the street. You don't care if they've got a gun, you don't care if they've got a knife, you just go in. That's what we need to do today. This is our family and we need to go out and support each other. Don't be afraid of what could happen. Just make sure you're helping each other out. When he tells those stories a couple of minutes before you go out, you want to run through brick walls for him. He's got a great way with words.

CHAPTER 11

Japan

'These are four individuals.
They are totally different people.'
Ange Postecoglou

WHEN ANGE Postecoglou warned against grouping his four Japanese signings together purely because they all hailed from the same country, he meant it. Celtic had just completed the triple Hogmanay signing of Daizen Maeda from Yokohama F. Marinos, Yosuke Ideguchi from Gamba Osaka and Reo Hatate from Kawasaki Frontale, with the trio arriving in Scotland less than six months after the acquisition of Kyogo Furuhashi from Vissel Kobe. Kyogo had become Celtic's talisman in the intervening period, netting 16 goals and leading the team to the League Cup during the first half of the season.

Historically, Celtic have tended to do their January business nearer the end of the month, so the announcement of Maeda, Ideguchi and Hatate on the day before the window opened was a sure-fire statement of intent. Celtic meant business for the second half of the season, and excitement was high. If the trio could make half the impact of their countryman, Celtic would have found three more valuable players. Postecoglou, meanwhile, was keen from the outset to dispel the myth that the four players were in any way connected beyond their nationality.

He told the written press after the triple signing:

> We have to be careful about just saying 'four Japanese
> players'. These are four individuals. They are totally
> different people. If you ever get the chance to meet them,
> you will see they are totally different people, totally
> different kinds of players. It is lazy for all of us to say I
> have just brought in four Japanese. I have brought in four
> quality players who I think can add to what I am doing
> here. They are all totally different, they all have different
> personalities, they have had different careers so far, and
> they offer something different to the club.

In time, supporters would come to see the four players as
individuals. One such person was Aisling Baker-Ford, a lifelong
Celtic fan who fell so much in love with the players that she
created a manga-style comic celebrating their success. *From
Yokohama to Glasgow: A New Era* tells the story of Celtic's
triumphant 2020/21 campaign from Postecoglou's uncertain
arrival to trophy day.

'Ange shocked us all when he came in,' she tells me. 'The
way he speaks is so captivating. My dad has been going to see
Celtic since he was ten, he's seen a lot of managers, but he's
fallen in love with Ange. He's trying to be him. He's even got
the jumper.'

Baker-Ford suffers from a condition called chronic fatigue
syndrome. It affects her mobility and keeps her up at night,
often without sleep. She found comfort late at night in creating
artwork of Postecoglou, Kyogo and more just as Celtic gained
momentum on the pitch.

> Through the night, I would be doodling and wondering
> how I could tell the story of Ange and the four Japanese
> players, especially Kyogo, who everyone immediately fell
> in love with. Then we were all at my house watching the

Ross County game when Ralston scored the late winner. I could just tell that was the turning point.

In my toughest times, I had the comic to focus on. I contacted my pal, a manga artist, and he made it more Japanese. It tells the story of Ange coming in, the initial scepticism and the journey to the end point where the whole stadium is singing his name. As Ange says, when you go to Celtic Park you don't need to worry about what's going on in your life. You can just focus on the game that's in front of you. There seems to be a massive change in the Celtic support, and I think part of that has come from the maturity Ange has brought.

Part of that is the perception of the four players we signed from Japan. We mustn't assume they're all the same because they're Japanese. They each have different personalities, skills and abilities. Even simple things like where they came from. It's easy to assume they were all born in Tokyo because they're from Japan. But they're all from different areas. Kyogo was the pivotal change. Hatate was exhausted when he came in, he'd just played a full season, but now we're seeing the best of him. Maeda is really underrated and has already given us so many goals and assists. It's just unfortunate that Guchi hasn't really had an opportunity.

In Postecoglou, the players had a manager who knew them from his time in Japan and would look after them, sometimes shielding them from the harsher aspects of Scottish life. With each player taking a leap of faith to join Postecoglou on the other side of the world, he felt a duty to protect them to let them flourish in the Scottish game. Celtic's boss would regularly bite back at any ignorance displayed towards the players.

After Hatate's man-of-the-match debut against Hibernian, BBC Radio Scotland's Chick Young drew comparisons with former Celtic star Shunsuke Nakamura. 'No, he's Reo Hatate, mate,' was Postecoglou's response. There didn't seem to be any malice in Young's question, nor was there in the grouping of the players from fans and the media. It was just a case of ignorance, something Postecoglou had to battle in his early days when answering questions like whether he'd ever heard of Heart of Midlothian. Yet, was Giorgos Giakoumakis compared to Georgios Samaras when he netted his hat-trick against Dundee in February? On the face of it, the Greek pair would seem to have as much in common as Hatate and Nakamura. It does make you squirm ever so slightly.

Perhaps even the fact that I've written this chapter, grouping all four players together, is more than a little hypocritical. The conclusion is that all four are Japanese and, therefore, are always likely to be lumped together to an extent. But any assumptions that they share anything else in common is just speculation. The players are all different, separate from the two Japanese players who preceded them at Celtic and the many who will follow them in years to come. Celebrating them as individuals who are part of a team, like in *From Yokohama to Glasgow*, is the way to go.

Joining the four players in Scotland is the unsung member of the entire operation: interpreter Akihito Ido. After arriving at the same time as Kyogo, as part of the attacker's agency, Ido has played an enormous role in the Japanese players' daily lives, helping them integrate into Scottish life with minimal fuss. It's a massive credit to him, Postecoglou, Celtic and the players themselves that three of the four signings have been tremendous successes. Unlike Nakamura, who was already playing in Europe before Celtic, the quartet were all signed directly from Japanese clubs. On the face of it, they seem to have taken well to life in Scotland, both on and off the park.

* * *

When Kyogo hit it up in his early months in Glasgow, attention quickly turned to who would join him in January. With the Japanese league season finishing in December, close-season moves made the most sense for all parties. By the time Celtic confirmed the deals for Maeda, Ideguchi and Hatate, most fans were familiar with all three. The speculation had been filling papers, podcasts and online slots for months, and footage of all three saying farewell to their clubs in Japan had practically confirmed that the moves would be happening.

Just like Kyogo months earlier, Postecoglou was well aware of his new signings. He'd worked with Daizen Maeda at F. Marinos, seen Reo Hatate at close quarters in battles with Frontale and even experienced Yosuke Ideguchi net a memorable goal for Japan against his Socceroos team in a World Cup qualifier.

Postecoglou: 'The reason I went down that road is: one, I have great knowledge of that market in that part of the world because that is where I have worked; and two, it is ideal for the January market because their season finishes in December. If we wanted to get players in early in the January window, that is a good part of the world to do business.'

The announcement of all three in a single tweet alongside the hashtag #JapaneseBhoys and the sight of them all hunched in front of a single camera during their media unveiling probably didn't go down too well with the manager. Although sitting that day, watching Hatate, Maeda and Ideguchi answer questions through their interpreter, it became apparent what Postecoglou meant. The trio gave off different vibes: Ideguchi, the mysterious figure; Hatate, the young joker; and Maeda, the experienced head. Even now it's hard to believe that just 32 days are separating the latter two.

As anticipated, Ideguchi's introduction to first-team action was slow, while Hatate and Maeda made a fast start. It took the latter less than four minutes to notch his first Celtic goal – a remarkable feat given the hype that had surrounded his debut. Yet, the early strike against Hibernian wasn't even the main talking point in the aftermath of the win. Hatate had stolen the show.

The 24-year-old son of an international baseball player completely ran the midfield on his first start, showing terrific balance, neat close control and an extensive range of passing. It was hard not to get a little swept up in the performance of such a young player in his first club match in Europe. His look of bemusement at being named the club's man of the match, with James Forrest having to inform him in the dugout, showed he had the character to match his talent too.

The spectacular goal that Hatate's early play had deserved arrived a week later in a crucial fixture against Hearts. Celtic went into the match without Callum McGregor, Tom Rogic and David Turnbull – the first-choice midfield from the first six months of the season. Hatate was thrown into the creative role alongside fellow new signing Matt O'Riley and leapt on to a Nir Bitton interception to strike a stunner past Craig Gordon. Some were critical of the former Celtic goalkeeper, but the ferocious power had been too much for him to handle. The noise of the ball striking the Tynecastle net, shortly before a delayed roar from the Celtic fans at the other end of the stadium, was the real beauty. Sky Sports commentator Ian Crocker's 'crash, bang, wallop' summed it up.

If Hatate's early performances excited Celtic fans, he properly announced his arrival in Glasgow with a stunning double in the 3-0 demolition of Rangers. The midfielder struck two goals and set up the third inside a breathless first half as Celtic went top of the league. Many eyes were on his sumptuous display with top-flight English football in the midst of a break. Liverpool's Scottish full-back Andy Robertson was one of the many to tweet. 'Hatate's a serious player,' was his report.

The rest of the campaign was more subdued for the former Kawasaki Frontale man. He managed just one more goal – the opener in the 7-0 mauling of St Johnstone – and looked to tire in the season's closing weeks with a non-stop 18 months catching up on him. Hatate was still able to contribute for Celtic throughout his first five months and, notably, he was kept in

Postecoglou's plans for every match other than the dead-rubber final-day clash against Motherwell.

Many signings from the other side of the world may have been content with contributing to a title success in their first months at a new club, yet Hatate was anything but. In the close season, he gave a fascinating insight into his mindset by penning a refreshingly honest article on the website From The Athlete. Hatate spoke openly about his dip in form at the end of the season, putting it down to fatigue and losing the surprise factor with opposition defences. Crucially, he wasn't listing excuses for the dip, only reasons why he felt the sparkling form from the early days hadn't continued right through. He promised more for the new campaign, which tied in perfectly with his manager's 'bigger and better' speech after the season's final match.

Hatate re-entered pre-season training earlier than most of his team-mates, having not been selected for international duty with Japan over the summer. He made a fast start to the campaign, impressing in the friendly matches and even appearing to score the club's first goal in the Champions League, against Shakhtar Donetsk, before the strike was awarded as an Artem Bondarenko own goal. Hatate's brilliance was evident in one early Champions League moment against Real Madrid when he volleyed a 40-yard switch to Jota from a Josip Juranovic throw-in. The technique, vision and awareness were all on show, and virtually no one inside was surprised.

When at the top of his game, Hatate is a joy to watch in the midfield alongside Callum McGregor and Matt O'Riley. He's been one of Postecoglou's very best acquisitions with little to be critical of, perhaps other than his inability to take part in the pre-game huddle correctly.

Reo, Reo Hatate, the Celtic get excited when we see you play
It's strange that this feeling grows more and more
But we've never loved a player like you before.

* * *

Despite netting just minutes into his debut, Daizen Maeda was a slow burner with the Celtic support. Perhaps it was the increased expectation after scoring so early into his Celtic career or the unhelpful standards set by Kyogo in his early months in Glasgow.

When Postecoglou moved to Celtic, many expected it to be Maeda rather than Kyogo who would join him that summer. The pair had worked together at Yokohama F. Marinos, with Postecoglou picking up Maeda shortly after his team had lifted the J1 League trophy. Like fellow arrival Ideguchi, Maeda had already sampled European football, with Portuguese outfit Marítimo, once playing in the same match as his future teammate Jota. Only two years had passed between that disappointing loan spell and the Celtic opportunity, yet Maeda had grown in stature to become one of Japan's most talked about talents.

At his best, the winger sets the tempo for Celtic's entire performance, with his pace and limitless energy closing down defenders before they have time to think. Shortly before his move to Scotland, the J.League posted a graphic highlighting the top ten 'most sprints in a match' entries in Japan's top flight that season. Kyogo was at number three, with Sagan Tosu's Kei Koizumi joint sixth. The other eight names on the list were the same: Daizen Maeda. In one match, he'd registered a staggering 64 sprints.

Most sprints by a player in a match (2021 season):

1	Daizen Maeda	64
2	Daizen Maeda	62
3	Kyogo Furuhashi	53
4	Daizen Maeda	48
=	Daizen Maeda	48
6	Daizen Maeda	46
=	Daizen Maeda	46
=	Daizen Maeda	46
=	Kei Koizumi	46
10	Daizen Maeda	45

'The key with Daizen, and it's the beauty of him, is his ability to repeat a sprint,' Postecoglou would later tell *Open Goal*. 'He's just elite level. I measured it even when I was in Japan, against the very best's ability to close down. He can sprint, recover super fast and go again.'

Maeda's unbelievable engine, which he likens to a Prius rather than a loud Ferrari, originated from a spell out of the picture at high school level. After being dismissed from the team for discipline issues, he took to the Japanese mountains to stay fit, telling *Number Web*, 'I learned that I couldn't do anything by myself, I could play with a lot of support, and the importance of running for the team.'

Maeda's early years saw him at Matsumoto Yamaga, where he made his J.League debut, before loan spells at Mito Hollyhock, Marítimo and Yokohama F. Marinos. When he arrived in Scotland, it took Celtic fans several weeks to realise what kind of player Maeda was and appreciate him for it. The obvious turning point was his goal and performance in the 3-1 win over Livingston in early March. The opening goal was Maeda's fifth for the club, but the all-action display was exactly what Celtic had needed against David Martindale's hard-working team.

Maeda's performance on the left in the vital Ibrox win that put Celtic on the brink of the title was even better. He wasn't involved in either of the goals but his tireless work rate to limit key Rangers threat James Tavernier, while also offering something in attack, was a critical factor. Yet, to allow just his work rate to define his game is to do him a disservice. In the 22 matches he played in season 2021/22, he netted eight goals and set up five more, providing a goal contribution (goal or assist) every 125 minutes he spent on the pitch. Maeda is wholly committed to Postecoglou's team, often doing the work that goes unseen and showing more emotion when his team-mates score than when he nets himself.

He's rarely looked happier in a Celtic shirt than during the celebrations on the final day of his maiden season. Sitting in the centre circle with his kids running around him, one wearing his medal and throwing confetti in his face, he had a look of genuine contentment. Maeda is a devoted family man, with his trademark *Anpanman* celebration a result of his days spent watching the cartoon show with his daughter. It's easy to see where she gets her boundless energy.

Occasionally, he can be accused of snatching at major chances, like the glorious opportunity he spurned shortly after coming on against Real Madrid. If Maeda can find a way to show more composure in the big moments while holding on to his unrivalled physical ability, Celtic will have another player wanted by teams in Europe's biggest leagues.

* * *

Celtic's final January signing from Japan has featured far less. Yosuke Ideguchi, or Guchi as he asked to be known in his early days in Scotland, has had to settle for sporadic appearances off the bench, behind Callum McGregor, Aaron Mooy and Oliver Abildgaard in the pecking order. A horror challenge from Alloa Athletic's Mouhamed Niang, in just his first start, set Guchi back, while a further knock sustained in July saw him miss out on the early portion of the new season. When Postecoglou left him out of the Champions League squad, it became clear that he had his work cut out getting into the Celtic team. Time will tell what contribution Guchi can make in a Celtic shirt. If it doesn't work out, it's unlikely to be down to a lack of trying.

* * *

Matt O'Riley, the attacking midfielder who joined on a four-and-a-half-year deal from MK Dons, completed the first-team January signings. It had become apparent during the month that Postecoglou was keen to recruit another advanced midfielder on top of Hatate, almost certainly as a replacement for the soon-to-be-departing Tom Rogic. Rogic's compatriot Riley McGree had been expected to sign but chose to move to Middlesbrough at the last minute instead. Postecoglou didn't lose much sleep, telling the press, 'I only want players who want to be here. I won't try to convince any player to come and sign for this football club.'

Just like Celtic's boss had benefited from Eddie Howe's decision not to join Celtic, O'Riley profited from McGree's choice. Initially, it seemed like Celtic wouldn't be seeking a McGree alternative, with Postecoglou telling the media, 'I wouldn't be expecting anyone else in.' Yet, ten days before the end of the window, the Denmark youth international was paraded around Celtic Park after signing for a reported £1.5m – a complete steal in an increasingly inflated English market. Somewhere in the making of the move was an enlightening phone conversation between O'Riley and Postecoglou, where both men got all of the answers they were looking for.

While virtually every young player is media trained to within an inch of their life nowadays, O'Riley bucks the trend. When he answers your question, you get the impression that he's already considered the topic you're looking to cover. Perhaps it's no surprise that his former manager at MK Dons, Russell Martin, tipped him to be a manager once his playing days are over. He doesn't stop short in his answers either. While always remaining respectful, he offers great insight into the camp, like when he told me to expect to see more late goals from Celtic due to opposing defences being increasingly worn down. Days later, Giorgos Giakoumakis scored a stoppage-time clincher against Hearts.

That deep thinking extends to his football too. O'Riley took his education at Fulham's academy, playing under Celtic favourite Peter Grant and alongside future signing and 'best mate' Moritz Jenz. Grant gave O'Riley his under-23s debut at the age of 16. 'There was no doubting his talent,' Grant told me for a *67 Hail Hail* interview. 'My big concern with Matt was his fitness levels. He always had a slight issue with his back. I think that was because he was growing so quickly. He's still got that funny gait when you see the way he runs. I was away by the time he left Fulham, but I was very surprised that other clubs hadn't picked him up quickly because there was no doubting his talent.'

O'Riley decided to leave Fulham in 2020 in search of more game time. As the world was battling the pandemic, he found himself keeping fit in the park without the security of a professional contract. He signed for MK Dons in early 2021 after around six months of training as a free agent and went on to flourish in a team intent on playing a passing game under Russell Martin and then Liam Manning.

More evidence of O'Riley's deep thinking was found in the reasons for his move to Scotland a year later. While many footballers are motivated by money or the bright lights, the main incentive for O'Riley to move to Glasgow was his suitability for Postecoglou's team, as he told me weeks after signing:

I always said my next move was very important. Just being my age, it was an important time for me to make the right step. I had other interest elsewhere but it wasn't necessarily the right thing for me in terms of my career. I spoke with Ange on the phone, and he explained the style of play to me and where I'd fit into the system, being one of the players who can hopefully create. From game one it's hopefully been pretty easy to see that I fit in well. I'm just someone who generally likes to play good football, and here is the perfect place to do that.

O'Riley's debut came against Hearts at Tynecastle on the night of Hatate's wonder strike. The biggest compliment you can pay the Dane, Postecoglou and the environment at the club is that seeing him put in such an assured display just days after signing, in such a hostile environment, wasn't even a surprise. A week later he experienced an even louder noise as Celtic battered Rangers 3-0 to move top of the table.

'I can't compare that to anything I've ever been in, no chance,' he told Celtic TV in the aftermath. 'I can't actually hear my own voice right now. That says enough. I'm actually struggling to put it into words, but in terms of fans, we've got to have the best in the world. I've never seen anything like that in my life. I've been to a lot of football games, Champions League games, but that was honestly crazy.'

Soon, O'Riley was sampling his own Champions League nights in Glasgow, starting in the team that went toe to toe with Real Madrid for the best part of an hour. Virtually every photo before the match caught O'Riley with a massive grin on his face. Like so many of his young Celtic team-mates, you sense the best is yet to come.

CHAPTER 12

The Journey, Part 3: Looking Down

*'I'm sure a lot of them walked in
with some problems in their life.'*
Ange Postecoglou

'YOU GUYS are crazy, mate. Fifteen degrees and your shirts are off.' Ange Postecoglou is addressing the media inside Celtic Park, having just watched his team move six points clear of Rangers at the summit of the Premiership. The Ibrox team have a game in hand, yet Celtic will head into the final international break of the season with at least a three-point lead, with the first match on their return a season-defining derby in Govan.

Someone should probably have reminded the crowd inside Celtic Park that the title was still on a knife-edge. They've spent the afternoon partying in the sunshine during a 4-0 humbling of Ross County. They're utterly convinced that the league title is returning to Celtic Park and have been singing about the triumph regularly over the past two hours. 'I had a feeling our supporters would be up for it today,' Celtic's boss says. 'It was important not just to win but to put on a performance. I really felt that was going to be important today for the whole club.'

When a media member asks him whether he'll be watching Rangers' trip to Dundee less than 24 hours later, his response is to lecture them on his TV schedule at home. 'My Sundays are dictated by my wife and kids, mate. If *Sing 2* is on or something, I'll have to fight for the remote control.'

Postecoglou and Celtic have little reason to watch events at Dens Park. They're amidst a 31-match unbeaten domestic run, with 27 of those fixtures won. They've gone from a team unable to find any consistency to a winning machine capable of churning out results even when not at their best. Celtic's entire camp has the laser focus Postecoglou finds so exhilarating in a new project:

> I've felt that for a while. There was no way we were going to embark on this run we've been on any other way. The starting point was fairly low in terms of how we started our season. For us to be in this position now means we've all had to be pulling in the same direction. We couldn't have people going off on their own or doubting what we were going to do. Credit to the players and the staff that, after the start we had, they were willing to go all in on the kind of team we wanted to be.

If the first part of the journey was about establishing an identity, and the second about dealing with a series of complications, then the months from January to March were where belief soared. Celtic returned from the winter break as the team chasing. Weeks later they were on top of the league, looking down on the rest. Things were about to go into overdrive. It all started with a bit of help from an unlikely place.

* * *

Celtic 1-0 Dundee United, Premiership, Celtic Park, Saturday, 29 January 2022

The roar outside Celtic Park could mean only one thing. It was around 2.20pm and supporters were making their way through the turnstiles for the home match against Dundee United. The afternoon was young, yet the Celtic support had already been put through the wringer with events elsewhere. Earlier there had been some murmurings of good news in the early kick-off between Ross County and Rangers, with the Staggies threatening an upset after taking a 2-1 lead. However, two second-half goals from the Ibrox team had them on course for a big win that would extend their lead at the top of the Premiership to seven points ahead of Celtic's match.

When the roar sounded at Celtic Park, it was unmistakable. A 96th-minute goal from Matthew Wright had earned a 3-3 draw for the Highlanders. It was also a huge goal for the green half of Glasgow. In times like these the true beauty of the Celtic–Rangers rivalry is showcased. While some fans like to maintain the facade that the other club is irrelevant to them, the truth is that the fortunes of one affects the other, like a giant see-saw. When news of County's equaliser fed through to Celtic Park, everyone's mood brightened, and with good reason too.

It was a crucial moment in the title race, perhaps the most significant turning point. Rangers had extended their lead to five points with the draw, but Celtic had a match in hand and a derby on home soil a few days later. If Celtic won both matches, there would be a new leader at the top of the Premiership, which would have been unthinkable less than two weeks earlier.

There was a buzz around Celtic Park that had rarely been felt in recent seasons. Sure, Postecoglou and his players had brought excitement in the first half of the season, but there had always been a sense that the campaign may be about building rather than winning, given the upheaval that had occurred at the club. The League Cup win in December and some swaying from Rangers in the early weeks of 2022 led many to believe that the season could bring about genuine success rather than just progress.

The upcoming derby – the first with fans at Celtic Park since 2019 – was on everyone's mind. But the players couldn't afford to take their eye off the ball against Dundee United, a team that had already come away from Celtic Park with a credible draw earlier in the season. Given the excitement in the air following events in Dingwall, and Postecoglou and Callum McGregor's pre-match tribute to recently passed former manager Wim Jansen, everyone expected a quick start from Celtic. It didn't arrive.

McGregor missed the match through injury, while Celtic were also without Tom Rogic and Daizen Maeda due to the pair being called up for their countries. Postecoglou had also decided not to start either Jota or Josip Juranovic, perhaps with the derby in mind. When he brought both on at half-time, they made an immediate difference to a left-hand side lacking under Liam Scales and James Forrest. First, Jota's cross was met by Matt O'Riley, only for Ben Siegrist to claw the ball away to his left. Siegrist was also the scourge of Giorgos Giakoumakis, who should have scored after more great work from Juranovic and Jota.

The feeling of it being one of those days heightened when Nir Bitton was sent off for a second booking for hauling down United substitute Declan Glass with just ten minutes to go. However, just like in Dingwall earlier in the day, there was to be late drama. Juranovic and Jota combined again, this time down the right, with the latter racing to the byline and digging out a brilliant cross to the back post, where Liel Abada was in space. The Israeli took one touch to control and another to smash the ball into the roof of the net to send Celtic Park into delirium.

As Abada whipped off his shirt and ran to the corner of the Main Stand and the Jock Stein Stand, Jota was experiencing his own celebration 40 yards away. The momentum of the assist had sent him into the advertising hoardings. Now he stood among the crowd, his arms raised and joyous supporters hugging him up from all directions. It was quite a sight.

Future Celtic signing Siegrist had his own memory of the moment and would share it with fan media shortly after signing in June: 'The lights started flickering and the whole crowd was going crazy. That was the moment when I thought this place was special. It made a huge impression on me, although I was gutted.'

The moment was huge for several reasons. Most importantly, Celtic had stopped history from repeating itself. When Giakoumakis had missed the penalty in stoppage time against Livingston months earlier, the team had passed up the opportunity to capitalise after a Rangers slip-up. Abada's goal signalled growth in the team. The next time Celtic met Dundee United on league duty there would be more room for error.

Celtic: *Hart, Ralston, Carter-Vickers, Starfelt, Scales, Bitton, O'Riley, Hatate, Abada, Giakoumakis, Forrest*
Subs used: *Jota, Juranovic, Doak, Taylor, McCarthy*

Dundee United: *Siegrist, Neilson, Butcher, McMann, Niskanen, Meekison, Levitt, Harkes, Spörle, Clark, Watt*
Subs used: *Graham, McNulty, Glass, Pawlett*

* * *

Celtic 3-0 Rangers, Premiership, Celtic Park, Wednesday, 2 February 2022

The image of Callum McGregor, wearing a protective face mask and snarling at Borna Barisic after the Rangers full-back refused to take him on, is perhaps the most defining of the entire season. It was the perfect encapsulation of this stunning February night and Celtic's physical and emotional battering of Rangers. Like the rest of his team-mates, Barisic would rather have been anywhere but Celtic Park when the Ange Postecoglou era got its first marquee result.

When Bobby Madden blew his full-time whistle, the Rangers players couldn't get off the pitch quickly enough. They'd been utterly blown away by the quality of Celtic's play and the vociferous atmosphere inside the stadium. Celtic had been possessed, and it all came from the captain.

While recent Rangers signing Aaron Ramsey chose to watch the match from the Main Stand at Celtic Park, McGregor sent a different message by declaring himself fit to play ten days on from a severe facial injury suffered at Alloa Athletic. With tabloids suggesting he could miss months, McGregor sat out just two matches, returning for the derby, wearing a mask and putting in a sensational performance. His commitment to the cause was matched by Daizen Maeda, who returned from playing in a World Cup qualifier for Japan on the other side of the world barely a day earlier to feature off the bench.

The pair's determination to play was symptomatic of Celtic's need to win at all costs. It had been 787 days since Christopher Jullien's controversial strike had won the League Cup Final at Hampden – Celtic's last victory in the fixture. Since then, seven derbies had passed, with all but one lost. Celtic had gone from being dominant against their rivals to being dominated. With that in mind and the opportunity to depose Rangers at the top of the Premiership, it became a match that Celtic had to win. The partisan crowd made up entirely of Celtic fans, and the rare spectacle of a derby under the floodlights, added credence to the notion that this was Celtic's time to strike.

'In my mind, that's the night we got ourselves in the position to be champions,' Postecoglou would tell fan media at the end of the season. 'It wasn't that we got to first place, but if we hadn't won, they probably would have got too far ahead of us. I didn't see them dropping too many games. That night was pivotal, and the manner in which we played, in terms of the players and their belief, they then got that extra bit of energy they needed to say, "Well, we can do this."'

The hero of this new fearless, all-conquering Celtic was Reo Hatate. After impressive performances against Hibernian and Hearts, he once again saved his best for under the bright lights. His opener, a deflected right-footed shot, sent Celtic Park crazy. His second, five minutes before the break, was a thing of beauty. Incisive build-up play from Josip Juranovic, Matt O'Riley and Liel Abada found Hatate on the edge of the Rangers box. With almost no backlift, he curled an impeccable strike into the right of the net beyond the despairing Allan McGregor. The lack of celebration was probably evidence of how natural it all felt.

The Celtic support couldn't be accused of a lack of celebrating when the third goal went in minutes later, although many were still basking in the glory of Hatate's strike. Again, the Japanese star was at the forefront, latching on to a quick Greg Taylor throw and crossing for Abada to nip in front of the hapless Barisic and send Celtic Park into ecstasy. By the time Duran Duran's 'Rio' was blaring at half-time, an apt choice, the match was over. Unbeaten in 13 matches under Giovanni van Bronckhorst, Rangers were heading for a season-defining loss.

For all of the tenacity and aggression of Celtic's first-half performance, the real beauty had been in the football they'd played. Rangers were chasing shadows from the first whistle, with several impressive McGregor saves preventing an even more considerable margin of victory. Van Bronckhorst making three substitutions at the break said a lot.

Celtic saw the job through in the second half with minimal fuss, with Joe Hart not forced to make a save. When the full-time whistle sounded and the Rangers players made their quick escape, Celtic Park could celebrate a derby win and a return to the top of the table after so long. The Oasis anthem 'Roll With It' – a popular song among the Celtic support – played, and Postecoglou and his players took the acclaim of their fans. McGregor, the heartbeat of the evening, had one last job, telling his team-mates not to over-celebrate in the aftermath of the victory. Celtic had won nothing yet.

Postecoglou had some post-match thoughts to perhaps even eclipse his team's performance. Speaking to BBC Radio Scotland after the biggest night of his Celtic career so far, he mentioned the role of the fans in the win and the importance of his players giving them something to smile about:

> We're upholding the values of this football club, not just in terms of winning but the way we play our football.

I want them to be proud of us. I hope they are proud on the journey home tonight. I am sure they will enjoy tonight. I don't know how work will go tomorrow for most of them. As I said to the players, we had 60,000 in tonight, and I'm sure a lot of them walked in with some problems in their life. For 95 minutes, we made them forget that and feel good. That's something special.

Celtic: *Hart, Juranovic, Carter-Vickers, Starfelt, Taylor, McGregor, O'Riley, Hatate, Abada, Giakoumakis, Jota*
Subs used: *Forrest, Maeda, McCarthy, Doak, Soro*

Rangers: *McGregor, Tavernier, Goldson, Bassey, Barisic, Kamara, Arfield, Aribo, Diallo, Roofe, Kent*
Subs used: *Balogun, Jack, Sakala*

* * *

Celtic 3-2 Dundee, Premiership, Celtic Park, Sunday, 20 February 2022

Single-handedly firing Celtic to a crucial league win over Dundee wasn't enough for Giorgos Giakoumakis. He was about to declare war on the rest of Scottish football. Okay, that may be a little strong. The forward was only saying what he believed to be the case and probably felt he had a little more licence to do so after his recent exploits.

Celtic had just extended their lead at the top of the Premiership after Rangers dropped more points earlier in the day, although it had been far from plain sailing against bottom-of-the-table Dundee. The Dens Park team had managed to net twice, doubling Celtic's entire league goals conceded at home in a single afternoon. Both goals had come from poorly defended set pieces, following on from two more in a recent win over Aberdeen.

Celtic had threatened to kick on after the win over Rangers, beating Motherwell 4-0 at Fir Park and leading the Dons by two at half-time. Stephen Glass's team had rallied in the second half, with Celtic having to battle for the win, while Ange Postecoglou had been audibly frustrated during a cup victory over Raith Rovers days later. The 3-1 loss at home to Bodø/ Glimt confirmed that his Celtic team were going through a dip. Giakoumakis aside, the display against Dundee hadn't been great either. The Greek international's perfect hat-trick – right foot, left foot, header – had secured a dramatic 3-2 win. He told journalists afterwards:

> We showed that we are a better team. We showed that we work harder on the field, and I think that we will win the championship. That is something we really want for us, the club and the fans. We work a lot, we work hard every day in the training centre and we show that in the games, and with this hard work, we can achieve many things. The squad is really good. I think it is the best in the league and I think we are a well-prepared team for every single game. I think we are better in every single part of the team.

While the journalists in attendance probably couldn't believe their luck, Celtic fans were initially split on whether this type of cavalier attitude was good, especially after such a narrow victory over the league's worst team. Many admired the confidence of Giakoumakis. Others claimed it would light a fire under Rangers ahead of the run-in. It's true that the comments reached Ibrox and upset some of their players, most notably midfielder Ryan Jack, who seemed visibly irritated and branded them 'disrespectful' on the eve of the next derby.

It's also true that Giakoumakis's words turned out to be prophetic, with Celtic proving their credentials as the best team in the country by going unbeaten from matchday seven of one season until matchday seven of the next. Giakoumakis had talked the talk, but he also walked the walk, netting five goals in his next three starts.

'I don't tell people what to think,' said Postecoglou when quizzed about the comments. 'The one thing I say to the players is you speak from the heart. You say what you feel is the truth in your own mind. It's not about saying things that might please or upset other people.'

Giakoumakis certainly had people on his side. Arriving as one of three deadline-day signings in the summer window, he'd initially taken his time to get up to speed in Glasgow. Despite being part of a VVV-Venlo club relegated from the Eredivisie, he'd notched a remarkable 26 goals in 30 matches, including eight penalties. When Celtic signed him for a reported £2.5m amid little apparent interest from the Netherlands' big three, some questions were asked.

With no proper pre-season under his belt, Giakoumakis took some time to get match-fit. Shortly after arriving in Glasgow, he contracted Covid, which further hampered his attempts to get up to full speed. When he wasn't injured, he was half-fit and had to settle for 10 or 15 minutes at the end of matches. When he did get his big opportunity from the start, he rarely looked convincing. A goal in his first start, against St Johnstone, was a positive step, but the last-gasp penalty miss against Livingston undid the good work. Such a miss may have spelled the beginning of the end for a lesser player.

When Kyogo Furuhashi limped off in Celtic's final match of 2021 and missed the first 14 weeks of the new year, Giakoumakis had the opportunity he'd been craving. While some lamented the timing of the winter break, it arrived perfectly for Celtic's No. 7, allowing him to push the reset button.

Goals in his first two starts of the New Year and a terrific battling showing in the 3-0 derby win over Rangers seemed to win the support over. Yet it wasn't until the perfect hat-trick against Dundee that Giakoumakis was catapulted to a new level of stardom. His remarkable knack of netting instinctively – his first 12 goals were all scored with a single touch – became a major talking point, as did his ability to thrive on the chaos of a packed penalty box.

Giakoumakis finished the season on fire, netting four goals in his final three matches, despite starting just one following Kyogo's return. He scored a stunning overhead kick on the season's final day against Motherwell, then repeated the feat twice more in the early weeks of the following campaign against Baník Ostrava and Kilmarnock. When Kyogo was forced off just minutes into the new season's first derby, it said much about Giakoumakis that many inside the stadium didn't think Celtic had any less chance of winning.

Remarkably, he finished his debut season as the joint-top scorer in the entire league, alongside Ross County's Regan Charles-Cook, with 13 goals to his name, despite only playing half of the campaign. 'It's a little weird because you're the top scorer, but you're not alone,' he told fan media. 'It's a nice feeling. I just wish we had some more time so I could be the only one. But the most important thing is that we won the league.'

> *Giakoumakis comes from Greece,*
> *When he plays he scores with ease*
> *He leads the line, he plays up top*
> *Our number seven gift from God*

Celtic: *Hart, Ralston, Carter-Vickers, Starfelt, Juranovic, McGregor, O'Riley, Hatate, Jota, Giakoumakis, Maeda*
Subs used: *Abada, Rogic, Bitton*

Dundee: *Lawlor, Daley-Campbell, Rossi, McGhee, Sweeney, Kerr, Anderson, Byrne, Mulligan, Mullen, McMullan*
Subs used: *McCowan, McGinn, Fontaine, Rudden*

* * *

Bodø/Glimt 2-0 Celtic, UEFA Europa Conference League, Aspmyra Stadion, Thursday, 24 February 2022

Celtic fans had just completed their crash course on the Conference League by the time Bodø/Glimt sent their team tumbling out of it. UEFA's new third-tier competition had offered Ange Postecoglou's men hopes of a deep run. At the very least the tie against the Norwegians gave them a terrific opportunity to win a post-Christmas knockout tie after almost 20 years of waiting.

However, dreams of a run to the Tirana showpiece weren't matched by reality, as Kjetil Knutsen's slick team stunned Celtic Park with a 3-1 win in the first leg. The Norwegian champions looked like everything Postecoglou wanted his team to be on the continent: strong defensively, meticulous in possession, lightning in attack and with a ruthless streak. Celtic had chances in Glasgow, but Glimt deserved their victory.

With the tie likely to be beyond Celtic, Postecoglou made his priorities clear with his starting line-up a week later in Bodø – a town of around 40,000 located just north of the Arctic Circle. Callum McGregor, Cameron Carter-Vickers, Josip Juranovic, Reo Hatate, Liel Abada and Jota didn't start in Norway. Months later, Postecoglou would tell *Stan Sport*: 'I'd made no bones of the fact I was concentrating on winning the league. I just felt that's where our biggest reward lay.'

Celtic's changed line-up never looked comfortable in the wintry surroundings nor on the artificial surface. When the impressive Ola Solbakken swept in Glimt's opener after nine minutes, the tie was as good as over. A second-half Hugo Vetlesen strike completed an emphatic 5-1 aggregate win for the hosts. The defeat was a deflating one for a Celtic team and fanbase who had built up real momentum together, and news of Rangers ousting German giants Borussia Dortmund in the Europa League didn't help.

Yet Postecoglou and Celtic had a get-out-of-jail-free card. Nobody would remember the two bleak matches in May if McGregor had the Premiership trophy above his head. With

11 matches to go and just a three-point gap at the top, Celtic still had work to do.

Bodø/Glimt: *Smits, Sampsted, Moe, Høibråten, Wembangomo, Vetlesen, Hagen, Saltnes, Solbakken, Espejord, Pellegrino*
Subs used: *Boniface, Konradsen, Mvuka, Sery, Koomson*

Celtic: *Hart, Ralston, Welsh, Starfelt, Scales, Rogic, Bitton, O'Riley, Forrest, Giakoumakis, Maeda*
Subs used: *Abada, McGregor, McCarthy*

* * *

Livingston 1-3 Celtic, Premiership, Almondvale, Sunday, 6 March 2022

Ange Postecoglou and his players have exited the scene, and yet the singing is still going on. In the corner of the North and East Stand at Almondvale, the Bhoys group is chanting in support of their manager. Time after time they belt out just one word, 'Postecoglou', to the tune of Eminem's 'Without Me'. As the stadium empties, their singing continues, getting louder and louder.

They have every right to enjoy themselves. Postecoglou's team have given them something to smile about on this bright but chilly afternoon in West Lothian. The team have passed a significant test of their title credentials with a 3-1 victory over David Martindale's stubborn team – their first win in Livingston in over 15 years. The Celtic support, who take over three sides of Livi's stadium every time they visit, are starting to believe that the title could be on its way back to Paradise.

It's hard to understate the size of the win. Celtic had failed to win in five visits to the challenging plastic surface since Livingston were promoted to the top flight in 2018. Three draws and two defeats – with the most recent loss coming in one of Postecoglou's early matches – made it a tricky venue for the team to visit. Livingston were one of the league's form teams, with only Celtic taking more points since the winter break.

To add even more pressure, Celtic went into the game level on points at the top after Rangers' narrow win over Aberdeen a day earlier. Postecoglou's team got away with dropped points at Hibernian a week earlier. They had to win here.

The Celtic boss made four changes from the relatively straightforward home win over St Mirren in midweek, with Anthony Ralston, Nir Bitton, Tom Rogic and James Forrest all coming into the starting line-up. 'I think they're going to be important in the run-in,' he told me after the Saints win. 'I thought Niro, Tommy and James came on and did exactly what I wanted them to do. Our squad depth will be really important in these games because you know most games will be pretty tight. I keep saying to the guys that whether you start or not, whether you play 90 minutes or half an hour, your contribution is going to be vital.'

The quartet had clearly been listening to their manager in the weeks leading up to Livingston, with all four playing a part in the win. Bitton gave Celtic some much-needed assuredness in the middle of the park, Rogic was heavily involved in the third goal finished by Forrest, while Ralston played a part in the opening two. It seemed no coincidence that the players performed so well after Postecoglou's midweek comments.

Their performances and important contributions from the likes of Daizen Maeda and Jota meant Celtic were never in danger of dropping more points at their bogey ground. Even when Callum McGregor missed a first-half penalty and another sitter a minute later, it was a matter of when and not if Celtic would score. Maeda's back-post header, an own goal from Livingston captain Nicky Devlin and Forrest's strike had the result out of sight before Andrew Shinnie netted a consolation.

When the stadium emptied and the singing finally stopped, Celtic found themselves in a strong position at the top of the Premiership. Having played 11 matches over five gruelling weeks, the team would face just four over their next five. With David Turnbull and Kyogo Furuhashi soon to return, and Celtic assured to be going into the next derby in top spot, the support could start to dream. They'd sing Postecoglou's name again very soon.

Livingston: *Stryjek, Devlin, Fitzwater, Obileye, Penrice, Omeonga, Holt, Pittman, Shinnie, Forrest, Nouble*
Subs used: *Anderson, Soto, Kelly, Sibbald*

Celtic: *Hart, Ralston, Carter-Vickers, Starfelt, Taylor, Rogic, Bitton, McGregor, Forrest, Maeda, Jota*
Subs used: *Abada, Giakoumakis, O'Riley, Hatate*

CHAPTER 13

Unsung Heroes

'When you have a good relationship,
you can speak more freely without
someone taking offence.'

Carl Starfelt

AS CELTIC ploughed forward in search of an unlikely title victory, pundits and supporters sent most of the credit in the direction of their attacking players. Guys like Kyogo Furuhashi, Jota and Reo Hatate had lit up the final third at various points in the season and made watching Ange Postecoglou's team an enjoyable affair. In fact, had your opinions been formed solely by reading and listening to the Scottish media, you may have concluded that the Celtic defence wasn't very good. When the team won matches, it was down to the brilliance of the attackers. When they lost, it was the fault of those at the back.

Of course, separating the attack and defence of any team is a mistake, even more so in Postecoglou's teams. In his set-up, goalkeepers and defenders become the team's deepest attackers, starting moves with courage on the ball. Equally, attackers are the most advanced defenders. They're free to do what they enjoy but only if they help the team when out of possession.

A look at the final 2021/22 Premiership table tells you that Celtic conceded 22 goals in 38 league matches, nine fewer than any other team. While they did ship some soft goals in the early portion of the season, most of the dropped points arrived due to a lack of goals being scored. Celtic's goals conceded per match average stayed pretty constant throughout the campaign. The big wins came when the team hit their groove at the other end.

While Postecoglou famously said he doesn't 'pop champagne corks for clean sheets', instead preferring to take a more general look at how his team has defended, he must have been encouraged by the growth of his men at the back. Joe Hart, Cameron Carter-Vickers and Carl Starfelt were the three tasked with providing the last line of defence for most of his debut campaign.

The trio were about as ever-present as you're likely to find in a Postecoglou team, starting 21 of Celtic's 24 matches after the winter break. When Postecoglou opted to change things in the cup, Stephen Welsh came into the fold and rarely let Celtic down. Nir Bitton and Christopher Jullien also had extremely short spells in the backline. Moritz Jenz, the charming German who shook every journalist's hand during his first press conference, joined the club after the title success and immediately played a part in both boxes. Vasilis Barkas and Scott Bain also had very short stays in goal.

Yet the defensive trio of Hart, Carter-Vickers and Starfelt have played the most significant part, with the early April victory over Rangers at Ibrox perhaps their best collective showing. After Carter-Vickers fired Celtic into the lead, the second half became about keeping Rangers out. Celtic dropped much deeper than usual and were well-drilled defensively, with Hart forced into just one notable save from a Fashion Sakala strike.

The assured showing was even more impressive because the players had all started nervously at Ibrox. Carter-Vickers and Starfelt had looked shaky in the intense atmosphere, while Hart's desire to play out from the back had led to several nervy moments. Once captain Callum McGregor drove the team forward to an equaliser, the defence grew into the match and ended up having a decisive say.

'We have a chemistry between each other,' Starfelt told me weeks later. 'Playing with each other more and more gives an understanding. Then also, outside of the pitch, we connect very well. We've become good friends, so we can speak very openly about situations on the pitch. When you have a good relationship, you can speak more freely without someone taking offence.'

* * *

Carl Starfelt was announced as a Celtic player, with the help of a David Bowie 'Starman' gif, barely an hour after the departure of Kristoffer Ajer to Brentford. Who knows whether the pair brushed shoulders in the Celtic Park foyer? If they did, Ajer's message might have been interesting.

Starfelt's arrival from Rubin Kazan – the first of three players signed from the Russians in 12 months – had been as good as confirmed 24 hours earlier when he shared an image of himself taking in Celtic's draw with Midtjylland while quarantining in a hotel room. Starfelt would have been watching as stand-in centre-back Nir Bitton was shown two yellow cards in six first-half minutes. He may also have squirmed at the soft nature of the goal that earned the Danes a draw on the night.

The Swede had a good profile, having impressed in Kazan, playing more minutes than anyone else for a club with the second-best defensive record in the 2020/21 Russian Premier League. He was also around the fringes of the international set-up, with his exclusion from Sweden's final squad for Euro 2020 a topic of debate in the country. At 26, he was far from the project signing Ajer had been years earlier.

At the time of his arrival, Celtic were short on defensive options. Ajer had been joined by Shane Duffy on the way out of the club, while Christopher Jullien was still at least six months away from making his return from injury. Hart and Carter-Vickers hadn't been signed yet, with only Liel Abada being introduced to the action as a first-team signing.

The signing of Starfelt arrived after the close of the Champions League registration window, so he was forced to watch on as Celtic were dumped out of qualifying in Denmark. Days later, over a week after his announcement, he was presented in front of the media. 'I've been here only one day, and I've already seen that there are a lot of leaders on the pitch,' he told fan media. The following day he started in the heart of the defence alongside Bitton as Celtic fell to an opening-day defeat at Tynecastle. It was a torrid debut, perhaps unsurprisingly, given his lack of training time.

Some shaky moments in subsequent fixtures, such as a penalty conceded in another match against Hearts and a disastrous own goal away to AZ Alkmaar, led many to believe that Starfelt wasn't up to the job. With Hart and Carter-Vickers being praised virtually from their arrival at the club, Starfelt's shaky moments made him the scapegoat in the media. Yet as Celtic settled under their new manager, so did the defender. The errors still occurred from time to time, but they were far less frequent and often came during solid performances.

The second half of the season was when he came on, forming a close defensive bond with Carter-Vickers. Celtic didn't lose a single league match with the pair playing together at the back. When their long unbeaten run eventually ended at St Mirren in September 2022, it was telling that neither was involved.

Starfelt had endured a tough start to the new season, with another hamstring injury suffered while on international duty forcing him to miss Celtic's entire pre-season schedule. When he returned to the squad as a substitute in an away match against Kilmarnock, he notched his first goal for the club. Remarkably, the strike arrived 21 minutes into his new season, having gone 4,397 minutes without a goal in 2021/22. 'It was the ugliest of the five, but probably the most significant,' Postecoglou said afterwards.

Starfelt is a vital member of the Celtic squad, even though his playing time has reduced a little since the signing of Jenz from Lorient. He's now appreciated by most supporters, with the feeling mutual. 'I think the supporters are absolutely amazing,' he told me midway through his first campaign. 'I've never experienced anything like it, I've never seen anything like it. So, of course, it's a big honour to go out every game and have a 60,000 full stadium. I am just really happy to be at this club right now.'

* * *

If the Swede's charming manner sees him sitting in front of the media frequently, Cameron Carter-Vickers is more of a mysterious figure. Signed initially on a season-long loan from Tottenham Hotspur, with the transfer made permanent a year later, it's hard to imagine Celtic winning the league without Carter-Vickers at the centre of defence. He goes about his business quietly, rarely missing matches through injury and seldom letting his team down. In fact, there's an argument he's the most underrated member of Postecoglou's squad.

The defender, born on the final day of 1997, sees himself as American and British. The Carter portion of his name is taken from his father Howard, a former basketball star who played in both the NBA and Europe, while his English mother Geraldine supplies the Vickers part. He plays international football for the United States because he feels it keeps him connected to the American side of his family. 'I have two last names, two parents, two homes,' he said in a 2018 video.

At that stage, CCV was on loan at Ipswich Town – one of six different loans he had at English Championship clubs while on Spurs' books. Before being picked up by the London club, he'd played Sunday league football with Essex-based Catholic United. Founded in 1959, the club has links going back decades with Celtic. In 1968, Celtic chairman Bob Kelly gifted jerseys to United, with the team wearing the Hoops ever since. When Carter-Vickers mentioned his boyhood club in his signing video, thousands of Celtic fans were made aware of the links.

'The last 48 hours have been truly remarkable for our club,' Catholic United chairman James Paviour said soon after in a statement. 'I simply cannot express the positive energy the incredible Celtic fans bring and what it has meant to our club, which is wholly run by volunteers.'

The defender had just returned from a loan spell with Bournemouth when it became clear that he wouldn't feature regularly in the plans of new Spurs manager Nuno Espirito Santo. When the Portuguese boss made 11 changes for a Conference League clash against Paços de Ferreira, and Carter-Vickers put in an error-laden performance, it was apparent he wouldn't be seen in a Spurs shirt again. After a summer of speculation, Celtic finally announced the season-long loan, with an option to buy, in the final minutes of August. Carter-Vickers became the club's 12th first-team signing of a hectic summer, perhaps their most important one.

He made his debut 11 days later, striding out from defence and netting the opener in a 3-0 home win over Ross County. He scored four times in his debut season, including crucial strikes against St Mirren and Rangers during the title run-in. However, it was his assured defending that led to him being one of the stand-outs as Celtic regained the league. Nicknamed 'The Fridge' by his team-mates, after former Chicago Bears star William Perry, Carter-Vickers doesn't resemble a typical modern-day footballer, but is deceivingly quick, rarely outmuscled and assured in possession. He's generally calm unless you do something to irk him, as St Johnstone striker Chris Kane found out after leaving the boot in during a Celtic Park clash. Joe Hart's 30-yard sprint to calm the defender down told its own story.

Postecoglou: 'He's been a fantastic addition and a great person to have in the dressing room. Cameron's really calm and belies his years in the way he conducts himself. When I did my research on him, Cameron looked like a type that could provide leadership, particularly at the back, and that's how it's proved.

There's still massive improvement in there. For a defender, he's still a young guy, and he wants to improve.'

That improvement was to come at Celtic after the club completed a reported £6m deal, with a further £4m to be paid to Spurs in add-ons. Carter-Vickers joined on a four-year contract and immediately took his spot in Postecoglou's team ahead of pre-season. Amid all the upheaval in the backline during the early weeks of the season, with Starfelt, Welsh and Jenz all getting playing time, it was Carter-Vickers who was the constant. Along with Callum McGregor, he's become Celtic's most consistent performer, rarely dipping below a 7 out of 10 and being appreciated by supporters.

* * *

When Joe Hart joined Celtic from Tottenham Hotspur, those looking favourably on the deal were in the minority. The goalkeeper, capped 75 times by England between 2008 and 2017, had endured a torrid few years since leaving Manchester City, gradually working his way down the food chain, from Torino and West Ham to Burnley and then as back-up at Tottenham Hotspur.

When Spurs hired Espirito Santo in June 2021, Hart's days were numbered. After just one meeting with his new boss, it became clear that he'd have to go elsewhere if he wanted to play football. He'd spoken to Celtic about a move 12 months earlier but, at the time, a lack of resale value had stopped the deal from getting off the ground. A year down the line, and after a horrendous season spent with Vasilis Barkas, Scott Bain and Conor Hazard between the sticks, Celtic made their move again.

On top of his experience, Hart had the presence Celtic had been lacking ever since Fraser Forster departed for the second time in 2020. Forster had been one of the many friends Hart asked about Celtic, with Stiliyan Petrov another canvassed for his opinion during the due diligence process. The consensus was that Celtic would be perfect for Hart, with his characteristics closely aligned to the club's.

'I just sensed in his voice that he needed a bit of love,' Postecoglou would later tell BT Sport's *Currie Club* podcast. 'He needed a bit of him being put in an environment where he could feel like himself again. He's very upbeat, very vocal. I got off the phone and thought, if he's bought into what I've just said, I think I've got a good one for the environment I'm setting up.'

Hart was immediately thrust into the Celtic line-up, starting in the Europa League win away to Jablonec just days after signing. His breakthrough moment came in the return leg in Glasgow a week later. With Celtic leading the tie 6-2 on aggregate, a rare mistake from Callum McGregor presented Jablonec forward Martin Doležal with a clear-cut chance. Hart sensed his opportunity, kept his frame big and diverted the shot wide of the post to send a packed Celtic Park wild. The noise got even louder 30 seconds later when he batted away another close-range effort from Milos Kratochvíl. It was a massive moment for the goalkeeper and a support who had been shorn of any defensive confidence for over a year.

From there his confidence grew and he quickly became one of the key people Postecoglou trusted to run the dressing room. For all the talk about the intangibles he brings to the squad, the quality of his goalkeeping is sometimes underappreciated. Hart regularly makes significant saves at critical times, while his ball-playing ability is less of a weakness than many like to portray. There have been occasional errors, but they could be counted on just a few fingers, and the reaction has always been strong.

Hart is tasked with starting Celtic moves, rapidly receiving balls from ball kids after wayward shots have passed his goal. It says a lot that his generally subdued exterior is only ever interrupted when opposition attackers attempt to disrupt him by standing in front of goal kicks or launching the ball away. That seems to irritate him even more than conceding goals.

A year, and two trophies after joining, Hart was handed the No. 1 goalkeeper's jersey. His playing style was also adapted during a summer free of European qualifiers, with Hart now playing in a more aggressive position when Celtic have the ball. The keeper regularly acts as another ball-playing centre-half when Celtic are building from the back, which he found uncomfortable initially but is warming to.

'That's always where he wants his goalie,' he told the press of Postecoglou during the close season. 'That's how he sees football. But he also understands you have to play with the players you have got. I couldn't just come in and play as high as that as I'd never done it before. So I had to learn, and I'm still learning. That's why I absolutely love being at Celtic and playing under the manager.'

When you think of Postecoglou's team's journey, Hart is often the first player who jumps to mind. Perhaps that's because of the low ebb his career was at when he moved to Glasgow, or the constant mentions of improvement in his weekly Instagram updates. Hart has taken to Postecoglou, Celtic and Scottish football like the seasoned pro he is. While similar big names have come to Scotland from the Premier League in the past, few have arrived with the same professionalism and respect for the Scottish game. From unsavoury incidents like looking for shards of glass in the penalty box at Ibrox to funnier ones like an Aberdeen fan coming on to the pitch mid-match begging for an 'it's deceeeent' catchphrase, Hart has embraced everything about his new surroundings.

That even extends to the media, although he often finds himself answering the same questions on past experiences. When tasked with looking back, Hart's response is almost always that he's 'just living in the moment'. When your moment is winning trophies or playing in the Champions League for Celtic, why would you want to do anything else?

Just like Starfelt and Carter-Vickers, Hart understands Postecoglou and Celtic. He best summed it up in the club's return to the Champions League, saying, 'I'm fully aware I've not got as much to look forward to as, for example, Jota career-wise. But I love stepping up and going into every game with excitement and not knowing what will come next. He is us, and we are him, so we are rolling as a unit.'

CHAPTER 14

Marinos

'He drives standards to the point where all you want to do is continue those standards because you know that is how the football club has to run.'

John Hutchinson

CELTIC COULD have picked a better day to show training under Ange Postecoglou in all its glory. The weather is the issue, but not as you might expect. Scotland is experiencing its highest temperatures since records began, with a reading of 34.8°C in the Borders surpassing the previous best set in the region almost 20 years earlier. While extreme heat like this is usually reserved for sun loungers and all-inclusive holiday bars, Celtic Park is everyone's destination today, with supporters having the easy job.

Celtic's stars are amid an intense pre-season schedule as they aim to improve on a debut season that brought a Premiership and League Cup double. They've already played four friendlies – including a first at Celtic Park two days earlier – and with a trip to the Polish capital to face Legia Warsaw coming up days later, things are heating up in more ways than one.

The 'Champions' Training Day' event is free to all season ticket holders from the previous campaign – one of the many perks used to entice supporters to renew when things seemed bleak. Celtic have organised similar events in the past but never like this. Under previous regimes, these occasions could be classified more as 'fun days' – an opportunity for supporters to watch the players away from the fierce pressure of matchdays. Fun isn't high on Postecoglou's agenda today. His players will be training at the same extreme intensity as always. No matter the fact they're at Celtic Park rather than Lennoxtown, nor the stifling heat.

What follows is an intense session that never seems to hit a lull. The changeover period between drills is short, with players even running to get water during breaks. Celtic go from warming up, to possession, to attacking in no time at all. Only at the end of the session, after McGregor and Postecoglou address the crowd, does any hint of fun arrive. Ten lucky kids are chosen to take penalties at Celtic's first-team goalkeepers – the lucky ones on this uncomfortably warm day.

Throughout the hour, Celtic's manager stands on his own with his arms folded, around 20 metres from the action. Postecoglou is engrossed in what's happening right in front of him. Much like on matchdays, he rarely shouts or gets involved in any meaningful way. Only occasionally does he interact with anyone. During the first 15 minutes, while the players are warming up, he's engaged in a lengthy conversation with his new coach Harry Kewell. The former Liverpool man is a fiery type, and the pair's conversation is animated.

Callum McGregor is one of the others to cross paths with Postecoglou during the session. While recovering from a physical friendly against Blackburn Rovers just days earlier, he has a discussion with his manager. Even when not taking an active role in training, Celtic's skipper wants to be involved. When the conversation is over, Postecoglou is left alone again. He's separated physically from the action but may as well be breathing down the players' necks. He just stands and stares while not missing a beat.

* * *

John Hutchinson worked with Postecoglou at Yokohama F. Marinos and knows all about the Ange stare. He laughs when I tell him my observations of the training day barely a week later. 'There are times when you're doing a drill and he's just staring at you,' he tells me. 'It took me a few weeks to get used to getting no feedback. After that, I didn't even know he was there half the time because I was so involved in the session. He wants full concentration to be on the players.'

Postecoglou has a reputation for keeping his distance from his players, and Hutchinson confirms that extends to members of his coaching staff:

> There were maybe four or five days in a row where I'd say 'morning boss', and I'd get a 'morning Hutch', and that was the extent of the conversation for days. Then other days he would start talking and you would just get your notepad out and start writing. Don't get me wrong, he oversees everything. You're kidding yourself if you think he's not watching or he's missed something. The detail is unbelievable. If you misspell something or get someone's name wrong, he's on to you immediately. In training, if you miss a detail or you're not preparing properly, or it's not up to a certain standard, you're going to be in a bit of trouble.

Postecoglou demands the same high standards from his coaches as he does his players. He regularly tells them to seize every day and never waste a session. A willingness to go out of your comfort zone is vital. While working in such an environment brings constant pressure, Hutchinson still enjoyed his time with Postecoglou immensely.

That was evidenced in his reply to my request for an interview. 'Always happy to chat about Ange. Absolute legend and inspiration.'

He rates Celtic's boss as the best Aussie coach of all time and felt that way even before his success in Scotland. As a young footballer, Hutchinson regularly travelled hours from home to watch Postecoglou's impressive South Melbourne team play. When he made it in the A-League with Central Coast Mariners, Postecoglou's Brisbane Roar denied them victory in a thrilling 2011 Grand Final that's still spoken about today. 'He never actually brought that up, which is a positive,' he jokes. Yet, if the 11-time Malta cap had a lot of admiration from a distance, the respect grew ten-fold when Postecoglou helped him out of a sticky position.

Hutchinson was in a difficult place, like most of the world, when the Covid-19 pandemic struck in early 2020. He was based in Washington, at Seattle Sounders, and found himself miles from home and needing some advice. He could never have imagined what a simple message would lead to:

Covid was taking over the world, my family were homesick and football was becoming a very small, lonely place for me. I wanted to reach out to someone I'd never spoken to but admired from afar. So I messaged Ange via LinkedIn, told him about my situation and asked him for some advice. I wasn't expecting a response, but I got one 24 hours later. I read the message and felt like I'd got a full energy charge from a guy I didn't really know.

A few months later, he reached out again, saying that there could be a position available at Yokohama F. Marinos. We interviewed on the phone for an hour, and he said the job was mine. I walked into the lounge room and told my wife we were moving to Japan. The first time I actually had a conversation with Ange in person was in Japan.

As unlikely as it seems, Hutchinson's story isn't unique. Postecoglou has a history of offering jobs to up-and-coming

Aussie coaches, providing them with a platform and an opportunity to learn before they embark on their career as a manager. It's his way of giving a little back to the game in his homeland.

When Harry Kewell was offered a coaching gig at Celtic weeks after they clinched the Premiership, some eyebrows were raised. Kewell had enjoyed a stellar playing career, perhaps Australia's greatest-ever footballer, and his managerial career had shown early promise while at Crawley Town. However, his coaching journey had stalled and he'd last been seen managing Barnet in the National League, where his tenure lasted just seven winless matches.

But just like Hutchinson and many others before him, Postecoglou sensed an opportunity. Celtic's coaching staff – John Kennedy, Gavin Strachan and Stephen McManus – was composed of former defensively minded players. Kewell would buck that trend and, as a former Champions League winner, offer valuable experience in Europe. That, coupled with the Aussie connection and the need for fresh impetus after a season of success, made it a no-brainer for all parties. Kewell was added to Celtic's first-team coaching staff, with McManus moving to the B team alongside Darren O'Dea.

'He's obviously one of Australia's greatest-ever footballers,' Postecoglou told club media early in pre-season. 'A guy who's worked really hard to try and get a coaching career going. The reports I've had on him are that he'll bring some really good qualities with his on-field coaching and his ability to mentor players. For me, it was really important that, when the players came back this year, they understood that nothing stands still. Seeing a couple of new faces in the staff is going to help that.'

Months later, Kewell told Fox Sports how the move came about. The pair had crossed paths briefly when Postecoglou took over at Melbourne Victory, just before Kewell left the club, although there wasn't much of a relationship to speak of. Like with Hutchinson, the offer came as a complete surprise. 'I was actually going in for another job at the time, and I thought the interview went really well, so I was waiting for a call back from that. Let's just say that happened on a Tuesday. I received a message from the manager around about Thursday or Friday. Within that message was enough for me to forget what I had been doing and come and learn from one of the best. I thought it was too good of an opportunity to pass by.'

Ante Milicic, the former forward best known for his time with Sydney United, is another who Postecoglou contacted when he least expected it. The pair had come into contact over the previous 30 years, but never for more than small talk before or after a match. In early 2014, just months out from the World Cup, Milicic was approached by Postecoglou. He was in a good role as number two to Tony Popovic at Western Sydney Wanderers but the lure of joining up with Postecoglou and coaching on the biggest stage in Brazil proved to be too alluring. He tells me:

> I remember one day just receiving a text from Ange out of the blue. I didn't have Ange's number, so it was pretty easy to think it was a gee-up at first. Now that I've spent time with Ange, I know his replies aren't basic three-word replies. They're so well written and there's always a thought behind them. His initial text sounded too intelligent for it not to be genuine. He said, 'Hi Ante, it's Ange Postecoglou. I'm wondering if you've got time for a chat?' And I'm thinking, *Wow, Ange is calling me wondering if I've got time for a chat.* Then he rang me and told me he was looking to restructure the national team coaching staff and that he'd been following my coaching career from a distance. He asked if I'd be interested in being part of the journey. I remember just getting off the phone, and I was so excited. After that initial call, I didn't hear from him for two weeks. Then he rang me up again,

and shortly afterwards, I started preparing for a World
Cup in Brazil.

Again, the theme is Postecoglou having his finger on the pulse,
being aware of Milicic's exploits without the former striker even
knowing it. There was no evidence of multiple candidates being
lined up for the role. Like with Hutchinson and Kewell, Milicic
was who Ange wanted, and that was who he got.

'I keep tabs on different young coaches in particular,' the
Celtic manager explained in an *Open Goal* interview. 'There was
a period in my career when I couldn't get an opportunity, and I
felt it wasn't right. I believed in myself and wanted someone to
give me a chance. It was a bit of luck and a bit of circumstance
that gave me the opportunity to coach again, and since then
my career has gone off. I just thought that there could be other
people out there like me. So I follow as many young managers
as possible to see how they're doing.'

* * *

Postecoglou didn't spend much time out of the game after leaving
as Socceroos boss. He announced his departure on 22 November
2017 and was paraded as the new manager of Japanese J1 League
outfit Yokohama F. Marinos less than four weeks later. After
tendering his resignation from Football Australia, Postecoglou
had made it clear he saw his immediate future away from the
country. After taking a fortnight's holiday with his family, he
was looking to get back into another managerial gig as soon as
possible. He wouldn't return to Australia until September 2022,
when promoting the Sydney Super Cup as manager of Celtic.

In this short period after leaving the Socceroos, Postecoglou
became an option for Rangers in a genuine Scottish football
sliding-doors moment. The Ibrox club had just parted company
with Pedro Caixinha and sat fourth in the Premiership, eight
points adrift of Brendan Rodgers' Celtic. Postecoglou's name
was heavily linked with the role before chairman Dave King

indicated a preference for a manager with experience in British football, eventually appointing Graeme Murty until the end of the season. By that stage, Postecoglou had found his new home in Japan.

Yokohama F. Marinos, the former club of beloved Celtic star Shunsuke Nakamura, are one of the better known names in Japanese football. The club, formerly known as Nissan FC and then Yokohama Marinos before a merger with Yokohama Flügels, are majority-owned by the car manufacturers, who have their headquarters in the city. They're also partially owned by the CFG – the global network of clubs headed by Manchester City. CFG, who own 20 per cent of F. Marinos, had been well aware of Postecoglou's credentials, having kept an eye on his progress for several years, something that would play to Celtic's advantage further down the line.

Postecoglou officially took over the club in February 2018, replacing the Frenchman Erick Mombaerts. His first season was in keeping with his previous experiences, with initial struggles endured while the building blocks for future success were put in place. Marinos were threatened with relegation throughout the 2018 campaign, although they didn't finish any matchday in the automatic relegation spots. A solid end to the season saw them rise to a 12th-place finish, while a runners-up medal in the J.League Cup showed further encouragement.

The potential was realised a year later when the club won its fourth-ever league title, a first since 2004. A 3-0 win against runners-up Tokyo FC sealed the triumph in front of over 60,000 fans at the International Stadium Yokohama as Postecoglou became the first Australian coach to win a major men's league title in another country. The size of the achievement wasn't lost on former Socceroos goalkeeper Mark Bosnich, who told Fox Sports that the achievement was 'easily the number one by an Australian coach'.

'Everywhere I've gone, there's a bedding-in process because we do things a little bit differently,' Postecoglou said after the triumph. 'We've had some ups and downs along the way but nowhere near as bad as last year. The last two months, it's really the players driving it now. They're really enjoying our football, we're scoring goals, and there's a real belief. Within the club, the players are loving playing like we are, the supporters are loving it, and other clubs here in the J.League and people following football are really enjoying it. For me, that's the greatest satisfaction.'

The attractive football also caught the eye of some key personnel at Manchester City in the summer of 2019. The reigning English champions visited Yokohama as part of an Asian tour and earned a 3-1 win through goals from Kevin De Bruyne, Raheem Sterling and Lukas Nmecha. After the match, Sterling seemed genuinely impressed by the Marinos performance, telling the media, 'They're probably one of the best teams I've seen play out from the back. They played some great football, so it was a great test for us.' His manager Pep Guardiola was also full of praise for their opponents.

Postecoglou had conquered Japan with a team many had expected to be scrapping to avoid relegation. Innovative playing styles such as the introduction of inverted full-backs had helped to upset the odds and bring about success. Marinos full-backs, mainly Ken Matsubara and Theerathon Bunmathan, would regularly move inside when play was being built from the back, offering an additional option to the ball player, while also freeing up more space on the flanks for the wingers. Postecoglou's style was evolving, and Celtic would benefit just as much as Marinos.

John Hutchinson may only have arrived at the tail end of Postecoglou's three-and-a-half-year spell in Japan, but the harsh introduction amid the struggles of the pandemic meant that it was a time to learn quickly. You don't tend to get too much of a honeymoon period under Postecoglou:

At first, I was running pre-season from Australia with another Aussie coach in Japan. I was organising training sessions on Zoom without any real contact with the players because of the language barrier. Ange was manager, I was head coach, and there were a few assistant coaches. We were doing double sessions, and it was chaos. Then the borders started opening, and I got to go to Japan. My first training session was crazy. We'd just finished the warm-up and were going into a rondo. Ange was 15 yards away, just staring at me, making sure the training session was going well. I had my head down, looking at a piece of paper, and I remember glancing up, and there were players everywhere. I'd struggle to tell you what I felt at that moment.

Training under Postecoglou would best be described as organised chaos, as anyone inside Celtic Park for that sweltering training session would know. Sessions are short but packed full of challenging drills. Mistakes are viewed as a good thing, with the manager's opinion that if mistakes aren't made, the session hasn't been challenging enough. Hutchinson learned numerous valuable lessons from Postecoglou during their time together in Japan, but training is perhaps at the top of the list. He took Postecoglou's methods with him to America with El Paso Locomotive.

Hutchinson: 'We train here for a maximum of about 65, 70 minutes because that's all the players can handle. I always had a belief in training hard, but he just takes it to another level. The players run. They run to get water, they run to the session, we have small breaks, and then we go again. We've all heard the slogan "We Never Stop"; that's training under Ange. From the moment players step on to the field to the moment they walk off, it's helter-skelter.'

Back at Celtic Park, Postecoglou watches as training rages on. Most of the session includes a ball, with quick, crisp passing evident in every routine. Drills start at a reasonable pace and increase in tempo as time passes.

Gavin Strachan, the son of former Celtic manager Gordon, takes a prominent role in the session. The former Peterborough United assistant had once been a derided figure among the Celtic support. During the dire 2020/21 campaign, Strachan was often seen on the touchline holding a laptop in an image that soon became a meme. When the club embraced the joke in the 2021 Christmas advert, it showed both they and Strachan had a sense of humour. Nowadays, it's an earpiece that's his chosen item of technology.

The squad appreciates Strachan, if some comments from Matt O'Riley on the team's improving set-piece return are anything to go by: 'Yeah, Gavin Strachan specifically,' O'Riley told club media after goals for the likes of Stephen Welsh and Moritz Jenz early in the new season. 'He does quite a lot of work with me and a few others on the training ground just to try and tighten up on a few things.'

Most importantly, Strachan is valued by Postecoglou. When the coach missed the Aussie's first manager of the month award in October 2021, his absence was noted. Postecoglou stood alongside John Kennedy, Stevie Woods and Stephen McManus for the presentation photo but was aware that someone was missing. When the manager's next award arrived after an impressive January, Strachan was alongside him in the picture.

For all the demands placed on the likes of Kewell and Strachan, Postecoglou appreciates their efforts immensely. After his October award, he told the media, 'It's great to be recognised in this way, but I'd like to thank the players, coaches and backroom staff for all of their efforts. Whatever we achieve, we do it together.'

That appreciation extends to non-coaching staff as well. As the monthly awards continued to roll in, attention was turned towards even more of the unsung heroes of Celtic's success. The recruitment and sports science teams were among those who got their spot in the limelight in February and March. By April's award, even legendary member of the Lisbon Lions and club kit man John Clark was in front of the camera. Virtually everyone included in the photographs was already at the club when Postecoglou arrived.

He told Darrell Currie and Chris Sutton on BT Sport's *Currie Club* podcast:

> I guess coming from Australia, I've been an outsider in football my whole career. Everything I've done in football has been as an outsider just because of geography more than anything else. I thought, there's a lot of people in this building who have had a lot of success, who went through a tough time last year. You learn a hell of a lot going through a tough time. Maybe they learned a lot last year. The reality is that if I had brought people in, it wouldn't have made the job any easier. It wouldn't have fast-tracked anything. It would have made me feel comfortable, but I'm not interested in feeling comfortable. I'm interested in being successful.

John Kennedy was the obvious backroom team member Postecoglou had to convince in his early days. Kennedy has been at Celtic in some capacity for most of his adult life, from player to coach. He initially broke through from the club's youth academy as a high-potential young centre-back, making his debut at 16 under Kenny Dalglish, before making real advancements under Martin O'Neill three years later. Around that time he earned international recognition with Scotland, where disaster struck in his debut against Romania. A horror challenge from forward Ionel Ganea midway through the first half of the friendly saw Kennedy suffer cruciate knee ligament damage, which virtually ended his career before it had really started. After years of operations, rehabilitation and unsuccessful return attempts, he called time on his career aged 26 in late 2009, moving into a coaching role at the club. He went from youth coach to reserve coach and then first-team coach when Ronny

Deila entered the building in 2014. Kennedy was a crucial part of the Norwegian's time in Glasgow and enjoyed a similar role under Brendan Rodgers and Neil Lennon. When Lennon left the club in early 2021, Kennedy led the team for the final ten matches of the season to disappointing results.

The short spell as caretaker manager doesn't seem to have damaged his reputation. Kennedy is regularly linked with high-profile Scottish managerial jobs, with Hibernian and Dundee United being mentioned as potential suitors over the past few seasons. The word also seems to have spread to Europe, with Denmark's Midtjylland linked with him early on in the 2022/23 season.

'He's worked with some fantastic managers, me aside,' Postecoglou said in a press conference at the time. 'He's built up his expertise through different areas of the game. He started in the junior ranks, he's done some scouting, and he's tried to make sure he's as well-rounded as he possibly can be. He's no different to anyone else at this football club. If people identify him as someone who can help their organisation, then it's up to the individuals to make those decisions. John is a really important part of what we do here. He's an important part of my set-up.'

Callum McGregor is another big fan of the former defender. 'Me and Kendo first worked together at the youth team,' he told fan media. 'Under-17s, 18s, 19s and then we both progressed to the first team at the same time. I've known him for a number of years now, and we know each other inside and out, which is great. He provides that continuity and what the club is about, so when any new manager comes in, or someone comes into the club, he's one of the first to let them understand what the club's about, what the expectation level is, and what the standards are like around the place.'

When Postecoglou does move on from Celtic, Kennedy is likely to be a contender to succeed him, assuming he hasn't been prised away by another club. At some stage, we'll learn much more about one of the unsung heroes of this glorious Celtic era.

* * *

Postecoglou's desire to not let anyone slip into their comfort zone extends to his coaches. Whenever John Hutchinson felt he had a grasp of his working environment, Postecoglou would move the goalposts. Whenever he felt settled, there would be a demand for more coming from above. Postecoglou, himself, craves the feeling of things being on a knife-edge. It's why multi-year contracts aren't important to him. Celtic's manager doesn't want long-term job security. He tries to avoid it if possible.

He keeps members of his backroom team focused by keeping their jobs simple. The likes of Kennedy, Kewell and Strachan are unlikely ever to have to worry about transfer dealings or press conferences. Postecoglou takes care of it all, allowing people such as Hutchinson to focus on their areas of expertise:

> When I was in Japan, every day was spent with the players and the staff, and that's all I had to worry about. Anything outside of that, I wouldn't even know what was going on. I didn't know who he was trying to sign. Sometimes we'd turn up to training, and there would be a new player. My sole role was to organise staff, organise training and take training. My everything was the players, and I couldn't wait to get on to the training park and get the guys going. I didn't deal with team selection. I didn't talk to agents. I didn't talk to scouts. Ange took care of anything outside of my bubble. He drives standards to the point where all you want to do is continue those standards because you know that is how the football club has to run. The journey's never straight, mate, it's a rollercoaster. That's what he told me. We're going to have ups and downs, great games, not-so-great games, and it's a rollercoaster. It stuck with me from that moment.

CHAPTER 15

Ange and the Media

*'You think you might be widely read on
any topic, and I almost guarantee you he's
already read that book.'*

Andy Harper

WHEN CELTIC fans took their crash course on Ange Postecoglou in June 2021, there were a few obvious findings. Their new leader was Australian, his teams played good football and, most notably, he took no prisoners when dealing with the media. Celtic fans yearn for a manager who regularly puts the country's press 'in their place'. It's one of the main things Martin O'Neill and Gordon Strachan had going for them in their impressive managerial stints. More laid-back figures such as Tony Mowbray and Ronny Deila didn't last quite as long in the Glasgow hotbed.

The Scottish sports media world is a demanding environment. Unlike in Australia, most of the coverage centres around one sport. Much of that concerns just two clubs. Throughout a season, similar tiresome themes develop time after time. Every visit to Livingston or Kilmarnock is met with days of build-up on artificial pitches and debates on whether they should be allowed in Scotland's top tier. At different intervals, discussions on winter breaks, post-split fixtures and allocations rear their head, while questions tend to be asked by most of the same faces. Every now and then, a smooth operator enters the scene, and press events suddenly become unmissable.

Ange Postecoglou was box office from his first dealings with the country's media. From his unveiling conference it became clear that journalists would have to do their homework before asking him a question. The BBC's Chris McLaughlin learned the hard way when he pondered the career step-up Postecoglou had taken in moving to Scotland. 'I've coached at a World Cup,' was the Australian's dignified response.

Many more have been scalded since. As his compatriot and close friend Andy Harper explains, you must have your ducks in a row before taking on Celtic's manager. 'Invariably, he's already thought about the topic you're looking to cover,' he says. 'He's already foreseen or tried to foresee and strategise around the potential potholes. What makes it endlessly humorous for him is that he's spent the time thinking about this stuff, and a lot of people asking the questions haven't. He doesn't say this, but it comes across in his answer: "Do your homework. If you want to ask a question of material substance, great, but make sure you've thought about it because I have."'

As we've already discussed in great detail, Postecoglou doesn't miss anything. Whether it comes to players, staff, board members or even future colleagues, his finger is always on the pulse. Harper knows about that better than most. Several years ago, the pair spent a 'whirlwind' period together at Harper's country home in New South Wales, writing *Changing the Game: Football in Australia Through My Eyes*. In the preface to the book, Postecoglou describes Harper as 'the only person capable of writing my words'.

Harper tells me:

The book, very much like my relationship with Ange, came out of the blue. We're not natural associates. He's from Melbourne, I'm from Sydney, and our paths crossed intermittently, at competitive football matches when I was playing and he was coaching or vice versa. The whole thing was pretty random, except it's not. Nothing with Ange is random. He'll have done it with you, he'll have done it with almost everyone at Celtic. He knows more about you than you know about yourself, and that's before he's even met you. That's one of the keys to his success. He's got a natural sense for the people and organisations that will work with and for him. He's done 90 per cent of the work before he's even physically been somewhere or met someone.

Ange doesn't suffer fools. He thinks deeply about stuff. You think you might be widely read on any topic, and I almost guarantee you he's already read that book. He's already read that book about self-improvement, leadership or the great coaches in any sport. We were having a coffee once, and someone recommended the biography of Pat Riley, the legendary LA Lakers coach in the NBA. I said, 'I reckon Ange would be interested in this.' Of course, he'd already read it.

* * *

Over the past few seasons, journalist Andrew Smith has dealt with Postecoglou on too many occasions to mention, yet not always in person. Smith is routinely tasked with phoning Celtic's manager to get quotes for the written press before sharing the transcript with his colleagues. It's how Celtic have conducted business since the start of the pandemic in early 2020. Smith and his associates used to be at Lennoxtown three times a week. Now he's not sure whether he'll ever get back.

He agrees when I put Harper's comments on Postecoglou's covert intelligence to him:

I get the sense he knows about the different journalists and where they're all coming from. The big thing about

Postecoglou is control. He's so incredibly controlled when dealing with us. Brendan Rodgers was similar, but Postecoglou does it in a smarter way. You could see the joins with Brendan. Ange is more nimble in how he engages or doesn't engage. I do think he likes us more than the broadcast media. He can see the bear traps with the broadcast because they're looking for a soundbite. I've found that you get value if you ask slightly different things. I try desperately to avoid the stuff where I know what he's going to say.

Postecoglou is also plainly much funnier than Rodgers. He often saves his best lines for Smith and the rest of the written press, even if the context is lost soon after:

I did the one when I put to him: 'You've only been behind three minutes in 1,035 of football.' And he said, 'I don't know what kind of sad life you're living if you're coming up with facts like that.' The two of us were chuckling away. Then I saw it appearing on all the websites with people saying, 'Great, he's put it to the journos again.' It wasn't like that at all.

The other one was when I asked him if he knew that you're expected to be an epidemiologist, a meteorologist and more in Scottish football. He said, 'I'm not an archaeologist mate, I'm not any kind of ologist, I'm a pretty simple guy.' This is just my opinion, but sometimes I feel that when he wants to get a message out and make sure it appears in the papers, he gives us one of the infamous 'mate' lines.

Smith has thoroughly enjoyed his dealings with Postecoglou and says most of his colleagues feel the same way, despite the relationship appearing frayed at times. However, things have become a little more challenging in his second season:

The thing about Postecoglou is he's pretty straight. He answers every question, even if his answer isn't really an answer. He always gives you something. We were filling our boots last year, but it's a little more difficult now. To be fair, what can you say about the seventh time playing Ross County? .

I do think he's changed since his first season. These managers, like Brendan Rodgers and Steven Gerrard, tire of us eventually, and you can't blame them. The Scottish media is quite a claustrophobic environment. There are so many games, and Postecoglou does every single press conference. Rodgers and Gerrard would delegate from time to time, but Postecoglou is always there taking our questions. League, League Cup, friendlies, you name it. It must be pretty draining because the narratives don't really change.

The other thing is that he doesn't need us nearly as much. Early on, he probably needed to get us on his side, which he did magnificently. Everybody warmed to him. Now he doesn't really need that. There doesn't seem to be the same colour in any of his stuff this season.

Postecoglou's broadcast conferences have become more taxing as time has passed. He's regularly found answering the same questions from the same people week after week. With Celtic limiting questions to two per outlet and most press conferences still taking place over Zoom, the events can often feel quite distant, although Postecoglou still has his moments.

It's no secret that Celtic's manager saves his best answers for when dealing with members of fan media. As supporters of the club, they naturally have a greater understanding of what's going on than journalists, and Postecoglou seems to enjoy being probed on less prominent matters. In my limited time spent with him as a fan media representative, he's spoken at length about several issues that would likely never be covered by more mainstream outlets. That said, sometimes difficult questions need to be asked, and they're more likely to come from those outside the Celtic bubble. Each type of media has its place.

Progress is being made between the club and fan media outlets. Virtually every Celtic press conference nowadays will have at least four questions from fans, while relations have also extended to in-person Champions League and new signing events. Positive steps have been taken, yet the club can do more to put fan journalists on a level playing field with reporters from mainstream outlets. Fan media is the future. Given his responses over the last two seasons, Postecoglou surely wouldn't be against that.

* * *

The Greatest Hits

Ahead of Celtic's league opener against Hearts, Postecoglou was asked whether he knew much about the Jambos:

'I'm still on the same planet, mate. I haven't come from outer space. You'd be surprised about how much I know about Hearts. We're preparing for it the same way, but you can ask me that question every week because it'll be my first time against every opposition.'

When told by a journalist all about Carl Starfelt's attributes following the Swede's arrival from Rubin Kazan:

'Yeah, that's why I signed him, mate.'

With ten matches in just over a month at the start of his Celtic career, Postecoglou was asked whether he was feeling any early fatigue:

'I'm all right, mate. I don't run around at all. I just sit down and do what I do.'

When Celtic reduced the gap at the top of the table to four points after winning at Motherwell while Rangers slipped up at home to Hearts, Postecoglou was asked about the significance of the afternoon:

'I thought the Premiership race was over, mate, so I'm not looking at the table anymore. We're just kind of doing our own thing.'

In the lead-up to Celtic's Europa League opener against Real Betis, he was quizzed about Celtic being the pot two team in the group and their opponents being in pot three:

'Mate, I stay out of the kitchen, so pots aren't my forte.'

Postecoglou was lamenting his luck when Giorgos Giakoumakis pulled up with a calf injury while warming up, adding to a raft of injuries to his squad:

'I don't know what it is, mate. I've definitely walked under a ladder.'

After back-to-back losses at the start of the Europa League campaign, journalists asked Postecoglou whether he'd change his approach to achieve better results:

'My view on that is, if you are a strict vegetarian, you don't drop into Macca's [McDonald's] just because you are hungry, mate.'

When Celtic got their first win on matchday three of the competition against Ferencváros, he was asked about the clean sheet that went along with the two goals:

'I don't pop champagne corks for clean sheets. It's how we defend that's more important.'

The match against the Hungarians kicked off at 3.30pm on a Tuesday due to a series of unfortunate events. After the match, Postecoglou had a message for the unfortunate employers who had lost workers due to the kick-off time:

'I apologise to all the employers who had little productivity today as they were missing people and schools may have been empty, but they come here, create an energy and we have to match that with our football.'

When Celtic released their annual financial results in September 2021, he was asked for his thoughts:

'I'm not an accountant, mate, I'm a football manager. When people start talking to me about finances, they miss the essence of what I'm about.'

When asked about Carl Starfelt's impending move from Rubin Kazan:

'I'm not a doctor, so I can't talk about medicals.'

Postecoglou on why he doesn't feel duty bound to comment on issues not within his direct control:

'I have never seen myself as an epidemiologist or archaeologist or any kind of ologist. I'm a pretty simple guy.'

When asked what it meant to go just two points behind Rangers after an impressive victory at Hibernian:

'It just means there's a long way to go, mate.'

Postecoglou to fan media on the warmth he'd encountered since moving to Scotland:

'You folk don't understand how friendly and welcoming you are compared to the rest of the world. I've been invited to numerous people's houses I've only just met.'

Ahead of the visit to Bayer Leverkusen, a member of the media decided to ask Celtic's boss about ticket allocations at Hampden Park:

'Nah, you're not going to ask me about ticket allocations. We're playing Leverkusen in a big game tomorrow night. Don't waste the opportunity. I have no desire or any inkling to get involved in ticket allocation. That's not my brief. I'll give you a freebie. Give me another question.'

After a 2-1 League Cup Final victory over Hibernian at Hampden secured his first trophy as Celtic boss:

'All of you were probably running a book on how long I'd last. A few of you probably had December, but that's now out the window.'

When asked about the narrative developing that Kyogo Furuhashi was a diver:

'Who are these brave people, these warriors, who are out there, who are accusing people? Kyogo is the size of a jockey, he is playing against guys who are almost a foot taller than him, and all these brave warriors on the outside are casting aspersions, are they?'

On the prospect of Kyogo and Tom Rogic being called up for international football and missing key Celtic matches as a result:

'There is a lot of violin playing around the place. We are not going to be one of them.'

When asked about modern metrics like expected goals (xG) following the appointment of former Benfica analyst Antoine Ortega in January 2022:

'The one that gets me is XL because that's all my clothes. I've got no idea, mate. That's why I've brought Antoine in. The analytics thing is well beyond me. Like you, I went through my schooling with a pen and paper.'

As the end of the January window approached, Postecoglou came face to face with a reporter looking for answers on any upcoming transfer business:

AP: 'I thought I was pretty clear.'

R: 'So, no more business at all, even if a few go out the door, then?'

AP: 'I thought I was pretty clear.'

When Rangers pulled out of the Sydney Super Cup amid fan pressure:

'Whatever ticket sales we lose out on, I'm sure my friends and family will pick up, mate. So we'll be alright.'

After the straightforward 2-0 win over St Mirren in early March, with BBC Scotland's Kenny Macintyre:

KM: 'That was a hard watch at times – is that fair?'

AP: 'It depends what you're looking for. Maybe you're disappointed with the way it went, mate.'

After Celtic moved six points clear at the top with a 4-0 victory over Ross County, Postecoglou was asked whether he'd be watching Rangers in action at Dundee 24 hours later:

'My Sundays are dictated by my wife and kids. If *Sing 2* is on, I'll have to fight for the remote control.'

An exchange on BBC Radio Scotland after the same victory over the Staggies:

BBC: 'It keeps this wonderful domestic run going, 31 games unbeaten, you're six points clear at the top of the league. It puts Rangers under pressure tomorrow?'

AP: 'All of those statements are true, yeah.'

When Rangers beat Borussia Dortmund, Braga, RB Leipzig and more on their way to the Europa League Final, Postecoglou was asked whether the run showed what Scottish clubs could achieve in Europe:

'If you want evidence of how well Scottish clubs can do in Europe, there's a trophy I can show you just down the road here, mate.'

With Celtic champions in waiting, he was asked by BBC Radio Scotland whether he'd prefer to win the league without winning, away from home with no Celtic fans or on the final day of the season at Celtic Park:

'Only you could make winning a championship feel like a downer. No, mate, any way it comes, thank you.'

When asked about the prospect of him parking the bus in the Champions League group stage, shortly after Celtic's qualification:

'I've never owned a bus, mate.'

On the uncertainty surrounding the future of Tom Rogic after his exit from Celtic two months earlier:

'I think Tom's fine. Has anyone spoken to Tom? No one spoke to him when he was here for ten years, either. That's Tom. I'd be more concerned if he was out there talking to people. Leave him alone. He's fine.'

On the deadline-day signing of Danish midfielder Oliver Abildgaard from Rubin Kazan:

'It's no secret he adds a bit of size to our team. Most of our side will struggle to get on any rides at Disneyland.'

Ange Postecoglou was formally unveiled as the manager of Celtic on Friday, 25 June 2021.

The 9,000-strong Celtic support gave their new manager a rapturous ovation ahead of his competitive debut against Midtjylland.

The Celtic players and fans celebrate a first away win in eight months after Jota's late winner at Pittodrie.

A half-fit Kyogo Furuhashi celebrates his stunning second goal in a dramatic League Cup Final victory over Hibernian.

Ange Postecoglou with his first trophy won as Celtic manager.

Callum McGregor, wearing a mask, was a huge part of Celtic's memorable 3-0 derby win over Rangers in February 2022.

Giorgos Giakoumakis wheels away after completing his vital hat-trick in the 3-2 win over Dundee.

The Celtic squad celebrates the regaining of the Premiership title after a 1-1 draw against Dundee United at Tannadice.

Yosuke Ideguchi, Daizen Maeda, Reo Hatate and Kyogo Furuhashi pose for the cameras on the night the league was won.

The Celtic starting line-up for the Champions League matchday two draw away to Shakhtar Donetsk in Warsaw.

Joe Hart raises a fist to the Celtic support after a quiet afternoon against Dundee United.

Jota celebrates his stunning goal in the 4-0 demolition of Rangers in September 2022.

Ange Postecoglou shows his appreciation for the Celtic support after another big win.

CHAPTER 16

The Journey, Part 4: Champions

*'Don't let any chaos out there derail
from what we're all about.'*

Ange Postecoglou

CELTIC'S ROLLERCOASTER campaign raged from late July to early May, with barely an opportunity to catch your breath. Momentum had been gathered with every passing month as supporters and their team battled to claim the prize on which the season would be judged: the Premiership title. Then, in the space of eight spectacular days, it was all over.

The three final matches of the season, against Hearts, Dundee United and Motherwell, saw Celtic all but win the league, officially win the league, and then get their hands on the trophy. Regaining the title from a 25-point deficit a year earlier was a significant achievement, further sweetened by it arriving in the first season for Ange Postecoglou and his new-look team. The triumph was major news, and not just in Scotland.

As Celtic were putting the finishing touches to their title victory at Tannadice on the second Wednesday in May, a small team of Australian broadcasters were high in the sky, ready to join the party and tell the story of the triumph to an unlikely audience. Given that the Aussie contingent offered so much hope and perspective in the early days, it was only right that they were along for the good times.

In Australia, football isn't the main sport. It lags behind Aussie Rules and rugby league in terms of attendance, while rugby union, cricket and horse racing are also watched in great numbers around the country. For football, especially overseas football, to make the news in Australia, something major has to have happened.

'We just wanted to be there to capture the moment of Ange lifting another piece of silverware,' renowned video producer Ben Coonan tells me. 'We had been wanting to get over there to cover the last few weeks of the season when it became apparent that he was going to have some success. We realised it was going to be Motherwell when he got his hands on the trophy, so we aimed for that.'

Postecoglou is big news in Australia, as was shown during the Sydney Super Cup, where he took his Celtic team to face Sydney FC and Everton. Celtic have always enjoyed a large following down under, but Postecoglou's time in Scotland has introduced thousands of new Aussies to Celtic. These people are committed to the cause, often getting up in the middle of the night just to see the team play on a dodgy internet stream. They live and breathe the club, despite living on the other side of the world. Most arrived for Postecoglou, but many will stay for Celtic when he eventually moves on.

'The story had a much broader cut-through with the general Aussie sports fan,' explains Coonan. 'If I were to survey my general group of friends, who aren't necessarily football people, they'd all know who Ange is and that he's doing a great job at Celtic. They might not even be able to tell you what colours Celtic play in, but they know that Ange Postecoglou is an Aussie and a top coach.'

Coonan and experienced broadcaster Michael Zappone were among the party that visited Celtic Park and Lennoxtown, with the Melbourne-based duo producing content for the nation's

Channel 10. 'We really wanted to show the people back home the impact Ange has had on Celtic and football in Scotland,' says Zappone. 'Even though we were watching him from afar and reading all the articles, the impact when we got there was much bigger than anyone could have imagined.'

By the time they touched down on Scottish soil, Celtic were champions and Postecoglou's face was on the front page of every newspaper, alongside royalty such as Kate Middleton. If Celtic's crowning moment was being presented with the Premiership trophy on the final Saturday of the season, then the real hard work had gone on in the months prior. Most of the season had been about not losing the league. The final weeks were about winning it.

* * *

Rangers 1-2 Celtic, Premiership, Ibrox, Sunday, 3 April 2022

If Celtic's derby win in February left Rangers battered and bruised, the April triumph virtually ended the title race as a contest. When Willie Collum's full-time whistle sounded, Ibrox was an empty place. The excitement and joy that had filled the arena hours earlier had dissipated, and all that was audible were 700 Celtic fans in the corner.

Like the February derby, this had been a major opportunity for the home team to dent their rivals' bid for the title. A Rangers win may well have turned the tide, planting a seed of doubt into the minds of an inexperienced Celtic squad. When Aaron Ramsey put them ahead after less than three minutes, it felt like the Celtic Park meeting. With Ibrox rocking and Celtic reeling, it was possible to foresee a similar outcome to the last clash between the teams, but in Rangers' favour. Surprisingly, the opposite happened.

A big part of Postecoglou's messaging is the need to stick to the plan in the face of adversity. Regardless of the scenario or the surroundings, Celtic's boss won't tolerate deviation from his principles. In the lead-up to the derby, Celtic had launched their 2021/22 season ticket campaign. Among the promotional material was an audio recording of Postecoglou addressing his players before the League Cup Final against Hibernian at Hampden. 'My message is the same here, don't play the occasion. Nothing changes,' Celtic's boss says. 'The basic principles of our game, that's what got us here, and that's what'll get us further, the things we can control. Don't let any chaos out there derail from what we're all about. That's the most important thing.'

Ibrox can be a chaotic place at the best of times, as Borussia Dortmund and RB Leipzig found out in the Europa League around the same period. It's easy to lose the run of yourself when the home support is buoyant and the hosts are inspired. Yet, amid the chaos, Celtic slowly worked their way into the match, sticking to the game plan and being led by Callum McGregor.

After collecting the ball inside the Rangers half, Celtic's captain saw an opportunity to put his stamp on the match. While his predecessor Scott Brown may have taken a more robust approach, McGregor did his talking with the ball at his feet. He drove past Ramsey, John Lundstram and Calvin Bassey before diverting the ball to Tom Rogic's feet. The Aussie's shot was blocked and rebounded for Reo Hatate, who forced Allan McGregor into a save before Rogic netted to silence Ibrox.

The goal was a killer for both the Rangers support and the players. Rogic had done the footballing equivalent of sticking a pin in a balloon. The noise inside Ibrox was never the same, as Rangers' insecurities came to the fore and Celtic's players exerted control on the match. When Cameron Carter-Vickers thumped in a scrappy second goal on the brink of half-time, most of the stadium was in full crisis mode.

The second half allowed Celtic's players to show how far they'd come. Defending narrow leads had been an issue in Europe in the early portion of the season, with the team getting deeper and deeper the nearer they got to full time. At Ibrox they were resolute, with Joe Hart only forced into one save of note from a left-footed Fashion Sakala strike. At the other end, Liel Abada had two golden chances to put the win beyond doubt, but his finishing wasn't decisive.

Until the Ibrox encounter, the title race had been too close to call. When the full-time whistle sounded, Celtic suddenly had one hand on the title, with a six-point lead going into the final six matches. With four of those at Celtic Park and Rangers still to visit in the last derby, it would take a significant collapse for Postecoglou's team not to be champions.

'It's not over, but this result makes it more difficult for us,' was Rangers boss Giovanni van Bronckhorst's response after the match. The image of an inconsolable Gers fan slumped in his seat, gesturing to his friend, painted a more accurate picture. You didn't have to be a lip-reading expert to work out what he thought of his team's chances in the title race. 'It's done,' was his message.

Rangers: McGregor, Tavernier, Goldson, Balogun, Bassey, Jack, Lundstram, Aribo, Ramsey, Kent, Roofe
Subs used: Sakala, Arfield
Celtic: Hart, Juranovic, Carter-Vickers, Starfelt, Taylor, McGregor, Rogic, Hatate, Jota, Giakoumakis, Maeda
Subs used: Bitton, O'Riley, Ralston, Abada, Turnbull

* * *

Celtic 7-0 St Johnstone, Premiership, Celtic Park, Saturday, 9 April 2022

If ever you needed a crash course on the togetherness of the Celtic squad, the club's 'unique angle' footage of the 7-0 demolition of St Johnstone is essential viewing. The team were on the highest of highs, having just won at Ibrox, and knew that four wins from their final six league matches would be enough to clinch the title. With such a healthy lead, the title race pressure had been relieved ever so slightly, and it showed in an emphatic performance.

The unfortunate visitors to the party on a sun-kissed spring afternoon at Celtic Park were relegation-threatened St Johnstone. Callum Davidson's team had been struggling to live up to the hype of the previous campaign – when they'd won both domestic cups – and didn't stand a chance from the eighth minute when Reo Hatate swept in the opener. Six more goals from five further scorers followed, with each strike celebrated by virtually every outfield player. At the centre of it all was Josip Juranovic.

Juranovic is one of the most vocal figures in the Celtic dressing room. He's one of the squad's biggest moaners when things aren't going his way but, most of the time, he's an infectious personality who leads by example. From mimicking Daizen Maeda's *Anpanman* celebration to jumping on Matt O'Riley's back after assisting him for a goal of the season contender, the club's St Johnstone video showed the smiley Croatian at the heart of every party, often the final one laughing and joking on the long walk back to the centre circle.

Celtic fans could probably have figured out that Juranovic would play this role even before his arrival in Scotland. When his £2.5m move from Legia Warsaw was nearing completion, the Polish club posted footage of a farewell speech given by Juranovic to his team-mates, including former Celtic hero Artur Boruc. The Croatian had spent just one season in Warsaw, yet his colleagues looked genuinely moved at news of his departure. 'Guys, what can I say?' was his message. 'I am here for only one year, and because of you, I play in the national team, and I make this transfer. Thank you so much.'

Like so many of his fellow summer arrivals, Juranovic had little time to adjust to his new surroundings before being thrust into the heat of battle. He made his debut in the early season derby loss to Rangers at Ibrox, putting in arguably the best display of any Celtic player that afternoon. An injury to Greg Taylor had seen him start the match in the unfamiliar position of left-back, and that's where much of his early football took place. He soon moved to right-back and became a quietly impressive performer who regularly chipped in with important goals, like the audacious 'Panenka' penalty in the Europa League clash away to Bayer Leverkusen.

His big breakthrough arrived in the early February derby win over Rangers when he completely man-marked Rangers winger Ryan Kent out of the match and offered plenty offensively. Around the same time, Celtic fans had discovered that Juranovic's name fitted perfectly into the main beat in the hit Pitbull dance tune 'Fireball'. When the chant went viral, the Cuban-American rapper shared a compilation of the full-back's derby exploits to his nine million Instagram followers.

Juranovic missed out on the season's final weeks after sustaining an injury in the cup loss to Rangers. His replacement Anthony Ralston covered impressively as Celtic got over the line to regain the title. 'Jura and myself support each other in every way,' Ralston said around the period. 'When Jura is playing, I support him to the max, and he does the same with me. We have a great relationship.'

Juranovic and Ralston are part of an immensely tight Celtic squad. Fans get limited glimpses of this during matches and on Instagram hours later. Juranovic is adored by his team-mates, as was shown by the reaction when he netted the fourth against St Johnstone. Celtic were in a terrific place, and it was down to players such as Juranovic excelling by buying into the manager's methods and showing respect to their colleagues.

Celtic found themselves six points clear with just five matches to go. The team were hurtling towards a major title win, yet the bigger picture was that they were improving with every passing match, something Glenn Middleton would find out to his cost. The winger was part of the Saints team that lost 7-0 at Celtic Park. When he faced the Hoops at the start of the new season, while wearing the orange of Dundee United, his team lost 9-0. Celtic were only getting better.

Celtic: *Hart, Juranovic, Carter-Vickers, Starfelt, Taylor, McGregor, Rogic, Hatate, Jota, Giakoumakis, Maeda*
Subs used: *Abada, O'Riley, Turnbull, Kyogo, McCarthy*

St Johnstone: *Clark, Rooney, Brown, Gordon, McCart, Booth, Davidson, Hallberg, Middleton, Crawford, Hendry*
Subs used: *MacPherson, Sang, Bair, May, Butterfield*

* * *

Celtic 4-1 Hearts, Premiership, Celtic Park, Sunday, 7 May 2022

'Check out Daft Punk's new single "Get Lucky" if you get the chance. Sound of the summer.' Scottish comedian Limmy tweets the words every Friday at lunchtime. Every single week, without fail, over half a million of the comedian's followers see the words appear on their Twitter feed. The words have become a long-running joke that gets dafter as time goes on. They're a sure-fire sign that the working week is nearing its end, and the weekend is once again upon everyone.

If the 2013 hit, also featuring Pharrell Williams and Nile Rodgers, is the 'sound of the summer' or every summer, then another Daft Punk hit was the theme tune for Celtic's first title success under Ange Postecoglou. As the Aussie and his players lapped the Parkhead surface after the resounding 4-1 win over Hearts that virtually secured the championship, another one of the French duo's hits blared from the heavens. Celtic Park had heard 'One More Time' before on joyous occasions, but not for several years.

The 2000 anthem, voted one of 'The 500 Greatest Songs of All Time' by *Rolling Stone* magazine, had provided the soundtrack to many a meaningful moment, yet the song had never felt more appropriate than when accompanying Postecoglou's all-conquering team.

'One more time, we're gonna celebrate. We don't stop. You can't stop. We're gonna celebrate.'

Had you rewound the clocks a couple of hours, you may have sensed some different emotions in the Glasgow air. Most of Celtic Park had still been sleeping when Ellis Simms put the Jambos ahead with a well-taken half-volley. Midday kick-offs can be a challenge for supporters to get up for, yet the weariness being shared by those on the pitch wasn't a good sign. Not that there was any real reason to panic. Celtic had earned some breathing space at the top of the table with their win at Ibrox. Subsequent victories over St Johnstone and Ross County, and a draw against Rangers at Celtic Park, when only a win would have sufficed for the visitors, meant that Postecoglou's team were in a commanding position.

That final derby of the season had been a strange affair. Celtic were dominant in the first half and deservedly led through Jota's back-post finish. But Rangers had stirred in the second period, equalising through Fashion Sakala, and perhaps deserved all three points in the closing stages. The scenes at full time were bizarre, with both sets of supporters appearing content in what must have been a derby first. Celtic had edged closer to the title, while Rangers had denied 60,000 home supporters a full-on party. Most Celtic fans saw the bigger picture despite the slight disappointment that the three points hadn't been won. The failure of Rangers to win meant it had become a case of when and not if Celtic would be crowned champions.

As those feelings changed, so did Postecoglou's messaging. Throughout the campaign, Celtic's boss hadn't been drawn into commenting on anything remotely related to the title race. As Celtic's glorious fate became clear, Postecoglou began pushing the need to finish the job in style. 'There are many ways to hit the finish line, but it is always nicer to burst through it, and that is what we plan to do,' he said.

The Celtic players heeded his message after falling behind against the Jambos. Daizen Maeda and Kyogo Furuhashi overturned the deficit before half-time, while further strikes from Matt O'Riley and Giorgos Giakoumakis put some gloss on a glorious afternoon. It was fitting that all four goals were scored by different players, part of a bigger team, and all brought to the club by Postecoglou. It was fitting that Celtic had won the match after a troubling start, which mirrored their entire league campaign. The opposition were fitting too. Hearts had beaten Celtic in the season's opening fixture in July when there seemed to be no light at the end of the tunnel.

The complexities of the league table meant that Celtic couldn't yet be declared champions. The win had moved them to 89 points, nine ahead of Rangers, who had just nine more to play for. However, Celtic's 22-goal advantage meant that a Rangers title win wasn't just improbable, it was nigh-on impossible.

The post-match comments all referenced there still being work to do, although the actions at full time told a different story. Joe Hart had the smile of a champion on his face, while TV cameras even caught Jota singing along to Daft Punk's tune. Like the background music, the images beamed worldwide couldn't have been more fitting. Among the tears of joy, the happiness on the faces of those inside the stadium told the true story. Postecoglou and his players had brought the smiles back. It was time to celebrate one more time.

Celtic: *Hart, Ralston, Carter-Vickers, Starfelt, Taylor, McGregor, O'Riley, Turnbull, Jota, Kyogo, Maeda*
Subs used: *Abada, Giakoumakis, Hatate, Rogic, Forrest*

Hearts: *Gordon, Atkinson, Moore, Kingsley, Cochrane, Haring, Sibbick, Ginnelly, Boyce, McKay, Simms*
Subs used: *Mackay-Steven, Woodburn, Thomas*

* * *

Dundee United 1-1 Celtic, Premiership, Tannadice, Wednesday, 11 May 2022

'I just wanna say thank you from the bottom of my heart for the support you've given me, the players and everyone else.

We'll enjoy tonight, we'll come back Saturday, and we'll enjoy it again.'

Ange Postecoglou probably didn't expect to be standing outside Celtic Park in the early hours of the morning, talking to thousands of supporters through a megaphone. He was learning that strange things happen when Celtic win the league.

The events leading to the pyrotechnic-filled scene had occurred hours earlier on the east coast of Scotland. Celtic had required a single point to be crowned champions against Tam Courts' impressive Dundee United. A combination of the home team's endeavour, a stunning Dylan Levitt strike and a nervy Celtic performance meant that it was just a point that they got. Not that it mattered.

Hours earlier, Postecoglou had surprisingly opted to change his entire front three for the match. Jota, Daizen Maeda and Kyogo Furuhashi all dropped out from the Hearts win, with Liel Abada, James Forrest and Giorgos Giakoumakis coming in and failing to deliver in the first period. Giakoumakis netted an emphatic header soon after the break before United equalised through Levitt. The hosts could have won the match too, and forced Celtic to wait until the final matchday, but Ryan Edwards couldn't direct his header on target when he looked more likely to score. Celtic also had a late chance to win but Maeda sliced wide.

'For the first time this year, I'm lost for words,' Postecoglou told match broadcasters Sky Sports at full time. 'I'm really proud of the players, the staff, our supporters, everyone involved. Nobody gave us much of a chance at the start of the year, and to do what they've done this year and achieve the ultimate is an unbelievable effort.'

While the Aussie gave the on-field interview, his players were partying in the background. They savoured the moment with supporters for half an hour, practically having to be dragged off the Tannadice pitch. Later in the evening, Postecoglou admitted the title success had taken 'every ounce' out of him.

After a long, hard season of squad overhauls, gruelling matches and media appearances, he was totally drained. Celtic's boss could probably have done with getting to his bed at a reasonable time but the supporters hadn't got the memo. As the team bus headed back from Dundee, it became apparent that the night wasn't over.

'We got word that there were a few people at Celtic Park,' Postecoglou told the press days later. 'When we got there we realised that it wasn't a few people. It was one of those spontaneous things that you don't organise. It was well beyond midnight, and there were thousands out there. It's great that we could share that moment with them.'

The scenes at Celtic Park were even more striking than the ones that had preceded them at Tannadice. Supporters lit flares, let off fireworks and sang songs about anything that made sense. As the players walked out of the main entrance, the majority filming events on their phones, the spectacle looked more like Istanbul or Belgrade than Glasgow.

Postecoglou addressed the crowd with a megaphone, although the chances of him being heard, even with the instrument, were about as slim as Josip Juranovic having a quiet one. The Croatian, still injured, celebrated the triumph by live streaming his drive home while blaring a Queen song from his speakers.

You didn't have to be a genius to work out which one he chose. Everyone was going to enjoy this one.

Dundee United: *Siegrist, Smith, Edwards, McMann, Freeman, Meekison, McDonald, Levitt, Niskanen, Clark, Macleod*
Subs used: *Mulgrew, Watt, Mochrie*

Celtic: *Hart, Ralston, Carter-Vickers, Starfelt, Taylor, O'Riley, McGregor, Hatate, Abada, Giakoumakis, Forrest*
Subs used: *Jota, Rogic, Turnbull, Maeda, Kyogo*

* * *

Celtic 6–0 Motherwell, Premiership, Celtic Park, Saturday, 14 May 2022

With the Aussie team of journalists now settling in Glasgow and their jetlag lessening, Celtic Park prepared for its big day. The club has had its fair share of Trophy Days – the final match of the season when the league prize is handed out – in recent years. Supporters got to enjoy one every May from 2012 to 2019, but a combination of the pandemic and not winning the league meant that 2020 and 2021 hadn't included end-of-season parties.

The event was already set to be special, with Callum McGregor getting to lift the Premiership trophy above his head for the first time as captain, as well as maiden trophy successes for the likes of Reo Hatate, Daizen Maeda and Matt O'Riley, not to mention Postecoglou enjoying his first league title.

Then Celtic took the emotion up a notch further in the days leading up to the match by announcing that long-term servants Tom Rogic and Nir Bitton wouldn't be extending their stay beyond the end of the season. The match against Motherwell would be the final one for the duo, who could boast a remarkable haul of 34 trophies between them. The farewells to Rogic and Bitton, two well-liked players, added to the desire in the Celtic dressing room to finish the season in style. For all the celebrating in midweek, Celtic had failed to show up on the night. The final match gave the squad a chance to end the season in style.

For a fixture with little riding on it, the atmosphere was electric as Celtic struck six goals without reply. A double from Kyogo Furuhashi was a fitting end to the season, while David Turnbull, Jota and a Giorgos Giakoumakis double completed the rout. Celtic finished the campaign with a goal difference of plus 70, 21 ahead of nearest rivals Rangers, but the real joy was found away from the numbers. Rogic and Bitton both got their perfect farewells, while Postecoglou was even able to bring on James McCarthy and Stephen Welsh for their tenth league appearances, making them eligible for a medal.

There were plenty of moments of satisfaction on the afternoon for Postecoglou, but maybe none more so than the final goal, struck by Giakoumakis in the very last minute of the season. The Celtic players had never stopped, just like their manager had demanded ten months earlier. Perhaps that thought was on Postecoglou's mind minutes later when he was handed the mic and asked to address a vibrant Celtic Park. The stadium had been rocking all afternoon but soon fell silent. 'Champions, that's who we are.' An eruption of noise. Unprompted, Postecoglou summed up the situation perfectly with his finale. 'I want everyone to enjoy today, enjoy the summer, and we will come back bigger, better because we never stop.'

Ben Coonan had one of the best seats in the house for the magical moment:

We couldn't stop watching Ange's speech. The noise made when he delivered that final line was something else. I remember thinking, this guy has got everybody here on the hook. They just cannot get enough, and they're willing to drop everything just to hear what he's got to say. To deliver such a rousing, gladiatorial speech with a line that lifts the roof off the place. I just thought, good on you Ange. This is where you belong.

In Australia, going to a football match can be like going to the theatre. People are engaged, but they're not totally immersed. At Celtic Park, there were 60,000 people there, but it's 60,000 people who have seen every press conference and know every player. They have bought into every single thing Ange had said throughout the season. And they seem to have that same respect that I, and a lot of people in Australia, have for Ange.

Given all that was happening at the club, with celebrations, high-profile departures and numerous media appearances,

Postecoglou would have been forgiven for not affording much time to the Australian visitors. That wasn't the case, though. Coonan and Zappone spoke to the boss at Lennoxtown and Celtic Park on several occasions, with an interview even scheduled for outside Postecoglou's house on the morning after the Motherwell match.

Coonan says:

> I had the privilege of working with Ange during his time with the Socceroos. As much as anyone gets the opportunity to know Ange in that professional environment, I got the chance. We had been in touch through text throughout his Celtic journey, but seeing him again was like catching up with an old friend. He gave us everything we asked for. He still gave us all the time in the world even though he's clearly moved on from that small-time Australian media attitude towards football. The fact that he hadn't forgotten where he came from was really heart-warming for us. He was so accessible all of the time. He found so much time for us when he didn't need to. We'll be eternally grateful for that.

Among all his Australian and Scottish media duties, Postecoglou also had a final meeting of the season with fan media in the hour after getting his hands on the Premiership trophy. He showed his class again, taking a question from everyone who wanted to ask one. The questions ranged from critical points in the season to Rogic and Bitton's perfect send-off and what was next for Celtic.

'I don't know,' he said in response to my question about the latter. 'I don't talk about the endings. I keep saying to the players that I don't want to sell us short. I didn't say this year that I wanted to be champions. What's important is the story, and if we can be a better football team next year than we were this year, and keep improving like we did, then we're going to be in a pretty good place. That's going to bring us moments like this.'

Celtic: Hart, Ralston, Carter-Vickers, Starfelt, Taylor, Rogic, McGregor, Turnbull, Neves Filipe, Kyogo, Maeda
Subs used: Giakoumakis, Ideguchi, McCarthy, Welsh, Bitton

Motherwell: Kelly, Mugabi, Lamie, Carroll, Nirennold, Cornelius, Goss, O'Donnell, Slattery, Shields, Efford
Subs used: Van Veen, Donnelly, Tierney, O'Hara

CHAPTER 17

Tom Rogic: When Lightning Strikes

'We've been top of the pile for the last decade.
It's a familiar position for us.'

Tom Rogic

EVERY CELTIC fan has a favourite Tom Rogic memory. When asked, many would plump for his momentous Scottish Cup-winning goal against Aberdeen in 2017, the last-gasp strike that clinched Celtic's incredible domestic treble without losing a single match. Others may go for a choice more personal to them, such as his late belters to beat Kilmarnock and Motherwell on league duty. Any of his six strikes against Rangers could be chosen, as could his majestic solo goal against Dundee United during Ange Postecoglou's first harsh winter. Everyone would have their favourite.

Rogic's contribution over nine trophy-laden years at Celtic will mean he's remembered about as fondly as anyone else in the 21st century. Complete legendary status is reserved for a select few, with Henrik Larsson and Scott Brown at the very top of the list in recent times. But the Aussie occupies the position one rung below those ultimate heroes, as a man who brought unbridled joy to many during his near-decade stay in Glasgow.

It seems foolish then that a man who delivered so many unforgettable moments doesn't even feel he's worthy of the adoration. If you bumped into Rogic in public and asked for a photo, he'd oblige but then wonder what all the fuss was about. He's a very private person, one of the nicest people you could ever hope to meet, with that serenity often revealing itself on the pitch. At Celtic, Rogic would frequently net goal of the season contenders then barely celebrate.

Now and again a figure like Rogic comes along. These players, capable of complete genius, often arrive without any real hype and their reputation is earned by the magic they produce on the pitch. The two players most fitting of that description in recent Celtic history are Lubomír Moravčík and Shunsuke Nakamura. Both created memories to last a lifetime, with magical moments aplenty during their stays in Glasgow. Rogic is the third name to throw into the mix as a Celtic genius of the 21st century.

Moravčík and Nakamura failed to get the send-off they deserved in Scotland, exiting the club with little fanfare. Moravčík had been a less prominent player in his final campaign, often brought on by Martin O'Neill as a calming influence in the closing stages of matches. Failure to get off the bench in the 2002 Scottish Cup Final loss to Rangers was the last memory Celtic fans were left with before he moved to Japanese outfit JEF United Chiba.

'I don't want to play in the last league game at Aberdeen, so I will be leaving Celtic and Scotland after the cup final,' he told the *Daily Record* at the time. 'I won't have any special message for the supporters at Hampden. There will be no T-shirts or anything like that.'

Despite the low-key nature of his departure, the Slovakian at least exited as a champion. Nakamura didn't even have that going his way when he departed for a short spell with Espanyol in 2009. The Japanese star had endured his most challenging campaign as Gordon Strachan's team missed out on the league title in his final year at the club. Nakamura left via the back door after a Celtic career spent in the limelight.

The moral of the story is that footballers rarely get to say the perfect goodbye. Football careers don't tend to play out like *Bend It Like Beckham* – just ask Scott Brown. The idea of riding into the sunset on a glorious spring evening to a standing ovation from thousands may exist in their minds, but it rarely plays out in reality. Players often leave after crushing cup final defeats, managerial bust-ups or gradual phasing out of the team. Social media has at least given them a chance to say goodbye to supporters away from the pitch, but it's still not the dream farewell they have in mind. Tom Rogic got the opportunity to say the perfect goodbye at Celtic as the curtain fell on his compatriot Ange Postecoglou's first campaign against Motherwell.

Rogic's departure had been announced by the club a day before the Motherwell clash, alongside fellow long-term servant Nir Bitton. The pair were off to seek a new challenge and were doing so after being a vital part of the Postecoglou revolution, something the manager was keen to point out. 'They have certainly made such a tremendous contribution to Celtic over such a long and successful period for the club,' Postecoglou said in a club statement. 'I understand that, in their minds, the time is right to move on. From a personal perspective, as well as being very talented players, both Tom and Nir are top guys who have supported me brilliantly this year in my first season. It is fitting that they leave Celtic as champions.'

Bitton's departure had been rumoured for much of 2022, while Rogic's exit was far more of a surprise. The gifted attacker had been a huge part of Postecoglou's maiden campaign, especially in the brutal winter months when everything had been conspiring against the team, and virtually everyone expected to see him back in the Hoops for another tilt at the Champions League after the summer. At 29, he'd surely missed his chance of a big-money move to a major European league, and it was far too early for him to head back to Australia.

On the Thursday before Celtic's final match of the season, Rogic took to Instagram to post a selection of images from his time at the club. The four-leaf clover accompanying the photos suggested that Rogic was trying to tell everyone something. Hours later, the news that fans had been fearing was confirmed. Rogic was leaving, but he was going out on top, and fans would have the chance to say a proper goodbye at Celtic Park.

Until the announcement, Trophy Day had been all about Callum McGregor getting his hands on the Premiership trophy, his first as captain. Now a new, more significant story was woven into the day as Rogic and Bitton said farewell.

Rogic started, the first time he'd done so in five matches. After 18 minutes he got his first big moment as Celtic Park got on its feet to show their appreciation in genuinely stirring scenes. If Rogic was too engrossed in the match at that stage to get emotional, the tears came later when he was substituted for the final time. Collectively, Celtic Park rose again. Every on-field Hoops player surrounded Rogic, despite many having spent just one season with him, signifying what a momentous occasion it was.

The only surprise was that he wasn't carried off the playing surface by his team-mates. Reputations at a club like Celtic are earned, and Rogic had earned every second of his reception.

* * *

There had been very little hype nine and a half years earlier when Celtic signed a little-known 20-year-old Rogic from Central Coast Mariners for around £400,000. Rogic was one of three players signed that month, alongside defender Rami Gershon on loan from Standard Liège and goalkeeper Viktor Noring from Trelleborgs FF. The Aussie's name hardly stood out amongst the pack.

At the time, Celtic were in a powerful position. With Rangers enduring their first campaign in the lower leagues of Scottish football, Neil Lennon's team were almost certain to win the league, and efforts could be focused on making progress in Europe. Celtic had done that in the months before Rogic's arrival, qualifying for the Champions League group stage with wins over HJK Helsinki and Helsingborgs and then finishing second in a tough group with Barcelona, Benfica and Spartak Moscow. As they headed for a last-16 meeting with Juventus, the squad was settled and Lennon made January acquisitions with the future in mind.

Rogic seemed to have a bright future ahead of him if his exploits in Australia were anything to go by. Like his unorthodox playing style, he didn't take the conventional route to stardom. After playing as a junior for Tuggeranong United in Canberra, his breakthrough came as part of Nike's 'The Chance' – a competition giving players from around the world an opportunity to showcase their abilities with the end goal of becoming professional footballers. Rogic, who had been playing futsal before the competition, was one of eight players selected from over 75,000 candidates worldwide and earned a spot in the famed Nike Academy as a result.

After being announced as a winner by Arsène Wenger and future Rangers boss Giovanni van Bronckhorst, who he'd torment years later, Rogic left his family to move to England and pursue a career in the professional game. He gained access to world-class coaches, nutritionists, psychologists and fitness conditioners and was given the guidance needed to allow his technical ability to flourish.

While in England, he trialled with Reading and was offered a professional contract, only to run into work permit issues. He returned to Australia and signed immediately for Central Coast Mariners, making his first-team debut those weeks later. On his second start for Mariners, he netted a long-range goal against Melbourne Victory, then added another belter a week later. He was named the A-League's young player of the month for February 2012, and his name began to be spoken about both at home and abroad.

John Hutchinson, Ange Postecoglou's former assistant in Japan, was Mariners captain when Rogic broke into the team and earned his move to Glasgow:

On the first day, this tall, gangly kid turned up. He had this funny walk with his big arms swinging. Normally a tall guy like him would be a central-defender or a number six, but I found out he was an attacking midfielder, and I had a few doubts. Then he received the ball and went on this run, and I was like, 'Oh my goodness.' We knew he wouldn't be with us for long. I always say I had the best seat in the house watching Tommy. I was a defensive-midfielder behind him, so all I did was give him the ball and sit back and watch. I wish I had a deck chair at times.

Hutchinson still seems pretty honoured to have even shared a dressing room with Rogic, with memories of the brilliance still fresh in his mind all these years later:

I'm fortunate enough to have played with some pretty good footballers. Mile Jedinak was a central-midfielder next to me, and he was pretty special. But Tommy was different. He had magic in his boots. There was a game against Sydney FC where we won 7-2 at home, and he was incredible. He did amazing things, but you wouldn't say it to him because you didn't want him jumping on clouds. I would laugh at training sometimes because of how easy it looked for him. I was there, every day, busting my ass at training, giving 100 per cent, and here was this kid who looked like he had the handbrake on, cruising around the football park doing whatever he wanted to do.

On the way home from training, Hutchinson regularly shared a car with a young Rogic. The pair exchanged few words at these times, but Rogic always came across well, even in some of his junior moments. 'He was a grumpy kid,' explains Hutchinson. 'He had a lot of aggro. He just wanted to be the best, and everything he did revolved around football. I always found him very humble and down-to-earth. I loved him to bits.'

Rogic's visa issues in England had been a bitter blow at the time, but the chance to play regular A-League football at a young age stood him in good stead as his big move approached. Celtic pounced in early 2013, with Rogic penning a four-and-a-half-year deal in Glasgow after impressing in a mid-season camp in Marbella. He made his debut a month later against Inverness Caledonian Thistle as Neil Lennon rotated virtually his entire team just days ahead of the first leg against Juventus. Rogic was impressive as Celtic came from behind to win 3-1, setting up a terrific Kris Commons opener and going close with a shot minutes later.

Despite that showing, he had to bide his time in Lennon's first spell. He struggled for playing time and was loaned back to Australia with Melbourne Victory in early 2014. At the time, then Socceroos boss Postecoglou had encouraged Rogic to leave Celtic on loan, telling the *Fox Football Podcast*: 'It's a World Cup year. There wouldn't be a player on the planet who is going to a World Cup who wouldn't for the next six months think the best move for him would be to play regular football.' Rogic's spell in Melbourne was hampered by a recurring groin injury that saw him miss out on the Socceroos squad for Brazil. He'd be part of the Aussie party for the following edition of the competition in 2018 though, after making his breakthrough at Celtic in the intervening period.

Rogic played under four permanent managers in his nine years at Celtic. All of them, bar Lennon, took his game to new heights, but it was under the tutelage of Ronny Deila that his breakthrough came. Celtic were enduring a fallow period. They were still dominating in the league but failure in the domestic cups, a lack of Champions League football and genuine competition led to vast swathes of Celtic Park lying empty for most matches.

It wasn't just some supporters who had left either. Many big names from previous years, such as Victor Wanyama, Fraser

Forster and Gary Hooper, had all moved on for big money to the Premier League, with Virgil van Dijk joining them after Deila's first season. There was no longer the same competition for a spot in the first team, so Rogic had a chance to benefit in Deila's second season. In August 2015 he was handed his first Celtic start in almost two years as Deila freshened up his team after a gruelling away clash against Azerbaijan's Qarabağ. The Aussie, in for skipper Scott Brown, netted a brilliantly improvised opener, his first of ten goals that season.

Rogic scored plenty of huge goals for Deila throughout the campaign. A belter against Hearts in a 2-2 Tynecastle draw stood out, as did the last-gasp screamer to beat Kilmarnock at Rugby Park. However, the abiding memory of the season was his skied spot kick in the Scottish Cup semi-final penalty shoot-out against Rangers. Rogic had scored an equaliser in extra time but his penalty miss sealed victory for the Ibrox team, who were still playing their football outside of Scotland's top tier. Deila announced his departure from the club three days later.

If the Norwegian had given Rogic the platform to thrive for Celtic, the thriving took place under his successor Brendan Rodgers. While the former Liverpool boss did add some key personnel in his early months in office, those signings didn't tend to be midfielders. Rogic's place in the first team remained, while a new three-year contract signed in August 2016 amid input from Rodgers, further stressed that he was in his new manager's plans.

Rogic regularly started matches under the Northern Irishman but rarely played the full 90 minutes. Nevertheless, he made a considerable contribution in Celtic's invincible treble achievement, finishing as the fifth-top scorer with 12 goals, behind Moussa Dembele, Scott Sinclair, Leigh Griffiths and Stuart Armstrong. That total was even more impressive when a 17-match lay-off for an ankle injury was factored in.

While every Celtic supporter has their favourite Rogic memory, the vast majority would be centred around the afternoon of Saturday, 27 May 2017. Celtic were going for the previously unthinkable feat of a domestic treble without losing a single match. Rodgers' team had navigated 46 league and cup matches, 42 of them won, just one more victory from completing a clean sweep of trophies.

The Hoops were tied 1-1 with Aberdeen in the closing stages at a drenched Hampden Park when Rogic received the ball from Stuart Armstrong, 40 yards from goal. The Aussie hadn't even started the showpiece occasion, only coming on as a first-half substitute when Kieran Tierney was forced off with a facial injury. The full-back was on his way back from A&E when Rogic drove at the heart of the Dons defence, outpacing Anthony O'Connor, wrong-footing Andy Considine and sliding the ball past Joe Lewis. Half of Hampden went into delirium and several journalists reported seeing a lightning bolt in the sky just as it all happened. Rogic had elevated himself to legendary status with six seconds of magic.

* * *

For all of Postecoglou's brilliance at Celtic, perhaps his most significant single achievement was reviving Rogic's career. It's probably all downhill from a 92nd-minute wonder goal to secure your team an invincible treble, but the following four seasons saw a gradual decline in Rogic's performances. He was still a player Celtic depended on at times, most notably in the 2017/18 campaign, but he often wasn't at his best in a Celtic shirt. By the time Brendan Rodgers had departed and been replaced by Neil Lennon, it seemed like Rogic's days in Scotland were numbered.

In August 2020, reports emerged that Rogic was set to move to Qatar for £4m. Thankfully, the deal fell through and he became a pivotal player in the initial stages of Postecoglou's reign. Under his compatriot, Rogic didn't just rediscover the form of the Deila or Rodgers days, he found a whole new level of excellence. He played an important role off the pitch too, as the one familiar face staring back at Postecoglou when he first addressed his players. He was also the point of contact for curious Celtic stars wanting to learn more about their new boss.

Rogic played a massive part throughout Celtic's title-winning season. He excelled in the winter months during an injury crisis, carrying Celtic through several vital matches. Rogic assisted or scored decisive goals in December wins over Dundee United, Motherwell, Ross County and St Johnstone, not to mention the assist for Kyogo Furuhashi's winner in the League Cup Final against Hibernian. His revival from the darkness of the previous campaign was stark, but it hadn't arrived as a result of anything other than hard work and a positive mentality.

His manager told *The Scotsman* months into the season:

> I am not the cuddles type. I try to provide an environment where they feel comfortable and can be the best they can be. That's what I try and create every day for everybody – players and staff. I just try to provide an environment where you hope players enjoy their football, understand they have responsibilities and work hard but get a huge kick at the end because the rewards are some success and enjoying their football. That's what's happening at the moment with Tom. He's enjoying the environment, the training and the way we play our football. So no cuddles, mate, just let's get on with it.

The results of Rogic enjoying his football were clear to see. He scored six goals and assisted a further ten in his only season under Postecoglou, although, as is often the case with Rogic, the numbers weren't what mattered. It was the moments of brilliance, like the goal at Tannadice, the sensational performance in the 4-0 win at Fir Park, or the crucial leveller at Ibrox in April. Rogic was starring again, and this time he was seeing out matches. Yet, none of this was a great surprise to his close pal and former international team-mate Ryan McGowan:

It's no coincidence that Tom's two best periods at Celtic were probably under Rodgers and Ange. The style of play suited him. He was the main man. Everything was set up for him to create things, and that's when he's at his best. You can only get your 90 minutes match fitness from playing 90 minutes. I'm not speaking for him, but when I was younger, if I was getting taken off after 70 minutes every game, my fitness level would drop to 70 minutes. Then when you play that extra 20 minutes, it's almost like extra time. His fitness was probably better from having a full pre-season and being able to train Monday to Friday. I personally know that in years gone by he had been going game by game, whether it be issues with his ankle, his knee or his groin, and putting off surgery at the end of the season because there were international games. Under Ange, he was probably playing pain-free.

Rogic tortured Scottish defences at times – just ask any of the four Dundee United defenders he bamboozled on the way to that sublime solo goal in early December. 'It's a lot better playing with him than against him,' says McGowan. 'There were a couple of times when I was at Dundee United and I got shifted into the midfield and played directly against him. People don't understand how big he is until you're standing next to him. He's strong, and he wears slippers when he's playing, so he's very difficult to play against.'

If Rogic was earning plaudits again for his performances on the pitch, his off-field displays weren't bad either. After netting a double in a win over Motherwell, he delivered a set of quotes that even Postecoglou would have been pleased with. Celtic had just thumped Rangers 3-0 in the rescheduled New Year derby to go top of the table for the first time in months. Days later, in a post-match interview, Rogic was asked about the pressure being back on his team's shoulders as league leaders.

'We've been top of the pile for the last decade,' he told Sky Sports. 'It's a familiar position for us. Last season was disappointing but it's been a brilliant season for a lot of us. We just need to keep working hard, keep our heads down, focus on the next game and not get too carried away. Everyone was watching us after that result. It was important to back it up.'

When news of his departure from the club became public knowledge, Aussie broadcaster Michael Zappone was in Glasgow, covering Celtic's title win:

> We were at the training ground when the announcement was made. We had requested an interview with Tommy weeks before, and he had agreed, which was great because he doesn't do many interviews. I got the sense that it was perhaps a little bit of a relief that he'd made the decision and his future was out there. After being at Celtic Park, it dawned on me how hard a decision that would have been. Playing at that level, at that intensity, in front of those crowds every week, 60 games a year. Perhaps he just thought it was time.

Rogic had made his mind up about leaving Celtic much earlier in the season, and it wasn't until the league had been tied up that the announcement was made public. He and Postecoglou had shared many conversations on the topic throughout the season, with the need for Rogic to go out on top mentioned regularly.

What followed at the season's end was a summer of speculation about who Rogic would next play for and, for a period, whether he'd find another club. When Rogic pulled out of Graham Arnold's Socceroos squad for the crucial World Cup play-offs in Qatar, there was concern for his well-being. Then, in mid-September, West Bromwich Albion announced he'd joined them on a one-year deal.

'I was looking for a change of scenery and a fresh challenge,' he said in the club's statement. 'I didn't just want to rush into anything. I think it was important for me to take my time and make sure my next club was the right club. I had time to reflect, and I now feel refreshed, re-energised, and excited about the future.'

* * *

Had Rogic not announced his departure at the same time, this chapter may have been dedicated to Nir Bitton, such was the Israeli's contribution in Glasgow. Bitton arrived at Celtic from SC Ashdod in the summer of 2013 as a replacement for the recently departed Victor Wanyama. His initial journey was more steady than Rogic's, although he did suffer difficulties in another department.

For his first year in Glasgow, Nir Bitton was Nir Biton. The single 't', an oversight on the club's part, wasn't corrected until travel was being booked for the player and his team-mates the following summer. The midfielder had been too shy to correct the error, putting up with his name being spelled wrong for a whole season, perhaps highlighting his diffidence in the early days at the club.

Bitton would become a huge figure in the Celtic dressing room in years to come, but only after some early struggles on the pitch. He was red-carded minutes after coming on as a substitute in one of his first matches, a Champions League group stage win over Ajax. The subsequent suspension and some injury issues restricted his playing time for the rest of the season but, unlike Rogic, he was always part of Neil Lennon's plans.

Bitton was another player who flourished in the Ronny Deila era, becoming a mainstay of the Celtic midfield alongside Scott Brown. His tidy passing was ideal for Deila's gameplan, and his knack of popping up with sublime long-range goals was a welcome bonus. As Celtic faltered under Deila in the second half of the season, Bitton's form dipped and his place at the club was arguably never the same again. When Brendan Rodgers arrived and transformed the club, he was one of the few players who didn't kick on. The emergence of Stuart Armstrong, Olivier Ntcham, Callum McGregor and Ryan Christie forced him on to the bench. When he did play, it was often in the unfamiliar position of centre-back and far too frequently in crucial Champions League qualifiers.

By the time Postecoglou entered the building, Bitton was viewed as more of a defender than a midfielder. Postecoglou changed that pretty early on, with a red card in a qualifier against Midtjylland spelling the end for him at the back. It was under Postecoglou that Bitton finally found his proper role in the squad, as a calm but physical presence in the base of the midfield. He was used throughout the campaign, playing in 38 matches and weighing in with two goals. He also played a pivotal role in helping his compatriot Liel Abada to settle into life in Scotland.

Bitton received an incredible ovation in his final match, against Motherwell, coming on as a substitute in the closing stages before a move to Maccabi Tel Aviv was announced weeks later. In nine years he'd gone from a shy 21-year-old boy to one of Celtic's most decorated players. The tears accompanying his goodbye interview on Celtic TV revealed more about what the club meant to him than any words could. 'I never thought this day would come,' he said. 'It's a really sad day for me. Basically, this club is all I know. I've been here for nine years. I came here as a young boy. If you'd have told me when I signed I'd stay here for nine years, win 18 trophies and make 270 appearances, I would bite your hand [sic]. I'm just glad I had the opportunity to play for this amazing club.'

History will remember both Rogic and Bitton very fondly. Both players had amazing days at the club and some less memorable ones. Their contributions to the Postecoglou era are still being felt.

CHAPTER 18

Liel Abada and Jota: Stepping Up

'I think the story was meant to be.'

Jota

WHEN KYOGO Furuhashi was forced off minutes into the first Glasgow derby of the 2022/23 season, more than a few nervous glances were being exchanged around Celtic Park. The Japanese forward is the talisman of Ange Postecoglou's team, the guy who makes it all click at the top end of the pitch. Yet the beauty of this Celtic squad that Postecoglou has built is that there's never an over-reliance on a single player. The Celtic support needn't have worried that afternoon against Rangers. Enter Liel Abada and Jota.

With Kyogo watching from the sidelines, Celtic's two wingers terrorised the Rangers defence. By half-time, they'd netted three goals between them. Rather fittingly, Abada had scored two from ghosting in at the back post, his favourite position. Even more fittingly, Jota's had been the one of real beauty.

* * *

When Liel Abada joined Celtic as Ange Postecoglou's first proper signing in July 2021, not many people took a great deal of notice. The signing felt like a significant gamble in a summer when Celtic had to recruit proven firepower. Sure, Abada had leapt on to the scene in his native Israel, netting 13 goals for Maccabi Petah Tikva in the previous season alone. Yet his lack of experience and association with Dudu Dahan – the Israeli agent who had supplied many a player to Celtic over the years – heightened the sense that the deal was a continuation of an old transfer policy rather than anything new. Abada signing at just 19 would turn out to be a little unusual, with Postecoglou choosing mainly to recruit players in the 23–27 age bracket. Yet with youthfulness came a fearless attitude that would steer Celtic through some stormy waters in the early days and beyond.

Abada didn't have to wait long for his first chance. He was the only new face in Postecoglou's first competitive outing – a 1-1 Champions League qualifying draw against Midtjylland – where he netted the first strike of the new era. Further goals and assists arrived in subsequent matches against Jablonec, Dundee and St Mirren. By the time the Buddies were sent packing, Abada and Kyogo were featuring in the first memorable fan chant of the new season.

We've got Abada, he's on the wing
We've got Kyogo, he's doing his thing
Ange is our leader
We're following Celtic all over the world.

The attacker continued to weigh in with big moments as the season progressed. Occasionally, when Celtic's striking options were decimated, he was asked to play up front, and he never let the team down. His two most memorable goals of the campaign arrived in the space of five glorious days at the start of 2022. They showcased everything good about his game: intelligent running, great spatial awareness and a knack of putting the ball into the net by whatever means necessary. Neither the last-minute winner against Dundee United nor the thrilling third against Rangers were likely to win any goal of the season competitions. Yet, if you asked every Celtic fan to list their ten favourite goals of the Postecoglou era, both would feature in almost every list. Abada finished a superb debut campaign with 15 goals and 11 assists from 54 appearances. He was also named the PFA Scotland men's young player of the year.

'I came with expectations of myself at Celtic,' he told Israeli outlet Sport 5 in the close season. 'Over time, I worked hard in training and games. I'm very happy about this season, personally and collectively. I'm a man who believes in himself and his abilities. I'm very happy with this season. A lot of people know about the rivalry with Rangers. Every game is important for the club and the fans. It's a crazy atmosphere. It's hard to explain in words. I don't want to compare this league to the league in Israel.'

Abada had to bide his time in the early weeks of his second season, with Daizen Maeda preferred by Postecoglou, but he remained among the league's top scorers. A hat-trick of back-post finishes in the 9-0 win over Dundee United was bettered a week later with two emphatic finishes in the derby win over Rangers. While technically not at the same level as Jota or Kyogo – Abada would have been unlikely to play the part of either in the amazing Ferencváros goal – his knack of finding a yard of space inside a packed penalty box is his most impressive attribute.

Abada doesn't enjoy the same adoration as his two attacking colleagues. The lack of media attention compared to most of his team-mates can often make it seem like he doesn't have much personality, either. Yet, when his compatriot and close friend Nir Bitton departed the scene after the 2021/22 season, he was happy to share how it made him feel: 'I think Niro ... he's like a big brother to me. I can speak with him about everything. He helped me a lot here last season with everything. Now we speak a lot on FaceTime. I wish him all the best and all of the family. I really love him, and I miss him.' In years to come, Abada may be remembered even more fondly than Bitton.

* * *

João Pedro Neves Filipe, or Jota as he was known from day one, arrived initially on a season-long loan from Benfica on the final day of the summer transfer window. A new-look Celtic were in the process of being formed and Jota, possessed with an immense grasp of the English language, was late to the party. He was keen to make an impression in his first media appearance.

His face lit up at my mere mention of previous Champions League meetings between Celtic and his boyhood club Benfica, almost as if he'd been waiting for the question to be asked. 'There's a really good story about the game in Lisbon,' he told me. 'I was in the stands watching the game, and at the end there were like three Celtic fans walking with me. I was 11 years old or something like that, and they asked me if I wanted to change scarves. You guys have the green-and-white scarf, and we have the red-and-white. I think I still have that scarf at home. I think the story was meant to be.'

Jota's journey from referring to Celtic as 'you guys' to wearing a Hoops top while having a kickabout in Cyprus a year later is a pretty special one. Given that Celtic faced Benfica so regularly in the early years of the 21st century, it's impossible to know which match he was referring to. It seems most likely that the trio of Celtic fans had just seen Neil Lennon's team go down 2-1 to Jorge Jesus's men amid their glorious run to the last 16 in season 2012/13. Little did the lucky Hoops supporters know that they'd just met a future Celtic star.

At that stage, Jota was a prodigious talent on Benfica's books. He signed for the Lisbon club when he was eight and worked his way through the various age groups and into the B team, playing men's football in the second tier. While progressing at club level, Jota was also impressive in the various Seleção youth levels. In 2018 he led his country to the 2018 UEFA European Under-19 Championship title, finishing as the joint-top scorer with five goals alongside compatriot Francisco Trincão. In a stunning final victory over Italy, Jota netted twice and set up two further goals, showcasing a big-match mentality that would benefit Celtic years later. At the time, Jota and the Braga attacker Trincão were the two hottest prospects from the 1999 age group. On occasion, Jota was rated even more highly at Benfica than forward João Félix, who was sold to Atlético Madrid for £113m in 2019.

Yet, while the careers of Félix and Trincão went from strength to strength, Jota was faced with an uphill battle just to get playing time. He made his Benfica first-team debut in a cup win over Sertanense in late 2018 but failed to play more under Bruno Lage. By the time the pragmatic Jorge Jesus arrived with his preference for experience, Jota was barely getting a look-in. The only option was a loan move away.

While Celtic imploded during the 2020/21 campaign, Jota endured an up-and-down spell at Real Valladolid in Spain's La Liga. He occasionally showed quality while playing for the club majority-owned by Ronaldo, scoring on his debut, but an ankle injury and subsequent contracting of Covid-19 stopped him in his tracks. With opportunities now even less likely at his hometown club and with just one Primeira Liga start to his name, Jota sought opportunities away from Portugal again. As a talented winger priding his game on entertainment, he wanted to find a home where supporters would love him.

Within weeks of his move to Celtic, he found the admiration he'd been craving. From his very first match, a 3-0 win over Ross County, his talent was clear to see. When he started adding goals and assists, like the crucial winner in the make-or-break match at Aberdeen, it became clear that the notion of him lacking end product was misguided. Jota loves to entertain. Yet to describe him as a luxury player is unfair. He has skill and quality but his off-the-ball running is underrated. He works hard for the team, a prerequisite of playing under Postecoglou, and benefits as a result.

After one of the Portuguese winger's finest early displays, the 2-0 home win over Ferencváros, Postecoglou was keen to hammer home the point that what Jota did without the ball mattered just as much as the stepovers and rabonas. 'He was great, but I look at the other side of things as well,' Celtic's boss told the media. 'The understanding that he needs to work hard defensively for us. The key with attacking players like him and the others we have brought in is that they need to invest in our football. They need to work hard in certain areas and, if they do, they will get their rewards with the way we play.'

Jota scored 13 goals and set up 14 more in his debut season in Glasgow. All but one of the goals came from inside the 18-yard box, proving that he was as much about substance as he was style. Talk of a permanent deal had been raging on for the best part of a year by the time his future was sealed in a reported £6.4m deal. Jota signed a five-year contract in Glasgow, joining Cameron Carter-Vickers as a permanent signing following a successful loan spell.

Immediately his displays showed the freedom of having his long-term future sorted for the first time in his career. His first two goals of the season were his two most spectacular yet, in league wins over Aberdeen and Kilmarnock. Replays of the latter showed Killie's Rory McKenzie yelling at Jota just before he sent a stunning 30-yarder into the net. It was the perfect encapsulation of how far clear the Portuguese star often is when playing in Scotland. Opponents were resorting to unsportsmanlike tactics and it still had no impact. Jota was wheeling away and dedicating the strike to Benfica legend Fernando Chalana, who had passed away days before.

He netted further early season goals against Dundee United and then in the derby when he ran in behind a static Rangers defence and dinked the ball over Jon McLaughlin's head to send Celtic Park wild. Like Abada, Kyogo and many of his Celtic team-mates, Jota plays the game with a big smile. He even enjoys some of the more mundane parts of the footballer experience, such as dealing with the media. Like many of his contemporaries, he speaks English fluently and, although he occasionally struggles with the broad Scottish dialect, he usually passes the test.

The winger is arguably Celtic's most talented winger in over a decade. Jota can bamboozle defences, assist and score goals, and help the team out defensively. He's yet another player suited perfectly to Postecoglou's playing style.

When you score you make the Celtic sing,
Jota on the wing, Jota, Jota on the wing,
Every time you're on the ball we know,
There's gonna be a goal,
Our superstar from Portugal

CHAPTER 19

Europe

'We've played quite a few big teams,
but probably the one most fans would
like is Real Madrid.'

Callum McGregor

'HE'LL WANT to make Celtic a force in Europe. That'll be his big goal. In his mind will be the Champions League and putting a mark on that with the way he wants to play.'

Ryan McGowan's words at the end of our interview stuck with me. You'd be hard-pressed to find a guy who thinks more highly of Postecoglou. McGowan, who has also enjoyed a successful career in Scottish football, seems to be as obsessed with his former boss as the rest of us. His assertion serves as a reminder of the man who was in charge at Celtic.

Postecoglou's close mate, not just a press conference 'mate', Andy Harper, agrees when I put McGowan's comments to him a few weeks later. 'He won't want Celtic's geography to be a de-limiter,' Harper says. 'He won't think he's succeeded until he's made a mark in Europe. It's going to be a hell of a ride, just don't expect it to be orthodox.' Orthodox isn't a word that has any relation to Celtic anymore. Even less so on a Champions League night in Glasgow.

* * *

It's no exaggeration to say that Celtic Park is the most renowned stadium in Europe for the big-match atmosphere. The world's finest players are routinely in awe of the noise and the colour when visiting Paradise on a Champions League night. Alongside the rivalry with Rangers and the Lisbon Lions' 1967 European Cup triumph, it's one of the things the club is most known for around the world. They even have a section on the official website devoted to the testimonies of greats who have played on the hallowed turf, such is the allure of Celtic Park under the lights.

Lionel Messi: 'Celtic Park is the best atmosphere in Europe, and we all want to experience that again.'

Wayne Rooney: 'Celtic Park is inspiring and intimidating. It's a stadium with a particular atmosphere you want to experience as a player.'

Xavi Hernandez: 'The atmosphere generated by the fans in Celtic's stadium for our visit was the most impressive I've ever witnessed.'

Paolo Maldini: 'Every professional footballer should seek to play at least one game at Celtic Park. I have never felt anything like it.'

Zlatan Ibrahimović: 'I have played in the biggest games in world football. But I have never experienced an atmosphere like I did at Celtic Park.'

The list goes on and on. The big-match atmosphere has become a virtuous cycle. Fans now arrive on major European nights with the intention of maintaining the reputation. When new stars such as Toni Kroos and Luca Modrić comment on the atmosphere, they look to enhance the reputation further.

The noise has aided Celtic too. Famous scalps in the 21st century include Barcelona's all-conquering team of Xavi, Messi, Iniesta and more, competition holders AC Milan, Sir Alex Ferguson's Manchester United, and Juventus. Bayern Munich and Manchester City are two other teams who came to Glasgow as favourites and failed to win.

In the first 13 years of the century, Celtic registered 57 points in Europe's premier club competition group stage, 53 of which were earned in Glasgow, with just four coming away from home. They won 16 of their 24 home matches, with five draws and just three losses. They went unbeaten in their three home matches in six of the eight seasons. Europe's best would regularly be left scratching their heads after a defeat at Celtic Park.

While Celtic's home form was outstanding, their record on the road was disastrous. In 24 away matches, they avoided defeat on just two occasions: a 1-1 draw with Barcelona in 2004 and a last-gasp 3-2 win away to Spartak Moscow in 2012. Players who had looked unbeatable under the Parkhead lights would turn into pretenders. It was the Celtic way in Europe.

In Celtic's two recent appearances before Postecoglou, things were almost flipped. The Hoops only registered a meagre six points from the 2016/17 and 2017/18 campaigns combined, but five of those were earned on the road. Manchester City were the only team that failed to win in the east end of Glasgow, as Borussia Mönchengladbach, Barcelona, Paris Saint-Germain, Bayern Munich and Anderlecht all departed with three points, often with a bit to spare. The fans were still singing, the atmosphere still the loudest in Europe, but the big scalps weren't coming anymore. The Celtic Park fear factor had seemingly vanished.

Despite being routinely embarrassed by Europe's best in those two campaigns under Brendan Rodgers – Barcelona 7-0 Celtic, Celtic 0-5 Paris Saint-Germain, Paris Saint-Germain 7-1 Celtic, Bayern Munich 3-0 Celtic – it was still far better to be in the competition than not.

Celtic have enjoyed and endured an up-and-down European journey this century. The highlights have undoubtedly been the three qualifications for the last 16 of the UEFA Champions League and the magical run to the 2002/03 UEFA Cup Final in Seville under Martin O'Neill. Yet all of those genuinely impressive achievements arrived in the first 13 years of the century, and progress has stalled. Since Neil Lennon took his Hoops to the knockouts of the Champions League, beating Barcelona on the way, the club has become one that tends to play its football in the Europa League.

In the eight seasons before Postecoglou's arrival, Celtic played in the Champions League group stage three times. Their cumulative total of nine points from 18 matches further emphasised how they felt more at home on a Thursday night. Every season started with promise but, more often than not, Celtic found themselves out of the competition before Europe's biggest clubs had even kicked a ball. In seven seasons, Celtic lost summer qualifiers to Maribor, Malmö, AEK Athens, CFR Cluj and Ferencváros. Ronny Deila's Hoops also lost a tie to Legia Warsaw before being reinstated, as the Polish team had fielded an ineligible player. Even in victory over Hapoel Be'er Sheva and Kazakh pair Shakhter Karagandy and FC Astana, Celtic were never totally convincing. Qualifiers had become something for Hoops fans to dread rather than embrace. The yearly sight of Nir Bitton, a central-midfielder utilised well by Postecoglou, playing out of position at centre-back added to the sense that Celtic weren't planning well for these crucial matches.

While the Europa League had become a more comfortable level for Celtic, the Hoops weren't exactly flourishing in UEFA's second competition either. Five appearances in the tournament group stage garnered 37 points, an average of just over seven points per season. With a total of nine widely seen as the benchmark for qualification, Celtic were falling short. When they occasionally made it to the knockout rounds, they cracked their heads on a glass ceiling. Ronny Deila, Brendan Rodgers (twice) and Neil Lennon all failed at the Europa League's round of 32. The team not having won a post-Christmas knockout tie since March 2004 against FK Teplice was a stick regularly used to beat the weary board.

When Rangers upstaged Celtic in Europe under Steven Gerrard and then Giovanni van Bronckhorst, the disappointment was even harder to take. The script at the top of Scottish football was pretty straightforward. When the domestic trophies were handed out, more often than not it was to a Celtic player but, in Europe, Rangers were the only team that looked capable of winning a knockout tie. Celtic could win a one-off match in the Europa League group stage, as Lazio, Stade Rennais, RB Leipzig and others all found out. But when the pressure was on in a knockout tie, the Hoops would be more likely to buckle than their Ibrox counterparts, in strong opposition to what happened domestically.

* * *

While Ange Postecoglou's maiden season was about winning the league title back from Rangers, European football couldn't afford to take a back seat. For all the chat about the league being all that mattered, Europe still provided the real excitement for Celtic fans, in the first half of the season at least.

Gone are the days when Celtic Park would be half empty for a Europa League clash. The stadium was packed to its limit when Real Betis and Bayer Leverkusen visited in late 2021. It would have been the same for the visit of Ferencváros, had that match taken place at a regular time. The fact that the Tuesday afternoon clash still attracted a larger crowd than St Johnstone's visit the following Saturday spoke volumes about where the Celtic support's minds were. The league was the most important thing, but the uncomfortable truth was that the Hungarian champions were more attractive than the double cup winners from the previous campaign. Celtic couldn't afford to take their eye off the ball in any competition.

Celtic's position isn't a unique one. Most significant clubs outside Europe's top five leagues want more European football. It's part of why UEFA launched a third club competition – the UEFA Europa Conference League – in 2021. Celtic found themselves involved in that tournament after Christmas, and the fallout after defeat to FK Bodø/Glimt lasted more than a few days.

Postecoglou's first season in European competition was hardly a roaring success, but labelling it a failure would be placing too much emphasis on 180 minutes against the impressive Norwegian champions. At times Celtic had sparkled, often performing above expectations only to be undone by a defensive mistake or a bit of quality from the opposition. On other occasions, things had been pretty bleak and defeats galling.

It became clear very early on that the team wouldn't change their game plan against any opposition. Celtic would attack the best in Europe with little fear, and matches would often become frantic. In their 14 European matches in 2021/22, there were 53 goals, an average of nearly four per match. Of those goals, 26 were scored by Postecoglou's men, with 27 conceded.

Celtic played teams from seven different European nations and became one of the first teams to play in all three UEFA competitions – the Champions League, Europa League and the Conference League – in a single season. Bowing out of all three in the space of seven months was another source of amusement to rival fans. Pundits and faceless social media accounts claimed Celtic were the first team to suffer such a scenario. As is often the case nowadays, the truth was very different, with Celtic one of many clubs to go out of all three competitions in that season alone. Slovan Bratislava, Cluj, Sparta Prague and HJK Helsinki had all suffered the same fate.

Celtic's maiden European campaign under Postecoglou started and ended with damaging two-leg defeats to Scandinavian opposition, leaving various people questioning things. The venues and conditions could hardly have been more contrasting, but the feeling was similar. When would Celtic get back to the big time in Europe?

* * *

Their next match in UEFA competition may qualify as a 'big time' encounter. Celtic's route back to the promised land of the Champions League group stage came courtesy of the Premiership success in Postecoglou's maiden campaign. Yet, winning the league alone wouldn't have been enough for automatic group stage participation in any of the previous ten seasons. Not since 2010/11 had the Scottish league winners been assured safe passage to the competition proper without the need for a single qualifier. In the decade since, Celtic had exited qualifying to the likes of Ferencváros, CFR Cluj, Malmö, Maribor and more. In just four of the nine seasons spent in the champions route – a path made by UEFA to make life easier for champions – had Celtic come out on top.

There was plenty of nonsense written about Scotland's ascent up the UEFA coefficient table, which guaranteed the automatic group stage berth. While it's true that Rangers outperformed Celtic in European competition for several years, it's the green half of Glasgow who supplied more points towards the 2022/23 automatic berth. In the five seasons between 2016 and 2021, which made up the total, Celtic contributed 34.000 points to Rangers' 31.250. Besides, the coefficient only decides which positions in the league will enter which competition in the following season. The real qualifying takes place during the actual league season, which Celtic won.

Their reward was a meeting with the competition's holders. Real Madrid were the team Celtic fans wanted to see most in Glasgow. Of Europe's truly major clubs, they were the only ones who hadn't tasted the Celtic Park atmosphere in the 21st century. Some had visited so many times that it had become a running joke – Barcelona six times, AC Milan five – while the likes of Manchester United and Benfica had also been seen in the east end of Glasgow on more than one occasion. Celtic's recent adventures in the competition had also seen 'new money' in the form of Manchester City and Paris Saint-Germain sampling the Paradise cauldron. Yet there was one obvious omission from the Celtic Park roll of honour.

Despite being in the same draw on 13 separate occasions – ten for the group stage and three for the last 16 – Celtic had miraculously avoided coming into contact with the Spaniards on every occasion. Number 14 is also a lucky number for the Madrid giants – the number of times they've lifted the European Cup/Champions League, including five times in the previous nine seasons. When Celtic last met them in 1980, Madrid had been on the far more modest total of eight wins. Then the teams had been drawn together in the quarter-final of the European Cup. Celtic, managed by the legendary Billy McNeill, had beaten the Spaniards 2-0 in the Glasgow first leg but went down 3-0 in the return fixture to crash out of the competition.

Of course, Celtic's entire first-team squad wouldn't have been born when that fixture occurred. Yet the allure of Madrid was still apparent in the camp in the lead-up to the draw. Captain Callum McGregor openly spoke about wanting to face Carlo Ancelotti's team: 'We've played quite a few big teams, but probably the one most fans would like is Real Madrid.'

Postecoglou was happy to defer to his captain when asked for a preference, but he too would surely not have had any other club higher on the list. He'd have grown up watching Madrid's glorious teams and even played under the legendary Ferenc Puskás in the early 1990s. 'He'd be awfully proud for sure,' was his response when asked about what the Hungarian, who died in 2006, would have made of the tie.

On Tuesday, 6 September 2022, Callum McGregor led his team out alongside Real Madrid captain Karim Benzema to a wall of noise and colour at Celtic Park. Celtic were back in the big time.

CHAPTER 20

The Journey, Part 5: Improvement

*'Just because you have had success or it
looks like things are going well, that's not
the time to stand still.'*

Ange Postecoglou

IT'S 4.05PM on a Sunday and Celtic Park is packed. The
stadium doesn't usually host matches at this time, but television
requirements have led to the late afternoon kick-off. Not that it
matters – the stadium would have been full at midnight.

It's the final match of the opening weekend of the 2022/23
Premiership season, as Celtic begin their title defence against
a much-changed Aberdeen. For the vast majority of supporters
inside Celtic Park, it's an opportunity to watch their team in
competitive action for the first time in over 11 weeks, as well
as a chance to take one last prolonged stare in the direction of
the season that's just passed.

There's still the best part of 30 minutes to go until kick-
off, yet not a single green seat is on show inside the stadium.
Musician Liam McGrandles starts the party with a popular
setlist, including 'Let the People Sing' and 'Grace'. Shortly
afterwards, Callum McGregor unfurls the championship flag,
a symbolic nod to Celtic's title win in Ange Postcoglou's maiden
campaign. Celtic's skipper conducts his business with minimal

fuss, looking unfazed by the occasion. It's not that he doesn't consider it an honour, more that he's itching to get the new season underway. The Celtic squad drew a line under their previous achievements on the first day of pre-season.

The backdrop to McGregor is the real beauty of the day. Ultras group 'the Green Brigade' have organised a full stadium tifo (a choreographed display where fans hold up material to form a large image) to mark the occasion. Such grand displays are a rarity, with Celtic Park seeing just three of them before. The group organised two before historic wins over Barcelona in 2012 and Hearts in 2017, while the club arranged a less successful one against the Catalans in 2013. The pre-Aberdeen display cost £22,227, paid for entirely by donations from the Celtic support. The ultras group planned and designed the tifo, which took around 38 hours to set up over the course of a week. The work was tireless and the final result priceless.

As McGregor walks out of the tunnel on this balmy July afternoon, 58,000 people around him hold up green, white, black or grey material. One half of the stadium is green, forming an image of the Premiership trophy, while the other is white and features the traditional championship winners' flag with the numbers '21' and '22' signalling the season of the triumph. On the vast North Stand is a giant four-leaf clover.

'Flag Day' isn't always like this. Matches in seasons gone by have been dull affairs featuring teams not fully up to speed and supporters still on their holidays. Nobody is missing the match today, as season two of the Ange Postecoglou era gets underway.

There's a strange feeling inside the stadium. It feels like the continuation of the previous season's momentum and the start of something new. The refreshed branding outside the stadium adds to the feeling that something exceptional is just beginning: 'We will come back bigger, better because we never stop'.

Postecoglou set the tone for this early season frenzy on the final day of the previous campaign. His promise of Celtic coming back 'bigger and better' after the break defined an entire summer of positive messaging about progress and improvement. There was never a hint of consolidation, just an understanding that the previous season had been memorable but that nothing stands still.

The addition of Harry Kewell to the coaching team reminded the players of that very message, while the permanent signing of Cameron Carter-Vickers from Tottenham Hotspur days into the summer window was a statement of intent. When Celtic announced Jota's permanent transfer from Benfica and the signing of young left-back Alexandro Bernabei from Club Atlético Lanús weeks later, they'd already achieved their three main window goals.

'People said we haven't really strengthened the first 11, but I think we have,' said Postecoglou of Carter-Vickers and Jota weeks later on *Open Goal*. 'I didn't want to bring them in permanently because they played well last year. I did it because their best football is ahead of them. Even if we didn't have them last year and they were on the market, I'd have said, "These two guys, I want in." For us, it was a no-brainer because not only are they great players, but they're brilliant characters. They fit in brilliantly, and they're great guys who train hard every day.'

The rest of Celtic's incoming business arrived in two short bursts. In mid-July, the club announced the double capture of Aaron Mooy and Moritz Jenz. Midfielder Mooy, known by Postecoglou from his time with the Socceroos, had briefly been training with Rangers to build fitness before joining Celtic after he departed from Chinese Super League club Shanghai Port. Centre-back Jenz arrived on a season-long loan from French top-flight club Lorient, with an option to buy included in the deal. Then, near the deadline, versatile winger Sead Hakšabanović and central-midfielder Oliver Abildgaard joined from Rubin Kazan.

The latter two signings weren't a necessity for Celtic, and most supporters wouldn't have grumbled had they not arrived. Postecoglou had his own plan, which involved not relying on a small group of players. He told the press: 'If we are going to play 60 games this season and try to compete in every competition, then we have to have a strong squad. Our whole recruiting process so far has been about making our squad robust. If we had some fragility last season, then it was around the fact it was too much of a burden on the individuals, and we ended up breaking down and losing key players for large chunks of the season.'

At the end of the window, Celtic had at least two viable options for every position.

Goalkeeper
Joe Hart
Ben Siegrist
Scott Bain

Right-back	Centre-back	Centre-back	Left-back
Josip Juranovic	Cameron Carter-Vickers	Carl Starfelt	Greg Taylor
Anthony Ralston	Stephen Welsh	Moritz Jenz	Alexandro Bernabei

Centre-midfield
Callum McGregor
Oliver Abildgaard
Aaron Mooy
Yosuke Ideguchi
James McCarthy

Attacking-midfield
Reo Hatate
Matt O'Riley
David Turnbull

Right-wing	Left-wing
Liel Abada	Jota
James Forrest	Daizen Maeda
	Sead Hakšabanović

Forwards
Kyogo Furuhashi
Giorgos Giakoumakis

The squad was undoubtedly more robust than it had been at the start of the summer. Carter-Vickers and Jota had been added, and while Bernabei got off to a slow start, his arrival did push Greg Taylor on to new heights. Goalkeeper Ben Siegrist seemed to be an upgrade on Scott Bain, Jenz would play more of a part than Christopher Jullien had, and Mooy was an improvement on the recently departed Nir Bitton.

Yet, for all the new signings, the most encouraging noises were from those already at the club. 'I always want more,' was Callum McGregor's message to Sky Sports in mid-June. 'I always want to be better as a person and as a football player and try to improve all the time. That's what keeps you hungry. In football, if you lose that hunger, you may as well not play.'

His fellow midfielder Reo Hatate had enjoyed a productive first six months at Celtic, yet he felt he was only getting started. 'I think my real challenge overseas will begin when I go back to Scotland this summer,' he wrote on the website From The Athlete.

With the McGregor and Hatate quotes dropping within hours of each other on a June afternoon, you'd be forgiven for thinking this was part of a coordinated strategy from the club's PR department to fill some slow news days. It's far more likely that two highly motivated players were just setting their stall out for what was to come. Their manager was at it later in the summer, too, saying, 'There's still work to be done. Just because you have had success or it looks like things are going well, that's not the time to stand still.'

Celtic's pre-season felt different from a year earlier. While the pandemic had played a part in the previous season's plans (Celtic had played most matches at training grounds or in front of few or no fans), Postecoglou was keen to avoid a repeat. There would be no European qualifiers for Celtic, so the challenge became trying to replicate those meaningful matches. Celtic played six friendlies, with all but the first proving competitive. Away matches in front of hostile crowds at Rapid Wien, Baník

Ostrava and Legia Warsaw provided a taste of what was to come in Europe, albeit against lesser sides, while the visits of English Championship teams Blackburn Rovers and Norwich City to Celtic Park brought different challenges.

'It was a cracking atmosphere,' Postecoglou said after the Baník Ostrava match, in which the Czechs celebrated their centenary. 'It gave the feel of a real contest. I didn't want just to play friendly games if they're not in main stadiums in front of crowds – it loses a little bit. The last two games have been perfect.'

Between the matches, Postecoglou spent a complete pre-season with his players in stark contrast to what had occurred 12 months prior. The lack of qualifying jeopardy and late transfer drama made the first couple of months a slow affair for supporters, with most of the hard work done out of the spotlight. Celtic focused their early efforts on the training ground and made a fast start to the league season. For the first time, things were calm under Ange Postecoglou. The serenity wouldn't last for long.

* * *

Celtic 2-0 Aberdeen, Premiership, Celtic Park, Sunday, 3 April 2022

It took Celtic 153 seconds to score at the start of the new season. Most of their supporters were still in the process of discarding their material from the pre-match display when Stephen Welsh rose above new Aberdeen signing Dante Polvara and headed into the corner of the net, from a floated Matt O'Riley corner. The academy graduate celebrated by sprinting to the corner, in front of the standing section, where so many of Celtic's big goals are celebrated. After striking with the final kick of the previous season, Celtic had netted almost instantly in the new campaign. It was like they'd never been away.

While Welsh may have been an unlikely contender to net Celtic's first competitive goal of the season, his contribution may not have been quite as unexpected for Postecoglou. Rather fittingly, Celtic's boss had spent the previous days talking up the growing importance and development of Welsh. Minutes into Celtic's league opener, it almost felt as if he knew a major moment was coming for the centre-back.

'Welshy has shown a lot of growth,' Postecoglou had told the written press in the lead-up to the match. 'I expect that from all the players. He has come back for pre-season and worked really hard through it. Because of our defensive situation, we have not had too many options at centre-back so he and Cam have played in the majority of games and his performances are improving all the time. We are challenging him all the time to take his game to another level. That's the nature of the beast, you have to keep improving whether you are established or not.'

Back on the pitch, a stunning long-range strike from Jota sealed the opening-day victory, his fifth goal in four meetings against the Pittodrie club, but only after Jonny Hayes had fluffed his lines with a major Aberdeen chance. Substitute Giorgos Giakoumakis missed an even better opportunity shortly before full time on a successful afternoon for Celtic.

Yet Postecoglou wasn't totally happy with how things had played out, telling Sky Sports, 'I thought we got a bit slack towards the end of the first half. Our passing got a bit lax. We weren't quite as aggressive in our press. In the second half, we addressed that. Overall, a decent performance, but I thought we were wasteful in front of goal or could have been a bit more clinical. You can be patient, but if there are chances, you take them.'

Postecoglou's message hinted at standards being raised again at the club. Celtic were already top of the league, as fans gladly boasted at full time, but the performances would have to be better if the season's goals were to be achieved.

Celtic: Hart, Juranovic, Carter-Vickers, Welsh, Taylor, McGregor, O'Riley, Hatate, Jota, Maeda, Kyogo
Subs used: Giakoumakis, Abada, Turnbull, Ralston, Mooy

Aberdeen: Roos, Richardson, Stewart, McCrorie, Coulson, Ramadani, Polvara, Kennedy, Besuijen, Hayes, Miovski
Subs used: *Luís Lopes, Roberts*

* * *

Dundee United 0–9 Celtic, Premiership, Tannadice, Sunday, 28 August 2022

Celtic had just netted their third first-half goal at Tannadice, yet Greg Taylor wanted more. After seeing his cross blocked for a corner, the full-back grabbed the ball with intent and sprinted to take the set piece. Dundee United were completely shaken and in a bad place, yet Celtic would be showing them no mercy. Postecoglou's Celtic aren't affected by the scoreboard. They just want to score goals.

At this stage, three, all from Kyogo Furuhashi, had been netted. Jota had set one up, Abada another, while the second goal had been a thing of individual beauty. When Matt O'Riley fed the Portuguese winger for number four minutes later, Celtic were in complete dreamland. The home team looked worn out and two stands of Tannadice were already empty before the interval.

With the match over as a contest, the intent shown by Taylor and his team-mates to keep the pressure up during a frantic seven minutes of stoppage time was a sight to behold. 'We Never Stop' was taking on an even greater meaning, while the vocal travelling support chanted some appropriate words:

Piling on the agony
Putting on the style
One, two, three, four, five, six, seven
Scoring all the while
I've never seen such football
I've travelled many a mile
As watching Glasgow Celtic
Putting on the style

After the break, Celtic's intensity remained, and five more goals followed to complete a remarkable 9-0 triumph – the biggest competitive away win in the club's entire history. Liel Abada joined Kyogo in the hat-trick club, while Josip Juranovic and Carl Starfelt also netted in the second half. The disappointment from the support and the players at not securing the double-figure victory said it all.

Taylor had once again been terrific in a unique position he was carving out for himself. His growth in a Celtic shirt had been a big talking point during the early weeks of Postecoglou's second season. When the previous campaign had concluded, the common consensus was that, beyond signing Jota and Cameron Carter-Vickers permanently, the main summer task was to upgrade the left-back position.

In late June, Argentine full-back Alexandro Bernabei joined on a five-year deal. At 21, he had a few years on Taylor and was widely expected to be Celtic's first choice over time, if not immediately. Yet Bernabei's signing seemed to spur Taylor on. The former Kilmarnock man had been steadily improving in a Celtic jersey under Postecoglou after the Aussie put immense faith in him in his early days, including with a new lengthy contract just months into the job. Early on it seemed as if Taylor didn't fully believe he was a Celtic player. By the time the 2022/23 campaign rolled around, that was no longer the case.

Taylor was immense in Celtic's first few matches of the season, most notably in the 5-0 success at Kilmarnock, after which Jota singled him out for praise live on Sky Sports. 'I think I should speak about Greg because he's been unbelievable this season,' the winger said. 'He's a top player delivering in every game, and his standards in every game are just unbelievable. I don't think he gets enough credit.' Taylor would later admit to being 'really touched' by Jota's words in a Celtic Twitter Q&A.

While he's an unsung hero as far as the media and the support are concerned, Taylor is anything but inside the Celtic camp. He's a massive personality in the dressing room. When players are asked about the biggest (or noisiest) presences in the Celtic squad, they regularly plump for one of two people: Josip Juranovic or Greg Taylor. Perhaps it's a full-back thing.

Yet Taylor can hardly even be considered a full-back anymore. Sure, that's the position he lines up in before kick-off but, once the match starts, he can be found virtually anywhere on the pitch. He has a pretty unique skill set for a modern full-back. Unlike most of his contemporaries, he isn't blessed with immense speed, in possession at least. He doesn't have the turn of pace of Jeremie Frimpong or the crossing or shooting of Kieran Tierney. He doesn't chip in with nearly as many goals as Josip Juranovic or Anthony Ralston and was one of the final first-team players to net in Postecoglou's debut season. In fact, if you were looking at all of Taylor's traits, you may conclude that he's more suited to midfield than the defence. That's where he plays under Postecoglou. What Taylor has going for him is immense stamina and an ability to accurately pass the ball into space, as was shown with his through ball for Daizen Maeda in Celtic's opener at Rugby Park. His tenacity and desire to win the ball back are also vital in a Postecoglou team.

When Postecoglou came to Scotland, it was essential that players like Taylor, who knew the club, bought into his way of playing. From day one the former Kilmarnock man has done that and his quality has eventually come to the fore. Had the cameras panned to the Aussie amid Taylor's sprint to the Tannadice corner flag, he'd surely have had a massive smile on his face.

Dundee United: *Eriksson, Freeman, Smith, Edwards, Graham, McMann, Meekison, Levitt, Harkes, Middleton, Fletcher*
Subs used: *Clark, McGrath, Sibbald, Niskanen*

Celtic: *Hart, Juranovic, Carter-Vickers, Starfelt, Taylor, McGregor, O'Riley, Hatate, Abada, Kyogo, Jota*
Subs used: *Forrest, Maeda, Mooy, Turnbull, Bernabei*

* * *

Ross County 1-4 Celtic, League Cup, Victoria Park,
Wednesday, 31 August 2022

The Celtic support is partying in Dingwall. Despite the match taking place in the most northern professional ground in Scotland on a chilly Wednesday night, and despite the home club allocating an entire additional stand to Celtic fans, there's still not a seat to be had.

With a derby coming up against Rangers in a matter of days, and then the small matter of Real Madrid three days after that, the Celtic support would have been forgiven for having other things on their mind. However, this evening deep in the Highlands they've taken a leaf out of their manager's book. 'Make the next game your best yet,' Ange Postecoglou regularly tells his players. The atmosphere may be one of the best Celtic have had under the Aussie.

It helps that the team are playing so well. Given that Postecoglou has made nine changes to the line-up that demolished Dundee United a few days earlier, you may have expected to see Celtic a little rusty. When Callum McGregor, one of the two kept in the team alongside Liel Abada, nets the opener from a corner and Giorgos Giakoumakis soon adds a clinical second minutes later, Celtic are as good as through.

Yet Ross County are made of stern stuff. Alex Iacovitti bundles in an untidy strike to reduce the deficit and make things a little nervier for the 4,000-strong Celtic following. Their worries don't last for long. Five minutes later, Daizen Maeda restores the two-goal advantage with a poacher's finish, and then James Forrest adds a fourth in stoppage time.

'Bring on the Rangers' chant the Celtic support, with the complete focus now on Saturday's mouth-watering derby. Celtic have progressed to the quarter-finals of the League Cup, yet the bigger takeaway on the night is the strength in depth Postecoglou now has at his disposal. Celtic changed virtually an entire team and still scored four goals away to a tricky top-flight team.

Even the Kessock Bridge being closed can't dampen the mood of the Celtic support right now. Those heading back to the central belt don't get home until around 3am.

Ross County: Eastwood, Johnson, Watson, Iacovitti, Purrington, Tillson, Loturi, Sims, Samuel, Harmon, White
Subs used: Cancola, Edwards, Hiwula, Paton, Olaigbe

Celtic: Siegrist, Ralston, Welsh, Jenz, Bernabei, Mooy, McGregor, Turnbull, Abada, Giakoumakis, Maeda
Subs used: Forrest, Starfelt, Hakšabanović, *McCarthy*

* * *

Celtic 4-0 Rangers, Premiership, Celtic Park, Saturday, 3 September 2022

Between September 2016 and September 2018, Celtic beat Rangers ten times in 12 matches. Brendan Rodgers' all-conquering team beat their rivals, 5-1, 1-0, 2-1, 2-0, 5-1, 2-0, 3-2, 4-0, 5-0 and 1-0 over a 24-month period that also saw the Ibrox club escape Celtic Park with two draws. Moussa Dembele, Scott Sinclair, Odsonne Edouard and Tom Rogic regularly tormented teams led by Mark Warburton, Pedro Caixinha or Graeme Murty. With trebles won at the end of every season, they were halcyon days to be a Celtic supporter.

Then the fightback from the other side began. The following six derbies were split with three wins apiece before the pandemic shut down the game. When football returned, the roles were reversed as Rangers won five of the next six derbies, drawing the other. Suddenly, Celtic were the team with mental baggage in the fixture.

Things were very even once Postecoglou and Giovanni van Bronckhorst got to grips with their new surroundings in early 2022. Celtic won two derbies, Rangers won one, and a draw in the other was shaded by the team wearing blue. Rangers' run to the Europa League Final, with impressive victories over Borussia Dortmund, Red Star Belgrade, Braga and RB Leipzig, catapulted them into the European limelight. If they'd beaten such good teams and weren't even top of the Premiership, Scottish football must be healthy. Comparisons to the early 2000s, when both clubs were extremely strong, didn't seem misguided.

When Celtic battered Rangers 4-0 at a boisterous Celtic Park in the opening derby of the 2022/23 season, it was a genuinely remarkable result. The Ibrox club had just seen off PSV Eindhoven to join Celtic in the Champions League group stage – the first time both had been involved in the same season since 2007/08. Two of Europe's elite 32 were battling it out in Glasgow. But Celtic were so far ahead.

The theme of the day was quick restarts. With minutes gone, Jota won a throw-in from Ryan Kent high up the pitch. While Kent and the nearby James Tavernier turned round to complain to referee Nick Walsh, Jota took the throw to Matt O'Riley, who crossed for Liel Abada to strike. If you pause the footage just as Jota is retrieving the ball, you see two Celtic players, O'Riley and Greg Taylor, making forward runs. At the same time, at least six Rangers players are on their heels. When the ball is crossed in by O'Riley, four of them are just watching as Abada strikes home. 'If the opposition wants to stop, that's good for us. We'll take advantage of it,' Postecoglou told his players in the infamous mic'd-up training session a year earlier. Many of a blue persuasion had mocked the video initially. They weren't laughing anymore. Their manager certainly wasn't.

Television pictures caught Van Bronckhorst's moment of frustration as he threw his arms out and crouched down, knowing how unforgivable an error his team had just made. Kent, Glen Kamara and John Lundstram had been the culprits, failing to stop Callum McGregor from taking a quick free kick after the latter had been called offside. McGregor found O'Riley in space, he fed in Jota and the former Benfica star dinked Jon McLaughlin from the tightest of angles. Jota didn't even see the ball cross the line – he was already away celebrating.

The noise around Celtic Park got even louder. Like in the February encounter, Abada banged in a third just before half-time. Again, he was unmarked at the back post. Again he finished emphatically. Unlike the match in February, Celtic added to their tally in the second half. Substitute David Turnbull leapt on to a horrendous error from the hapless McLaughlin to side-foot in a fourth. The Rangers players couldn't get off the pitch quickly enough at full time. Celtic had proven themselves to be the best team in Scotland by a country mile. This was the next best facing them, and they'd been utterly blown away.

Yet the players weren't getting carried away. Again, Callum McGregor's message was to keep the celebrations relatively low-key. The Celtic players knew better than anyone about the dangers of writing a team off early in the season. 'No, come on,' Jota said when BBC Scotland asked about the title race afterwards. 'This is September. Last season, you kept saying they were in front of us, and the championship was done. Things don't work like that. This is football. It's game after game, and until May there's plenty of football to play. So just chill.'

Once again, Celtic had done their talking on the pitch.

Celtic: Hart, Juranovic, Carter-Vickers, Starfelt, Taylor, O'Riley, McGregor, Hatate, Abada, Kyogo, Jota

Subs used: Giakoumakis, Jenz, Turnbull, Maeda, Mooy

Rangers: McLaughlin, Tavernier, Goldson, Sands, Barisic, Davis, Lundstram, Tillman, Kamara, Kent, Coluk

Subs used: Wright, Arfield, Morelos, Jack, Sakala

* * *

Celtic's stunning derby victory over Rangers is where this part of the journey ends. In many ways it's a satisfying place to finish. When Ange Postecoglou entered Celtic Park for the first time in June 2021 he was arriving at a club in a desperate state – 25 points adrift of Rangers the previous season and with little hope for what was to come. The upturn in Celtic's fortunes has been immense. The 4-0 success over the Ibrox club at a buoyant Celtic Park showed just how far everyone had come.

Only time will tell where the actual ceiling sits for this spectacular Celtic squad he's assembled. Will the team be able to crack the Champions League in years to come? Or will that prove too much of a challenge, even for Postecoglou? It's a mystery that no one can answer yet. That's what Postecoglou loves most about football.

What we do know is that Celtic will continue to push forward while the Australian is in charge. Over the coming years, players will leave and replacements will be signed. Expectations will continue to rise and rise. More trophies will be won and the Celtic support will sing as they always do.

Postecoglou will move on one day, probably to a major job in one of the world's biggest leagues. Celtic Park will be a slightly worse-off place without his presence. Postecoglou, too, will be missing a little something he once had in his life. All that will be left are the memories.

Until that day, the journey will continue. Celtic are unlikely to stop.

Bibliography

A special thanks to the following ...

Celtic TV
Currie Club BT Sport
From The Athlete
KeepUp.co.au
Number Web
Open Goal
Tokyo Weekender
Virgin Media Sport
Vissel Kobe